VEGETABLES & SALADS

LAROUSSE
GASTRONOMIQUE
RECIPE
COLLECTION

VEGETABLES & SALADS

With the assistance of the Gastronomic Committee
President Joël Robuchon

hamlyn

First published in Great Britain in 2004 by
Hamlyn, a division of Octopus Publishing Group Ltd
2–4 Heron Quays, London E14 4JP

ISBN 0 600 61161 2
EAN 9780600611615

A CIP catalogue record for this book is available from the British
Library

Printed and bound in Italy

10 9 8 7 6 5 4 3 2 1

Gastronomic Committee

President

Joël Robuchon

Members of the Committee

Michel Creignou, *Journalist*

Jean Delaveyne, *Chef, founder of Restaurant Le Camélia, Bougival*

Éric Frachon, *Honorary president, Evian Water SA*

Michel Guérard, *Chef, Restaurant Les Prés d'Eugénie, Eugénie-les-Bains*

Pierre Hermé, *Confectioner, Paris*

Robert Linxe, *Founder, The House of Chocolate, Paris and New York*

Élisabeth de Meurville, *Journalist*

Georges Pouvel, *Professor of cookery; consultant on cookery techniques*

Jean-François Revel, *Writer*

Pierre Troisgros, *Chef, Restaurant Pierre Troisgros, Roanne*

Alain Weill, *Art expert; member of the National Council of Gastronomy*

Contributors

Marie-Paule Bernardin
Archivist

Geneviève Beullac
Editor

Jean Billault
Member of the College of Butchery

Christophe Bligny
Paris College of Catering

Thierry Borghèse
Chief Inspector of Consumer Affairs

Francis Boucher
Confectioner

Pascal Champagne
Barman, Hotel Lutetia; Member, French Association of Barmen

Frédéric Chesneau
Project manager

Marcel Cottenceau
Former technical director, College of Butchery

Robert Courtine
President, Marco-Polo Prize

Philippe Dardonville
Secretary-general, National Union of Producers of Fruit Juice

Bertrand Debatte
Officer of the Bakery, Auchamps

Jean Dehillerin
President and managing director, E. Dehillerin SA (manufacturers of kitchen equipment)

Gilbert Delos
Writer and journalist

Christian Flacelière
Journalist

Jean-Louis Flandrin
Professor emeritus, University of Paris VII; Director of studies,

E.H.E.S.S. *(College of Social Sciences)*

Dr André Fourel
Economist

Dominique Franceschi
Journalist

Dr Jacques Fricker
Nutritionist

Jean-Pierre Gabriel
Journalist

Thierry Gaudillère
Editor, Bourgogne Aujourd'hui (Burgundy Today)

Ismène Giachetti
Director of research, C.N.R.S. (National Centre for Scientific Research)

Sylvie Girard
Cookery writer

Catherine Goavec-Bouvard
Agribusiness consultant

Jo Goldenberg
Restaurateur

Catherine Gomy
Agribusiness certification officer, French Association of Standardization

Bruno Goussault
Scientific director, C.R.E.A. (Centre of Food and Nutrition Studies)

Jacques Guinberteau
Mycologist; Director of studies, I.N.R.A. (National Institute of Agriculture)

Joseph Hossenlopp
Director of studies, Cemagref (Institute of Research for Agricultural and Environmental Engineering)

Françoise Kayler
Food critic

Jacques Lacoursière
Writer

Josette Le Reun-Gaudicheau
Teacher (specializing in seafood)

Paul Maindiaux
Development officer, Ministry of Agriculture

Laurent Mairet
Oenologist

Jukka Mannerkorpi
Cookery editor

Pascal Orain
Manager, Bertie's Restaurant

Philippe Pilliot
Secretary-general, Federation of French Grocers; Editor, Le Nouvel Épicier (The New Grocer)

Jean-Claude Ribaut
Cookery correspondent, Le Monde

Isabelle Richard
Bachelor of Arts

Michel Rigo
Deputy head, National Federation of Fruit Brandies

Françoise Sabban
Master of ceremonies, E.H.E.S.S. (College of Social Sciences)

Jacques Sallé
Journalist

Jean-Louis Taillebaud
Chef, Ritz-Escoffier (French School of Gastronomy); Ritz Hotel, Place Vendôme, Paris

Claude Vifian
Chef and professor, College of the Hotel Industry, Lausanne

Leda Vigliardi Paravia
Writer and journalist

Jean-Marc Wolff
College of the Hotel Industry, Paris

Rémy Yverneau
Secretary-general, National Federation of Makers of Cream Cheese

Contents

Useful information

How to use this book

The recipes are divided into two main chapters: Vegetables and Mixed vegetables & salads. Within these chapters entries are grouped by main ingredient in A–Z order. The third chapter, Basic recipes & classic additions, has recipes for the batters, pastry, sauces and so on referred to in the first two chapters.

When an entry refers to another recipe, it may be found by first referring to the relevant section and then to the food or dish type. A comprehensive index of entries lists the entire contents.

Weights & measures

Metric, imperial and American measures are used in this book. As a general rule, it is advisable to follow only one set of measures and not to mix metric, imperial and/or cup quantities in any one recipe.

Spoon measures

Spoon measures refer to standard measuring utensils. Serving spoons and table cutlery are not suitable for measuring as they are not standard in capacity.

¼ teaspoon = 1.5 ml
½ teaspoon = 2.5 ml
1 teaspoon = 5 ml
1 tablespoon = 15 ml

Oven temperatures

Below are the standard settings for domestic ovens. However, ovens vary widely and manufacturer's instructions should be consulted. Individual ovens also perform differently and experience of using a particular appliance is invaluable for adjusting temperatures and cooking times to give the best results. Those working with commercial cooking appliances will be accustomed to using the higher temperatures attained. Many chefs' recipes refer to glazing or cooking in a hot oven for a short period: as a rule, the hottest setting for a domestic appliance should be used as the equivalent.

Temperatures and timings in the recipes refer to preheated ovens.

If using a fan-assisted oven, follow the manufacturer's instructions for adjusting timing and temperature.

Centigrade	Fahrenheit	Gas mark
110°C	225°F	gas ¼
120°C	250°F	gas ½
140°C	275°F	gas 1
150°C	300°F	gas 2
160°C	325°F	gas 3
180°C	350°F	gas 4
190°C	375°F	gas 5
200°C	400°F	gas 6
220°C	425°F	gas 7
230°C	450°F	gas 8
240°C	475°F	gas 9

Introduction

Larousse Gastronomique is the world's most famous culinary reference book. It was the vision of Prosper Montagné, a French chef who was responsible for the first edition published in Paris in 1938. His aims were to provide an overview of 20th-century gastronomy and its history, as well as a source of reference on the more practical aspects of cookery. Twenty-three years later the first English edition was published and it immediately became the culinary bible of chefs, cooks and food aficionados.

A new English edition of this monumental work was published in 2001. Completely revised and updated, it reflected the social and cultural changes, together with advances in science and technology, that have dramatically influenced our ideas about food, the way we cook and how we eat.

Distilled from the latest edition, in one convenient volume, is this collection of over 600 vegetable and salad recipes, together with over 80 recipes for sauces, dressings, pastry, butters and stocks. Whether your interest is in the great traditions of French cuisine or in the wide spectrum of food as the international subject it has become, the recipes reflect the diversity of the world of cooking in the 21st century.

Vegetables

Artichokes, globe

To prepare

Break off the stalk of the artichoke by bending it until it comes away from the base; the stringy parts will come away with the stalk. Using a very sharp knife, cut the base flat and then remove the tough outer leaves. Neatly trim the outside of the artichoke, then cut off the top and remove the choke. Rub with lemon to prevent it going black, even if it is to be used immediately.

Arles salad

Slice some boiled potatoes and quarter some boiled artichoke hearts. Mix together and dress with vinaigrette, sprinkle with chopped chervil and tarragon, and garnish with curly endive (frisée) and tomato quarters. Garnish with drained canned anchovy fillets arranged in a criss-cross pattern, with a stoned (pitted) black (ripe) olive placed in the centre. Pour some vinaigrette (seasoned with very little salt) over the garnish just before serving.

Artichoke fritters

Trim some small, young globe artichokes (harvested before their chokes have formed). Blanch for 5 minutes until just tender, then drain and cut each artichoke into four pieces. Sprinkle with plenty of lemon juice and a little olive oil, season with salt and and a few turns of pepper and leave to marinate for 30 minutes. Drain the artichoke pieces. Dip them in batter, deep-fry in hot oil, drain again and serve on a napkin. (Brussels sprout fritters are prepared in the same way.)

Artichoke hearts à la florentine

Slowly cook some artichoke hearts and some spinach in butter in separate pans. Stuff each artichoke heart with a heaped tablespoon of prepared spinach and coat with Mornay sauce. Sprinkle with grated cheese and brown in a preheated oven at 240°C (475°F, gas 9).

Artichoke hearts à la piémontaise

Cook some artichoke hearts in melted butter. Prepare a risotto *à la piémontaise* and garnish each artichoke heart with a dome of 2 tablespoons risotto. Sprinkle the artichoke hearts with grated Parmesan cheese and a little melted butter and brown in a preheated oven at 240°C (475°F, gas 9). Serve with tomato sauce.

Artichoke mirepoix

Prepare 12 small young artichokes. Place 200 ml (7 fl oz, I cup) fondue of vegetable mirepoix with some butter in a sauté pan and add 2 tablespoons finely diced lean ham. Arrange the artichokes in the sauté pan and cover with a lid. Cook very gently for 5 minutes, then moisten with 4 tablespoons dry white wine and reduce. Add 100 ml (4 fl oz, ½ cup) veal gravy, cover the pan once more and cook for 35 minutes.

Arrange the artichokes in a vegetable dish, pour the mirepoix over the top of them and sprinkle with chopped parsley. Serve immediately.

Artichoke omelette

Slice 4 artichoke hearts and sauté them in butter until they are half-cooked, without letting them brown. Add the artichoke slices to 8 eggs and beat together; cook the omelette as usual. It can be garnished with a row of sliced sautéed artichoke hearts and surrounded with a ribbon of reduced veal stock.

Artichoke ragoût

Prepare 2 kg (4½ lb) small artichokes. Heat some oil in a large flameproof casserole and toss the artichokes in it. Brown them, stirring constantly, for 5 minutes. Add sufficient water to cover, season with salt and pepper and, without covering the casserole, simmer very gently for 15 minutes. Sauté 2 kg (4½ lb) small new potatoes in a little oil. Blanch 150 g (5 oz) lean diced bacon and add to the potatoes. Cook for 5 minutes to brown. Drain and add to the artichokes, cover and complete the cooking without stirring (this takes about 20 minutes).

Artichokes à la barigoule

Prepare the artichokes for stuffing. Clean and chop 75 g (3 oz, 1 cup) mushrooms for each artichoke. Mince (grind) 50 g (2 oz) fat bacon and the same quantity of ham. Mix these ingredients together with chopped parsley, salt and pepper. Fill the artichokes with the mixture, cover with fat bacon, tie up with string, and braise in white wine with a little olive oil. Thicken the cooking liquor with a very small amount of softened butter.

Artichokes à la bretonne

These are boiled artichokes accompanied by a white sauce prepared from the cooking liquid and enriched with crème fraîche; butter is added to the sauce just before serving.

Artichokes à la cévenole

Blanch the artichokes and gently cook them in butter. Garnish with chestnut purée flavoured with Soubise purée. Sprinkle with grated Parmesan cheese and melted butter and brown in the oven or under the grill (broiler).

Artichokes à la duxelles

Blanch the artichokes and cook gently in butter, then stuff with finely chopped mushroom duxelles.

Artichokes à la lyonnaise

Choose medium-sized artichokes with long spread-out leaves, either the green or the violet variety. Break off the stalks, chop the artichokes into four, cut the leaves down to two-thirds their length and remove the choke. Plunge the artichokes into a saucepan of boiling water, half-cook them and then drain them thoroughly.

Heat a mixture of equal parts of oil and butter in a flameproof pan and soften a chopped onion in it. Add the artichokes, season with salt and pepper and cook over a moderate heat until the vegetables begin to brown. Add 1 tablespoon flour and about 300 ml (½ pint, 1¼ cups) stock. When the artichokes are cooked, arrange them on a vegetable dish and keep them hot. Add a little more stock to the pan and reduce. Add some chopped parsley and then stir in a good-sized piece of unsalted butter and the juice of ½ lemon. Pour the sauce over the artichokes and serve.

Artichokes à la niçoise

Blanch the artichokes and sauté in olive oil. Garnish with thick tomato sauce, sprinkle with white breadcrumbs and olive oil, and brown in the oven or under the grill (broiler).

Artichokes à la portugaise

Gently cook the prepared artichokes in oil with chopped onion. Add 2 peeled seeded chopped tomatoes, a little grated garlic and some chopped parsley. Cover and cook over a very low heat. Garnish with a well-reduced tomato sauce and sprinkle with chopped parsley.

Artichokes aux fines herbes

Lightly blanch the artichokes, then sauté them (either whole or sliced) in butter. Arrange in a vegetable dish and sprinkle with chopped chervil and parsley. If the artichokes are very tender, the raw hearts may be sliced, rubbed with lemon and sautéed in butter.

Artichokes Clamart

Clean a lettuce and cut it into long thin shreds. Wash 12 small young globe artichokes; break off the stalks and cut away the large leaves. Butter a flameproof casserole and arrange the artichokes in it. Add 500 ml (17 fl oz, 2 cups) shelled fresh green peas, the lettuce, some salt, 1 teaspoon caster (superfine) sugar and 3 tablespoons water. Cover and cook very gently. Serve in the cooking dish, adding 1 tablespoon butter at the last minute.

Artichokes cooked in butter or à la crème

Prepare and trim the artichoke hearts. Rub them with lemon and blanch for 10 minutes in boiling salted water with a few drops of lemon juice. Drain the hearts, arrange in a well-buttered sauté pan and season with salt and pepper. Sprinkle with melted butter and cook, covered, for about 20 minutes. The artichoke hearts may then be served *à la crème* by covering them with hot crème fraîche that has been reduced by half. They may be cut into slices if they are too large.

Artichokes Crécy

Prepare 12 very small fresh artichokes and put them in a generously buttered sauté pan. Turn 800 g (1¾ lb) small new carrots and add them to the sauté pan. Season with salt and a pinch of sugar. Moisten with 4 tablespoons water, cover, and cook slowly for about 40 minutes. Add 1 tablespoon unsalted butter just before serving.

Artichokes Soubise

Blanch the artichokes and steam them in butter. Garnish with Soubise purée. Sprinkle with a little Parmesan cheese and brown lightly in the oven or under the grill (broiler).

Artichoke velouté soup

Prepare a white roux with 40 g (1½ oz, 3 tablespoons) butter and 40 g (1½ oz, 6 tablespoons) flour. Moisten with a generous 750 ml (1¼ pints, 3¼ cups) chicken consommé. Blanch 8 small artichoke hearts, cut into slices, and simmer in 40 g (1½ oz, 3 tablespoons) butter for about 20 minutes. Add them to the consommé, bring to the boil and cook until the vegetables break up. Reduce the mixture to a purée in a food processor or blender. Dilute with a little consommé to obtain the desired consistency and heat. Remove from the heat and thicken the soup with a mixture of 3 egg yolks beaten with 100 ml (4 fl oz, 7 tablespoons) double (heavy) cream. Finally, whisk in 75 g (3 oz, 6 tablespoons) butter. Reheat but do not boil.

Boiled artichokes

Using scissors or a very sharp knife, trim off the top third of the outer leaves of the artichokes and wash the heads in plenty of water. Break off the stalk level with the leaves (do not cut it); the stringy parts will come away with the stalk. Tie up each artichoke with string so that the head retains its shape during cooking and plunge the vegetables into acidulated boiling salted water. Keep the water boiling vigorously. The cooking time (average 30 minutes) depends on the size and freshness of the artichokes. (Allow 10–12 minutes after the steam begins to escape when using a pressure cooker.) The artichokes are cooked when the outside leaves come away when pulled upwards. Drain the artichokes by placing them upside down in a colander, remove the string and serve immediately. If they are to be eaten cold, put them under the cold tap as soon as they are cooked and then drain them; do not untie them until the last moment. To serve, take out and discard the centre leaves which hide the choke and remove the choke by scooping it out with a small spoon.

Artichokes may be eaten hot with melted butter, a white sauce (prepared with the cooking water enriched with fresh cream), a cream sauce (or simply cream flavoured with lemon and heated), a hollandaise sauce or a mousseline sauce. Cold artichokes may be served with mayonnaise, mustard sauce, soy sauce, tartare sauce, or vinaigrette and flavoured, if desired, with chopped parsley or chervil.

Braised stuffed artichokes

Trim and tie large artichokes. Blanch for 5 minutes in boiling water, cool under the tap, drain and remove the small central leaves and the choke. Season with salt and pepper. Fill the artichokes with a meat stuffing (made, for example, with 4 parts sausagemeat to 1 part onion softened in butter, and some chopped parsley). Wrap them in thin slices of fat bacon and tie them. Butter a sauté dish and line the base with bacon rashers (slices), and sliced onions and carrots. Place the artichokes on top, season with salt and pepper, and add a bouquet garni. Cover and begin cooking over a low heat. Moisten with a small quantity of dry white wine, and reduce. Add a few tablespoons of veal stock, cover and cook in a preheated oven at 180°C (350°F, gas 4) for about an hour, basting frequently. Drain the artichokes, untie them and remove the bacon rashers. Arrange the artichokes on a round dish. Strain and skim fat from the cooking liquor, add some demi-glace or any other reduced sauce, and use to coat the artichokes.

Casseroled artichokes

Choose small Italian or violet Provençal artichokes, and trim the leaves to two-thirds of their length. Blanch the artichokes, drain, remove the centre leaves and choke, and fill them with a stuffing made from breadcrumbs, chopped garlic, capers, parsley and salt and pepper. Arrange the artichokes close together in a casserole, moisten with a generous quantity of olive oil and season with salt and pepper. Cook in a preheated oven at 180°C (350°F, gas 4), uncovered, for about 50 minutes, basting from time to time. To serve, arrange the artichokes on a dish and pour the cooking juices over them.

Noisettes Beauharnais

Braise some small artichoke hearts in butter. In another pan, sauté some lamb noisettes in butter, arrange them on fried croûtons and keep hot. Prepare some noisette potatoes and a béarnaise sauce, and pour the sauce over the artichoke hearts. Deglaze the meat pan with Madeira, boil down to reduce and add some chopped mushrooms. Arrange the noisettes on a serving dish with the artichoke hearts and the noisette potatoes and cover with the sauce.

Scrambled eggs with artichokes

Cook the artichokes in water until tender and remove the leaves and the choke. Slice the artichoke hearts crossways and sauté them in butter. Make the scrambled eggs and add half the artichoke hearts. Arrange the mixture on a dish, garnish the top with the remaining slices of artichoke and fried croûtons, and surround with a ribbon of concentrated veal stock.

Young whole, trimmed artichokes

These may be braised without stuffing, devilled, cooked *à la lyonnaise* or *à la mirepoix*, or used in any of the recipes for artichokes.

Asparagus

To prepare

Lay the asparagus stalks flat on a chopping board and cut them all to the same length. Peel them, working from the tip to the base, and clean the tips with a pointed knife if necessary. Wash the asparagus in plenty of water but do not soak. Drain and tie into bunches or small bundles.

Plunge the bundles of asparagus into boiling salted water – 1½ teaspoons salt to 1 litre (1¾ pints, 4⅓ cups) – water and cook for 20–30 minutes depending on the thickness. Remove the asparagus as soon as it is tender, and drain either on a plate covered with a napkin or on a draining rack. There are special cylindrical pans for cooking asparagus. The stalks are held upright and water is added to cover the stems but not the tips. The lid is replaced during cooking. The tips are more tender if they are cooked in the steam.

At the end of the season, asparagus becomes a little bitter. Blanch for 5 minutes and drain it, then complete cooking in fresh water.

Asparagus à la flamande

Cook some asparagus in salted boiling water. Serve hot with melted butter to which sieved yolks of hard-boiled (hard-cooked) eggs and chopped parsley have been added.

Asparagus à la polonaise

Clean some asparagus and trim to the same length. Tie into small bunches and cook for 25 minutes in plenty of boiling salted water (to which may be added 1 tablespoon flour to help the asparagus keep its colour). Drain thoroughly and arrange in a long buttered dish, in staggered rows, so that the tips show clearly. Sprinkle with sieved hard-boiled (hard-cooked) egg yolk and chopped parsley. Lightly brown some breadcrumbs in noisette butter and pour over the asparagus. Serve immediately.

Asparagus aspic

Coat the base and sides of ramekins with aspic jelly. Cut asparagus tips to the height of the ramekins and arrange them so that they stand upright around the edge, closely pressed together. Fill the centre of the ramekins with a purée of foie gras. Cover with aspic and leave to chill in the refrigerator for several hours before serving.

Asparagus au gratin

Cook the asparagus in boiling salted water, drain and arrange on an ovenproof dish, staggering the layers in order to expose the tips and hide the stalks. Coat the tips with a layer of Mornay sauce. Place a strip of foil over the uncoated parts. Sprinkle with grated Parmesan cheese, drizzle over melted butter and brown in the oven or under the grill (broiler). Remove the foil just before serving.

Asparagus charlotte

Trim 1 kg (2¼ lb) very fine green asparagus. Cook it in a generous quantity of salted water and then drain. Set aside 6 asparagus tips and pass the remainder through a fine sieve or a blender. Pour the resulting purée into a small saucepan and dry it out over a very gentle heat.

Plunge 12 cherry tomatoes into boiling water, peel and halve them, and remove the seeds. Soften them over a gentle heat and add salt and pepper. Peel 12 small pearl (button) onions, brown them in butter, add some stock and cook them until they are very tender. Make a zabaglione with 1 egg yolk, omitting the sugar.

Beat 2 eggs in a bowl with some salt and pepper. Add the tomatoes, asparagus purée, onions and half the zabaglione. Stir gently with a wooden spoon until thoroughly mixed. Warm 100 ml (4 fl oz, 7 tablespoons) double (heavy) cream, whisk it slightly, and then add it to the vegetable mixture.

Pour the preparation into a buttered charlotte mould. Place it in a preheated oven at about 160°C (325°F, gas 3) and cook for just under 1 hour. Heat the 6 asparagus tips in a bain marie. Turn out the cooked charlotte on to a serving dish and surround with a rosette of asparagus tips. Coat with the remaining zabaglione.

Asparagus mousse with orange butter

Cook 200 g (7 oz) trimmed green asparagus spears in well-salted boiling water. Cool down quickly in a bowl of iced water, drain and dry on a cloth. Place in a blender with 2 whole eggs, 1 egg yolk, 50 g (2 oz) uncooked white chicken meat and 2 tablespoons crème fraîche. Add 7 tablespoons pouring cream, 2 tablespoons truffle juice, salt and pepper. Purée in a blender until the mixture is smooth.

Butter 4 stainless steel rings 6 cm (2½ in) in diameter and 4 cm (1½ in) high. Place on a roasting tin (pan) which will act as a bain marie. Cook 100 g (4 oz) green asparagus tips, 5 cm (2 in) long. (Check that there are sufficient asparagus tips to line the sides of the rings.) Carefully arrange them vertically at regular intervals around the edge of each ring. Next fill the rings to the top with the asparagus mousse so that the asparagus tips stick out by 1 cm (½ in). Pour water into the tin up to one-third the height of the rings. Cook in a preheated oven at 110°C (225°F, gas ¼) for 20 minutes.

In a small sauté pan, reduce the juice of an orange with the blanched, finely shredded zest of ½ orange. (Reserve the remaining blanched zest for garnishing.) Whisking continually, add 100 g (4 oz, ¼ cup) butter cut into small pieces. Season with salt and pepper. Put aside in a warm place. Carefully transfer each stainless steel ring to a serving dish, slide a thin knife blade round the ring to loosen the mousse and remove the ring. Pour the orange butter around the mousse. Garnish with orange segments and blanched zest.

Asparagus ragoût with young garden peas

Take equal quantities of shelled young garden peas and peeled asparagus. Cut the asparagus into 2 cm (¾ in) lengths. Sauté some small onions in a pan with butter, oil or, ideally, goose fat. When they have browned, add the asparagus and peas, cover, and sweat for 5 minutes. Add salt, pepper, a little sugar and enough chicken stock to just cover. Cover the pan and cook over a low heat for 15 minutes. Arrange the ragoût in a vegetable dish and serve.

Asparagus tart

Cover a pastry case (pie shell), baked blind, with a layer of creamed chicken purée. Garnish with asparagus tips that have been gently cooked in butter. Coat with cream sauce or suprême sauce. Sprinkle with fried breadcrumbs and brown in the oven.

Asparagus velouté soup

Prepare a white roux with 40 g (1½ oz, 3 tablespoons) butter and 40 g (1½ oz, 6 tablespoons) flour. Moisten with a generous 750 ml (1¼ pints, 3¼ cups) chicken consommé. Cut 400 g (14 oz) washed asparagus into pieces, blanch for 5 minutes in boiling water, drain and then simmer with 40 g (1½ oz, 3 tablespoons) butter for about 10 minutes. Reduce to a purée in a food processor or blender and add to the consommé. Dilute with a little consommé to obtain the desired consistency and heat. Remove from the heat and thicken the soup with a mixture of 3 egg yolks beaten with 100 ml (4 fl oz, 7 tablespoons) double (heavy) cream. Finally, whisk in 75 g (3 oz, 6 tablespoons) butter. Reheat but do not boil. Garnish with cooked asparagus tips and chopped parsley.

Buisson of asparagus in pastry

Buisson is the term for a traditional method of arranging food, especially crayfish and asparagus, pressed together in a pyramid. The term is now also used for fried smelts and *goujonnettes* of sole arranged in a dome with a garnish of fried parsley.

Cook some very thick white asparagus tips in salted water, keeping them slightly firm. Drain and wipe dry. One by one, coat them in a little mayonnaise stiffened with gelatine. Bake a thin pastry case (pie shell) blind and half-fill with a salad of green asparagus tips and very fine slices of truffle. Arrange the white asparagus tips on top in a pyramid.

Canapés with asparagus

Spread some thickened mayonnaise on rectangular slices of bread. Arrange very small asparagus tips on each canapé and 'tie' each bunch with a thin strip of green or red sweet pepper.

Cream of asparagus soup

Shred and blanch 400 g (14 oz) asparagus tips, then cook them in 40–50 g
(1½–2 oz, 3–4 tablespoons) butter. Prepare 750 ml (1¼ pints, 3¼ cups) white
sauce using 900 ml (1½ pints, 1 quart) milk to a white roux of 25 g (1 oz,
2 tablespoons) butter and 40 g (1½ oz, 6 tablespoons) plain (all-purpose)
flour and purée with the cooked asparagus in a food processor or blender.
Reheat and season the soup, then thin with a little cream before serving.

Royale of asparagus

Cook 75 g (3 oz) asparagus tips and 5 or 6 fresh spinach leaves in boiling
water for a few minutes, then drain them thoroughly. Add 1½ tablespoons
béchamel sauce and 2 tablespoons consommé. Press through a sieve. Bind the
mixture with 4 egg yolks, pour into buttered dariole moulds and cook in a
bain marie in a preheated oven at 200°C (400°F, gas 6) for 30 minutes.
Unmould and serve.

Aubergines (eggplant)

To prepare

Traditionally, the slightly bitter taste of aubergines (eggplants) was minimized by sprinkling the sliced or cut up flesh with salt and leaving it for 30 minutes to draw out bitter juices. The aubergine was then rinsed and dried before cooking. This process of degorging is no longer necessary as commercially cultivated aubergines are no longer as bitter as they used to be.

Aubergines may be stuffed in two ways depending on their size and shape. They may be cut in half lengthways and the flesh scooped out of each half. Alternatively, the top may be removed and the aubergine hollowed out inside. Use a sharp knife to remove the flesh, leaving a thickness of 5 mm (¼ in) around the edge, and scoop out the remainder of the flesh from the base with a grapefruit knife. Sprinkle the empty case and the flesh with lemon juice to prevent discoloration.

Aubergine caviar

Cook 3 big, heavy, whole aubergines (eggplants), in a preheated oven at about 200°C (400°F, gas 6) for 15–20 minutes until tender. Hard boil (hard cook) 4 eggs, cool under a cold tap and shell them. Peel and seed 2 tomatoes and chop the flesh. Peel and finely chop an onion. Cut the aubergines in half, remove the flesh and chop it up with a knife. Mix the tomatoes, aubergine flesh and onion in a salad bowl. Season with salt and pepper and slowly work in 1 small glass olive oil, stirring as for mayonnaise. Alternatively, purée the mixture in a blender. Place in the refrigerator until ready to serve. Garnish with quarters of hard-boiled eggs and tomato slices.

Aubergine fritters

Peel some aubergines (eggplants), slice them and marinate for 1 hour in olive oil, lemon juice, chopped parsley, salt and pepper. Mix together with a fork (or in a blender) some hard-boiled (hard-cooked) egg yolk, a little butter and some chopped parsley. Spread the mixture on the aubergine slices. Dip the slices in batter, deep-fry in hot oil, drain and serve on a napkin. The same method may be used for broccoli, cardoons, celery, celeriac (celery root), courgettes (zucchini), cauliflower, marrow (squash) flowers, salsify, tomatoes and Jerusalem artichokes.

Aubergine omelette

Add 2 tablespoons diced aubergines (eggplants), sautéed in oil, to 8 eggs and beat together. Cook the omelette.

Aubergine papeton

Prepare 500 ml (17 fl oz, 2 cups) very reduced tomato fondue. Peel 2 kg (4½ lb) aubergines (eggplants), cut them into cubes, sprinkle with fine salt and leave them to exude their juice for 1 hour. Wash the aubergine cubes in cold water, wipe them thoroughly, then sprinkle lightly with flour and cook very gently in 4 tablespoons olive oil until soft. Season with salt and leave to cool, then purée in a food processor or blender.

Mix 7 large eggs, beaten as for an omelette, with 100 ml (4 fl oz, 7 table-spoons)milk, 2 finely crushed garlic cloves, some salt, pepper and a pinch of cayenne. Stir in the aubergine purée and pour into a buttered manqué mould or soufflé dish. Place this mould in a bain marie, bring it to the boil on the top of the stove, then transfer it to a preheated oven and cook at 180°C (350°F, gas 4) for 1 hour. Turn out on to a warmed serving dish and coat with the hot tomato fondue.

Aubergine soufflés

Cook 3 big, heavy, whole aubergines (eggplants), in a preheated oven at about 200°C (400°F, gas 6) for 15–20 minutes until tender. Cut the aubergines in half, remove the flesh and chop it up with a knife. Press the flesh through a sieve or purée in a blender and add an equal quantity of reduced béchamel sauce. Bind with egg yolks and season with salt, pepper and grated nutmeg. At the last moment, fold in very stiffly whisked egg whites. Fill the aubergine cases with the mixture and arrange them in a gratin dish. Sprinkle with Parmesan cheese, if desired, and cook in a preheated oven at 200°C (400°F, gas 6) for about 10 minutes.

For aubergine soufflés *à la hongroise*, add 2 tablespoons chopped onion softened in butter to the filling and season with paprika.

Caponata

Peel 4 aubergines (eggplants), cut into large dice and sprinkle with salt. When they have lost some of their water, wash and wipe them and fry in oil. Cut the following ingredients into very small pieces: 100 g (4 oz, ¾ cup) olives, a head of celery scalded in salted water, 4 desalted anchovies and 50 g (2 oz, 3 tablespoons) capers. Slice an onion and brown in oil. Heat up 200 ml (7 fl oz, ¾ cup) tomato passata (purée) with 50 g (2 oz, ¼ cup) sugar until it is well reduced and darker in colour, then add 3 tablespoons vinegar and leave to simmer for a few minutes. Season with salt and pepper, add some chopped parsley, then mix the sauce with the aubergines and other ingredients. Allow to cool thoroughly. Arrange in the shape of a dome in a vegetable dish.

Gratin languedocien

Half-cook in oil 4 peeled and sliced aubergines (eggplants), seasoned with salt and pepper, and 12 halved, seasoned tomatoes. Arrange them in alternate layers in a flameproof dish. Cover with a mixture of breadcrumbs, chopped garlic and parsley. Sprinkle with olive oil. Begin cooking on the top of the stove, then bake slowly in a preheated oven at 180°C (350°F, gas 4) until the top is well browned.

Imam bayildi

A Turkish dish of stuffed aubergines (eggplants) whose name means 'the imam fainted'. According to legend, when aubergines prepared in this way were offered to a certain imam (priest), he was so moved by the fragrant odour of the dish that he fainted from sheer gastronomical joy!

Soak 200 g (7 oz, 1 cup) currants in a little tepid water. Wipe 4 long aubergines (eggplants) and, without peeling them, slice them in half lengthways. Carefully remove the pulp without piercing the skin, cut it into small dice and sprinkle with lemon juice. Peel and chop 4 large onions; peel, seed and crush 8 large tomatoes; and chop a small bunch of parsley. Heat 4–5 tablespoons olive oil and brown the diced aubergine, tomato pulp, chopped onion and parsley. Add salt, pepper, a sprig of thyme and a bay leaf. Cover the pan and cook gently over a low heat for about 20 minutes. Then add 2 crushed garlic cloves and the drained currants. Mix everything together thoroughly and cook for a further 5 minutes. Grease an ovenproof dish remove the thyme and the bay leaf, arrange the aubergine halves in the dish, and fill them with the mixture. Pour some olive oil around the aubergines and add a little fresh thyme and some crumbled bay leaf. Cook in a preheated oven at 160°C (325°F, gas 3) for 2 hours. Serve hot, warm or cold.

Rougail of aubergines

Remove the stalks from 2 or 3 aubergines (eggplants) weighing in total about 300 g (11 oz) and cook them for 20–25 minutes in a preheated oven at 220°C

(425°F, gas 7). Meanwhile, in a food processor, purée 1 small new onion, a small piece of fresh root ginger, ½ red chilli pepper, ½ teaspoon salt, the juice of ½ lemon and 3–4 tablespoons olive oil. Halve the aubergines and remove the pulp with a spoon. Mix this pulp with the other ingredients and blend well to obtain a fine paste. Chill until ready to serve.

Sautéed aubergines

Cut the aubergines (eggplants) into 2 cm (¾ in) cubes and coat with flour. Sauté the cubes in olive oil in a frying pan. Arrange in a vegetable dish and sprinkle with chopped parsley.

Stuffed aubergines

Cook 6 small aubergines (eggplants) in a preheated oven at about 200°C (400°F, gas 6) for 15–20 minutes until tender. Cut the aubergines in half, remove the flesh and chop it with a knife. Sprinkle each hollow shell with salt and 1 tablespoon olive oil and arrange in an ovenproof dish. Cook them in a preheated oven at 220°C (425°F, gas 7) for 15 minutes. Place all the diced flesh in another dish, cover and cook it in the oven at the same time. Meanwhile, stone (pit) and finely chop 100 g (4 oz) large black olives and put them in a large bowl. Heat 1 tablespoon olive oil in a frying pan, add 6 anchovy fillets and mash them to an oily purée. Pour this purée into the bowl of olives and add the cooked crushed aubergine flesh and 1 crushed garlic clove and some thyme. Season with salt and pepper and mix well. Fill the aubergine shells with the mixture and flatten with a fork. Heat thoroughly in the hot oven.

Stuffed aubergines à la catalane

Cut 2 good-sized aubergines (eggplants) in half lengthways to form boat shapes. Leaving a 1 cm (½ in) rim around the top, scoop out the flesh without damaging the skin. Chop the flesh together with 2 hard-boiled (hard-cooked) eggs, 2 crushed garlic cloves and some parsley. In olive oil, lightly cook 2 large chopped onions per aubergine, add it to the egg and aubergine mixture, and fill the aubergine boats. Arrange in an ovenproof dish, sprinkle with fresh breadcrumbs and oil, and cook in a preheated oven at 220°C (425°F, gas 7–8).

Stuffed aubergines à l'italienne

Cook 6 small aubergines (eggplants) in a preheated oven at about 200°C (400°F, gas 6) for 15–20 minutes until tender. Cut the aubergines in half, remove the flesh and chop it with a knife. Mix the chopped flesh with an equal quantity of risotto seasoned with chopped parsley and garlic. Fill the aubergine shells with this mixture and sprinkle breadcrumbs over the top. Sprinkle with olive oil and brown in the oven or under the grill.

Avocado

Alienor salad

Mix 2 tablespoons grated horseradish with enough crème fraîche to give a smooth sauce with a strong flavour. Trim 2 smoked trout and remove the fillets, taking out all the bones. Cover 4 plates with lettuce. Cut a large avocado – stone (pit) removed – into thin slices; arrange the slices on the plates and sprinkle them with lemon juice. Arrange 2 fillets of trout, coarsely shredded, on each plate. Coat with the horseradish sauce. Sprinkle with a few flaked (slivered) almonds and complete with slices of gherkin.

Avocado and prawn barquettes

A barquette is a small boat-shaped tart made of short-crust pastry (basic pie dough) or puff pastry, baked blind and then filled with various sweet or savoury ingredients.

Mix some mashed avocado to which some lemon juice has been added with an equal volume of mayonnaise. Season with salt and pepper and add a little cayenne. Fill the cooked barquettes with this mixture and garnish with shelled prawns (shrimp).

Avocado salad archestrate

Cut the heart of a head of celery into thin strips. Dice 3 cooked artichoke hearts and 3 peeled and seeded tomatoes. Halve 4 avocados and carefully remove the flesh, keeping each half intact. Slice the flesh and sprinkle with lemon juice. Season the avocado and vegetables with vinaigrette, arrange in a salad bowl and sprinkle with chopped herbs.

Avocado salad with crab

Cut 3–4 avocados in half and scoop out the flesh with a small spoon. Mix the flesh with crumbled crabmeat, diced tomato flesh, slices of hard-boiled (hard-cooked) egg, pepper and a little tomato purée or ketchup. Sprinkle with chopped herbs and serve cold.

Avocado salad with cucumber

Assemble equal quantities of avocado (halved, stoned, peeled, diced and sprinkled with lemon juice) and halved, seeded and sliced cucumber in a salad bowl. Dress with vinaigrette, flavoured with mustard, and sprinkle with some chopped mixed herbs.

Avocado sauce

Blend together avocado flesh with lemon juice in the following proportions: 2 tablespoons lemon juice to a medium-sized avocado. Mix with an equal volume of whipping cream. Serve very cold with hot or cold meat or poultry, with quarters of lemon.

Avocados stuffed with crab

Prepare a mayonnaise and season it with mustard and cayenne pepper. Crumble some crabmeat (fresh, canned or frozen). Halve the avocados and scoop out the flesh in large pieces, then cut it into even-sized cubes. Sprinkle the flesh and the insides of the avocado shells with lemon juice and season them with salt and pepper to taste. Mix the mayonnaise with the crabmeat and carefully stir in the chopped avocado flesh. Pile the filling into the avocado shells. If you like, the avocados can be garnished with mayonnaise flavoured with a little tomato purée (paste) piping it with a star (fluted) nozzle. Dust with paprika.

Avocados stuffed with shrimps

Prepare a mayonnaise and season it with mustard and cayenne pepper. Mix the mayonnaise with shrimps (fresh, canned or frozen). Sprinkle the flesh and the insides of the avocado shells with lemon juice and season them with salt and pepper to taste. Mix the mayonnaise with the shrimps and carefully add the chopped avocado flesh. Pile the filling into the shells. If you like, the avocados can be garnished with mayonnaise flavoured with a little tomato purée (paste) piping it with a star (fluted) nozzle. Dust with paprika.

Californian avocado salad

Peel 2 grapefruit, removing all the pith, then cut the segments from between the membranes. Place the fruit segments in a salad bowl. Halve 3 avocados, remove the flesh, dice it and sprinkle with lemon juice. Add to the salad bowl together with 150–200 g (5–7 oz) shelled shrimps. Sprinkle with 2 table-spoons gin or brandy and add 3–5 tablespoons mayonnaise flavoured with a little ketchup and cayenne pepper. Garnish with slices of lemon.

Cornmeal pancakes with avocados

Make a pancake batter with 250 g (9 oz, 2 cups) cornmeal, 3 eggs, salt, pepper, 2–3 tablespoons oil or melted butter and 500 ml (17 fl oz, 2 cups) warm milk, or a mixture of milk and water. Beat the ingredients together until smooth then set the batter aside. Purée the flesh of 3 avocados in a food processor or blender, adding cayenne, salt, pepper and 3 tablespoons olive oil. Cover with cling film (plastic wrap) and put in a cool place. Add some chopped tarragon to the cornmeal batter and make the pancakes, then allow them to cool. Spread the pancakes with avocado purée, roll them up and hold them together with cocktail sticks (toothpicks). Serve cold, with a tomato salad sprinkled with snipped chives.

Grilled avocado with mozzarella

Mix 4 finely chopped spring onions (salad onions) with 100 g (4 oz) finely diced mozzarella cheese and the grated rind (zest) from 1 lemon. Peel, seed and dice 2 tomatoes. Halve and stone (pit) 2 firm but ripe avocados, then arrange them in a fireproof tin (pan) or dish, supporting them with crumpled foil. Sprinkle with lemon juice and trickle with olive oil. Grill (broil) until hot and lightly browned. Divide the tomatoes between the avocados, sprinkle with seasoning, then top with the mozzarella mixture. Continue grilling until golden brown and bubbling. Serve at once.

Guacamole

Finely chop ¼ small onion and mix with 2 peeled, seeded and diced tomatoes, 1 seeded and finely chopped green chilli, 1 finely chopped large garlic clove, the juice of ½ lime and a little grated zest from about a quarter of the lime. Mash the flesh from 2 large ripe avocados in a mixing bowl, then add the vegetable mixture and gradually beat in 2 tablespoons olive oil. Stir in 2–3 tablespoons chopped fresh coriander (cilantro) and seasoning to taste.

Iced avocado velouté soup

Using a melon baller, scoop out some balls of pulp from a small peeled and seeded cucumber. Blanch them rapidly in boiling water. Peel a firm ripe tomato after dipping it in boiling water, and cut the flesh into very small dice. Halve 3 avocados, remove the stones (pits) and scoop out all the pulp with a spoon. Put the pulp through a food processor or blender, adding the juice of 1 lemon, 4 tablespoons crème fraîche and 100 ml (4 fl oz, 7 tablespoons) milk. Season with salt and dust with cayenne pepper. Place in the refrigerator to chill. Pour the soup into 4 bowls and garnish with the cucumber balls, the diced tomato and 6 finely chopped mint leaves. Serve ice cold.

Barley

To prepare

Pearl barley is the hulled and milled grain, pot barley is unhulled; both are used chiefly in soups, broths and stews, such as oxtail soup, *cholent* and Scotch broth. Pearl barley can be boiled and served as an alternative to rice.

Consommé with pearl barley

Wash 100 g (4 oz, ½ cup) pearl barley in warm water and add it, with 1 celery stick, to 2.5 litres (4¼ pints, 11 cups) clarified beef stock. Simmer for 2 hours, then remove the celery and serve the soup in cups.

Cream of barley soup

Wash 300 g (11 oz, 1½ cups) pearl barley and soak it for 1 hour in warm water. Add the drained barley and 1 sliced celery stick to 1 litre (1¾ pints, 4⅓ cups) clear white stock and simmer for 2½ hours. Rub the soup through a fine sieve and dilute with a few tablespoons of stock or milk. Heat the soup through again and add 200 ml (7 fl oz, ¾ cup) double (heavy) cream.

Polish kasha with barley

Pick over 350 g (12 oz, 1⅓ cups) pearl barley and blanch in boiling water for 2 minutes. Bring 3 litres (5 pints, 13 cups) milk and 65 g (2½ oz, 5 tablespoons) butter to the boil, then add the barley. Bring to the boil, reduce the heat so that the mixture simmers and cook, stirring frequently, until the barley is soft – about 1 hour. Take the pan off the heat and add 200 g (7 oz, 1 cup) butter. Cool for about 10 minutes before stirring in 6 lightly beaten eggs and 100 ml (4 fl oz, 7 tablespoons) soured (sour) cream. Pour the mixture into a buttered charlotte mould and cook in a preheated oven at 200°C (400°F, gas 6) until set and golden on top. Serve it in the mould with double (heavy) cream served separately.

Beans, fresh & dried

To prepare dried beans

Dried beans are usually soaked before cooking, as this reduces the cooking time. Soaking also allows the skins to rehydrate and the beans to plump up, preventing both from separating during boiling. Overnight soaking in plenty of cold water is best, though soaking in boiling water will reduce the time. Beans should not be left in warm water or in a warm room and they should not be soaked for more than 24 hours, as they may ferment and produce poisonous substances. For this reason always use fresh water for cooking.

Boil beans rapidly to destroy natural toxins, then reduce the heat to keep the water just on the boil. Cook for 45 minutes to 1½ hours, or longer for soya beans to become tender. A bouquet garni, 1 onion studded with 2 cloves, 1 garlic clove and 1 diced carrot can be added during cooking. Do not add salt, as this will prevent the beans from becoming tender or will even harden part-cooked beans. Season beans when they are thoroughly tender. The old way was to include a pinch of bicarbonate of soda (baking soda) in the cooking water to speed cooking, but this is not advised now, for nutritional reasons.

To prepare podded fresh haricot beans

Remove the fresh beans from their pods. Cook in boiling salted water with a bouquet garni and vegetables to flavour (such as carrots, turnips, leeks and diced celery).

Alternatively, cook either 1 sliced onion and 1 sliced carrot or the white parts of leeks and some sliced celery sticks in butter until soft. Then add sufficient water to amply cover the beans when they are put in, together with a bouquet garni and a 300 g (11 oz) blanched and drained piece of lean green bacon. Cook for 30 minutes, add the beans, and simmer until they and the bacon are cooked (the time required will depend on the freshness and tenderness of the beans).

Broad beans with savory

Shell, skin and cook some broad beans in salted boiling water with a bunch of savory. Drain them well and heat in a shallow frying pan for a few moments until thoroughly dry. Add a generous knob of butter and a little cream. Mix gently over a low heat for a few seconds, taking care to ensure that the beans do not break.

Cabécou figs en coffret with bean salad

Coarsely chop a small bunch of chives. Cook 400 g (14 oz) very fine green beans in salted water, keeping them al dente. Soak 65 g (2½ oz, ⅓ cup) sultanas (golden raisins) in 60 ml (2 fl oz, ¼ cup) vinaigrette until very soft.

Cut 2 Cabécou goat's cheeses into quarters. Cut 8 figs 1.5 cm (¾ in) from the top, reserving the tops, and remove one-third of the flesh. Fill each fig with one quarter of Cabécou. Using a pastry (cookie) cutter with a fluted edge, cut out 6 cm (2½ in) rounds of very thinly rolled puff pastry and brush with beaten egg. Place a fig on each piece of puff pastry and bake in a preheated oven at 200°C (400°F, gas 6) for 20 minutes. After 15 minutes, replace the tops of the figs.

Toss the green beans with the sultana vinaigrette and add the chives. Arrange 2 figs in puff pastry on each plate and add some of the bean salad. Sprinkle with toasted flaked almonds and serve at once.

Cockle salad with fresh broad beans

Heat some cockles until they open, remove the walnut-sized pieces of flesh and keep warm. Peel some fresh broad (fava) beans, blanch them for 5 minutes in boiling salted water, then rinse in cold water. Pour some vinaigrette mixed with chopped herbs into a salad bowl. Add the beans and the cockles, toss quickly and serve.

Crab and beansprout salad

Clean and cook 2 large crabs. Wash, scald and cool 500 g (18 oz, 4½ cups) bean sprouts and dry them. Mix 4 tablespoons mayonnaise, 1 tablespoon ketchup or very concentrated sieved tomato purée and at least 1 tablespoon brandy. Mix the crabmeat, the bean sprouts and the sauce and serve on a bed of lettuce leaves. Sprinkle with chopped herbs.

Estouffat of haricot beans à l'occitane

Estouffat is a Languedoc dialect word for a dish that is stewed very slowly. In that region it is used mainly for a stew of pork and haricot (navy) beans, flavoured with garlic, onions and tomatoes.

Brown a diced carrot and a sliced onion in either goose fat or lard in a pan. Add 1.5 litres (2¾ pints, 6½ cups) water and a bouquet garni, bring to the boil and simmer for about 20 minutes. Add 1.5 litres (2¾ pints, 6½ cups) fresh white haricot (navy) beans and cook until almost tender, then drain. Cut

250 g (9 oz) slightly salted belly bacon into cubes, blanch and brown in goose fat or lard. Add to the pan 150 g (5 oz, ¾ cup) chopped onions, 2 large tomatoes (peeled and crushed) and 1 crushed garlic clove, and cook for a further 10 minutes. Then add the drained beans, cover the pan and gently simmer until cooking is completed.

If liked, 200 g (7 oz) rind from preserved pork may be added to the bean cooking liquid. When cooked, the rind is cut into squares and added to the beans in the serving dish.

Feijoada

A Brazilian speciality whose basic ingredient is the black bean (*frijol negro*). It is a complete dish served on special occasions: a mixture of meat and beans is poured into the centre of a plate and surrounded by rice *au gras*, green cabbage (thinly sliced and fried) and a few slices of orange (peel and pith removed). A mixture of grilled (broiled) manioc flour, onion and other ingredients, together called *farofa*, is sprinkled over the whole plate. The dish is served with a very spicy sauce, *molho carioca*, made with cayenne pepper, vinegar, the cooking liquid from the beans, chopped tomatoes and onions.

Soak 1 kg (2¼ lb) black beans in cold water for 12 hours and, in another container, 1 semi-salted pig's tail and 500 g (1 lb 2 oz) lean, smoked bacon, changing the water in both containers several times. Peel 5 garlic cloves. Drain the beans and put them in a large braising pan. Cover with plenty of water and season with salt. Add 4 garlic cloves and 3 bay leaves. Bring to the boil and simmer gently for 1 hour. Drain the meats and boil for 10 minutes, then set aside. Seed 2 sweet (bell) peppers and cut into strips. Scald 500 g (1 lb 2 oz) tomatoes, peel, seed and crush. Finely chop 1 small bunch parsley and 1 small bunch chives. Heat 3 tablespoons oil in a frying pan. Add 1 chopped onion and fry until golden. Add the peppers, tomatoes, the remaining garlic clove and the parsley. Cook for 20 minutes over a medium heat, stirring all the time. Season to taste. When the beans can be crushed between the fingers, remove a ladleful of them and a ladleful of cooking liquid. Purée the beans and return to the pan. Sprinkle with chives and set aside. Slice 6 small fresh sausages, 6 small smoked sausages and 1 chorizo. Add the various meats to the pan. Season with salt and paprika. Cook for a further hour, stirring in the tomato and onion purée halfway through cooking.

Prepare the farofa. Soak 100 g (4 oz, ⅔ cup) raisins in lukewarm water for 10 minutes. Melt 40 g (1½ oz, 3 tablespoons) butter in a frying pan and fry 1 large chopped onion. Add salt and 100 g (4 oz, 1 cup) manioc flour, then 40 g (1½ oz, 3 tablespoons) butter to obtain a kind of light, sand-coloured mixture. Add 1 sliced banana, the drained raisins and 50 g (2 oz, ½ cup) grilled (broiled) cashew nuts.

Serve with rice mixed with slices of orange and onion, allowing each person to sprinkle over more farofa.

French bean salad

Cook the beans just long enough for them to remain slightly crisp. Drain them and dry off any remaining water. Cut them in two and leave them to cool. Add a few chopped spring onions (scallions) and some well-flavoured vinaigrette. Mix and sprinkle with chopped parsley. Alternatively, the beans can be tossed in olive oil, sprinkled with pine kernels, and arranged in a lattice with long strips of marinated red peppers.

French beans à la lyonnaise

Cook the beans in boiling salted water and drain them well. For every 800 g (1¾ lb) beans, prepare 225 g (8 oz) sliced onions and cook gently in butter in a sauté pan until golden brown. Add the beans, season with salt and pepper, and sauté until the beans are slightly browned. Add 1 tablespoon vinegar and mix well. Turn into a dish and sprinkle with chopped parsley.

French beans in tomato sauce

Boil the beans in salted water until they are three-quarters cooked, and drain thoroughly. Cook them gently in butter for about 5 minutes, add a few tablespoons of concentrated tomato sauce and simmer. Turn into a dish and sprinkle with chopped parsley or basil.

French beans sautéed à la provençale

Cook the beans and drain them thoroughly. Heat some olive oil in a large saucepan and brown the beans lightly. At the last moment add some chopped garlic and parsley; use 1 garlic clove and a small bunch of parsley for every 800 g (1¾ lb) beans.

French beans with cream

Boil the beans in salted water until they are three-quarters cooked, Drain. Cover with single (light) cream and simmer until the cream is reduced by half. Add salt and pepper and transfer to a serving dish. A sprinkling of chopped parsley can also be added.

This dish can be prepared *à la normande*: for every 450 g (1 lb) beans, add 1 egg yolk and 40 g (1½ oz, 3 tablespoons) butter after removing the pan from the heat.

Green beans bonne femme

Partially cook 1 kg (2¼ lb) green beans in salted water. Blanch 250 g (9 oz, 1½ cups) diced unsmoked streaky (slab) bacon. Brown the blanched bacon in a frying pan, then add the drained beans and 150 ml (¼ pint, ⅔ cup) rich meat stock. Taste and adjust the seasoning, cover the pan and cook until the beans are tender. Dot them with butter and sprinkle with chopped parsley before serving.

Haricot bean salad

Cook the beans, allow them to cool and then drain. Add a chopped mild onion to the beans, mix with a well-flavoured vinaigrette, and sprinkle with chopped herbs (parsley, chervil and chives).

Haricot beans in tomato sauce

Cook the beans with 500 g (18 oz) lean bacon in one piece for each 1 kg (2¼ lb) beans. When the beans are cooked, drain them and mix with 300 ml (½ pint, 1¼ cups) tomato sauce. Drain the bacon, dice it and add it to the beans. Simmer for about 10 minutes and serve very hot. This dish can also be browned in the oven.

Haricot beans with onions

Cook and drain the beans. Cook some sliced onions gently in butter – allow 200 g (7 oz) onions for each 1 kg (2¼ lb) cooked beans. Add the beans, cover the pan, simmer for 6 minutes and serve sprinkled with chopped parsley.

Haricots à la crème

Cook the beans, drain them and warm them gently in a saucepan until nearly all the moisture has evaporated. Cover with crème fraîche, warm through again, add some chopped savory and serve very hot.

An alternative method is to butter a gratin dish, pour in the cooked beans mixed with cream, sprinkle the dish with white breadcrumbs and melted butter, and brown in a very hot oven or under the grill (broiler).

Maître d'hôtel French beans

String and slice the beans and place them in a large pan of boiling water. Cook at a rolling boil, uncovered, and season with salt halfway through cooking. Drain thoroughly and mix in 50 g (2 oz, ¼ cup) maître d'hôtel butter per 450 g (1 lb) cooked beans. Serve with a little chopped parsley.

Mixed green beans

Take equal quantities of French beans and flageolets and cook them separately. Drain well and mix together. Blend in some butter or cream and sprinkle with chopped *fines herbes*.

Purée of French beans

Half-cook the beans. Drain them thoroughly and then cook gently in butter for 7–8 minutes, allowing 50 g (2 oz, ¼ cup) butter for every 800 g (1¾ lb) beans. Purée the beans in an electric blender or rub them through a fine sieve. (A quarter of its volume of mashed potato can be added to the bean purée.) To serve, warm through and add more butter.

Purée of fresh broad beans

Shell and skin 500 g (18 oz) fresh broad beans and simmer in a covered pan with 7 tablespoons water, 50 g (2 oz, ¼ cup) butter, a sprig of savory, a pinch of salt and 1 teaspoon sugar. Pureé in a blender. Add some consommé to the purée if liked.

Purée of fresh podded haricot beans

Cook the fresh white beans using the basic method (page 39). Drain them, then rub through a sieve to remove the skins. Pour this purée into a saucepan and warm gently, stirring with a wooden spoon until the mixture is smooth.

If it seems to be too thick, add a few tablespoons of boiling cream or milk. Just before serving, blend in 50–100 g (2–4 oz, ¼–½ cup) butter for each 1 kg (2¼ lb, 4½ cups) purée.

Red beans à la bourguignonne

Soak and drain red kidney beans, then boil them for 10 minutes and drain. Cook the beans with a little streaky bacon in equal quantities of water and red wine until tender. When the beans are cooked, drain them a little and place in a deep sauté pan. Cut some bacon into dice, cook gently in butter, then add to the pan. Thicken with beurre manié and season to taste.

Shellfish and soya bean sprout salad

Cook a large crab in stock and 200 g (7 oz) prawns (shrimp) in salted water. Shell the crab and the prawns and flake the crabmeat. Place 500 g (18 oz, 4½ cups) soya bean sprouts in cold water, remove the debris that comes to the surface, drain and blanch for no more than 1 minute in salted boiling water. Drain and refresh in very cold water, then wipe them.

Place the flaked crab, prawns and bean sprouts in a salad bowl. Finely slice 2 spring onions (scallions) and add ½ teaspoon soy sauce, ½ teaspoon mustard, a pinch of sugar, 1 tablespoon brandy or sherry, 1 tablespoon vinegar, 2–3 tablespoons oil, pepper, a little salt and a few drops of Tabasco (or a small pinch of cayenne pepper). Pour the sauce on to the salad, mix well and sprinkle with chopped fresh coriander (cilantro).

Sobronade

Soak 800 g (1¾ lb, 4½ cups) dried haricot (navy) beans in cold water for 12 hours. Peel 2 turnips and cut into thick slices. Brown one third of these in a pan with 100 g (4 oz, ½ cup) chopped fat bacon. Drain the beans and put

them into a large saucepan, cover completely with cold water and add 250 g
(9 oz, 1¼ cups) diced ham and a piece of fresh pork (fat and lean), weighing
about 800 g (1¾ lb). Bring to the boil and skim; add all the turnip, 1 bouquet
garni, 1 onion studded with 2 cloves, 4 carrots, 2 sliced celery sticks, 1 bunch
of parsley and 2 chopped garlic cloves. Boil for about 20 minutes, then add
250 g (9 oz) thickly sliced potatoes and leave to cook for about 40 minutes.
Garnish a soup tureen with slices of dried bread and pour the soup on top.

Soissonnais soup

Soak 350 g (12 oz, 2 cups) dried white haricot (navy) beans in cold water for
12 hours. Put them in a saucepan with 1.5 litres (2¾ pints, 6½ cups) cold
water and bring to the boil. Add 1 onion studded with 2 cloves, 1 peeled diced
carrot, 1 bouquet garni and 75 g (3 oz, ⅓ cup) slightly salted belly of pork or
unsmoked streaky (slabs) bacon, blanched, diced and fried in butter. Cover,
bring to the boil and cook until the beans break up. Remove the onion and the
bouquet garni. Put the beans and some of the liquid through a blender or
food processor. Return the purée to the saucepan, dilute with stock or
consommé and adjust the seasoning. Bring to the boil and whisk in 50 g (2 oz,
¼ cup) butter. Serve with croûtons fried in butter.

Soya bean sprout salad

Place 500 g (18 oz, 4½ cups) soya bean sprouts in cold water, remove the
scum that comes to the surface, drain and blanch for no more than 1 minute
in salted boiling water. Drain and refresh in cold water, then dry them and
lightly fry with 3 tablespoons hot oil. Hard boil (hard cook) and shell
4 eggs. Put the bean sprouts in a salad bowl and dress with a spicy vinaigrette
seasoned with a little cayenne. Add a few slices of white chicken meat or cold
roast duck. Mix and garnish with the quartered hard-boiled eggs.

Beetroot (beet)

To prepare

Beetroot (beet) can be eaten raw (peeled and grated) but it is usually cooked. Trim leaves and roots, leaving short lengths attached to the beetroot as the root will 'bleed' and lose colour if cut before boiling. Boil in salted water or bake wrapped in foil or in a covered dish in a preheated oven at 180°C (350°F, gas 4). Cooking time depends on size and age: small young beetroot are boiled for about 30 minutes. Larger and/or older vegetables require 45–60 minutes boiling or longer. Baking time is about 1–2 hours. Drain and peel while hot when the peel slips off easily.

Beetroot à la lyonnaise

Parboil some beetroot (beet) in salted water, peel and slice. Cook until tender in butter with thinly sliced onions. Add a little thickened brown stock or bouillon to which 10 g (⅓ oz, 1 teaspoon) of softened butter has been added. Heat through and serve.

Beetroot salad à l'alsacienne

Peel some baked beetroot (beet) and slice or dice. Make a vinaigrette dressing with mustard and add some finely chopped shallots and herbs. Pour over the beetroot and marinate for 1 hour. Garnish with sliced saveloy before serving.

Beetroot salad à la polonaise

Peel some cooked beetroot (beet) and cut into thin slices. Season with a highly spiced vinaigrette, pile in a salad bowl and sprinkle liberally with chopped parsley and sieved hard-boiled (hard-cooked) egg yolk. Thin apple slices sprinkled with lemon juice may be added to the salad.

Braised beetroot with cream

Parboil some beetroot (beet) in salted water, peel and slice. Cook in a little butter in a covered pan until tender. Remove the beetroot and keep hot. Boil some double (heavy) cream, add to the cooking liquor and reduce to half its volume, seasoning with salt and pepper. Remove from the heat and stir in 25 g (1 oz, 1 tablespoon) butter. Pour this sauce over the beetroot slices.

Cold beetroot soup

Wash thoroughly 1 kg (2¼ lb) small raw beetroots (beets), cook gently in salted water, then add the juice of 1 lemon and allow to cool. Cook 3–4 egg whites in a small flat-bottomed dish in a bain marie. Wash and chop a few spring onions (scallions), including the stems. Peel the cold beetroot and slice into thin strips. Add with the diced egg whites, 2 diced Russian gherkins and the chopped onions to the liquid in which the beetroot was cooked, together with a generous pinch of sugar and 150–200 ml (5–7 fl oz, ⅔–¾ cup) crème fraîche. Stir well and place in the refrigerator. Just before serving, sprinkle chopped parsley over the soup.

Cream of beetroot soup

Cook 200 g (7 oz) beetroot (beet) in a preheated oven at 180°C (350°F, gas 4). Finely shred 50 g (2 oz) of the cooked beetroot and set it aside. Purée the remainder in a food processor or blender. Press through a sieve into a large saucepan and sprinkle with lemon juice. Prepare 500 ml (17 fl oz, 2 cups) white sauce by adding 600 ml (1 pint, 2½ cups) milk to a white roux of 25 g (1 oz, 2 tablespoons) butter and 40 g (1½ oz, 6 tablespoons) plain (all-purpose) flour and add this to the saucepan with the same amount of milk. Cook for 10 minutes. Add 100 ml (4 fl oz, 7 tablespoons) single (light) cream and heat without boiling. Add the reserved beetroot and adjust the seasoning before serving.

Gratin of beetroot in verjuice

Slice 1 kg (2¼ lb) raw beetroot (beets) and cut into sticks. Cook in a white stock and drain without cooling. Gently heat 200 ml (7 fl oz, ¾ cup) single (light) cream without boiling, whisking all the time. Remove from the heat. Mix together half a glass of verjuice (obtained by pressing a large bunch of sour white grapes), 2 egg yolks, 1 tablespoon chopped parsley, salt and pepper. Gradually add this mixture to the cream. Arrange the vegetables in a baking dish and cover with the sauce. Sprinkle with grated Cantal cheese, add very small knobs of butter and cook *au gratin* by placing the dish in a very hot oven for a few minutes until the top is browned.

Scandinavian beetroot salad

Peel some baked beetroot (beet) and cut into cubes. Peel and slice some onions and separate the rings. Hard boil (hard cook) some eggs and cut into quarters. Cut some sweet smoked or unsmoked herring (a speciality of Scandinavia) into pieces. Sprinkle the beetroot with highly seasoned vinaigrette and place in a salad bowl. Garnish with the herrings, hard-boiled eggs and onions, and sprinkle with chopped parsley.

Ukrainian borsch

Fry 2 chopped onions and 200 g (7 oz) raw sliced beetroot (beet) in lard, cover and continue to cook gently. Bring 1 kg (2 lb) stewing (chuck) steak to the boil in 2.5 litres (4¼ pints, 11 cups) water, then skim. Add 500 g (18 oz) shredded white cabbage, 3 carrots, a bunch of parsley, small trimmed celery sticks, and the beetroot and onion. Season with salt. Cook 4 ripe tomatoes in a little water, sieve and add them to the soup. Cook for 2 hours, then add a few potatoes, cut into quarters. Prepare a roux with lard and flour, mix with a little stock and pour it into the borsch with 2 tablespoons chopped fennel. Boil for a further 15 minutes and serve.

This Ukrainian borsch is served with a bowl of fresh cream, garlic cloves (which should be eaten between spoonfuls of soup), buckwheat kasha with bacon, and *piroshki*, little dumplings filled with meat, rice and cabbage.

Broccoli

Broccoli à la crème

Prepare 1 kg (2¼ lb) broccoli, then blanch it in 2 litres (3½ pints, 9 cups) boiling salted water for about 30 seconds. Drain the broccoli and chop very coarsely. Lightly brown 50 g (2 oz, ¼ cup) butter in a frying pan and add 150–200 ml (5–7 fl oz, ⅔–¾ cup) double (heavy) cream. When the cream is coloured, add the broccoli. Season with pepper and again with salt if necessary. Simmer for about 10 minutes. Serve the broccoli very hot with roast or sautéed meat or with certain types of fish, such as bass, cod or hake.

Broccoli, potato and bacon pot with soup

Soak a piece of unsmoked streaky bacon about 500 g (18 oz) in cold water, then place in a large saucepan with 2 litres (3½ pints, 9 cups) cold water; simmer for about 1½ hours. Add 1 kg (2¼ lb) prepared broccoli, 2 crushed garlic cloves, with a little salt. Add 575 g (1¼ lb) quartered potatoes and boil for 15 minutes.

Drain the meat and vegetables. Chop the broccoli coarsely and heat with 40 g (1½ oz, 3 tablespoons) butter. Cut the bacon into slices and brown in 25 g (1 oz, 2 tablespoons) butter. Slice the potatoes. Layer the broccoli, then the potatoes and finally the slices of bacon in a heated dish. Sprinkle with the butter used for cooking.

Add 25 g (1 oz, 2 tablespoons) butter to the water in which the bacon and vegetables were cooked. Pour this stock into a soup tureen over thin slices of wholemeal bread dried in the oven. Sprinkle with chopped parsley and serve the soup before the hotpot.

Brussels sprouts

Brussels sprout purée

Purée some cooked buttered Brussels sprouts in a food processor, see Purée of Brussels sprout soup (page 54). Then pour into a saucepan and heat, stirring to lose some moisture. Add a quarter of its volume of potato purée and double (heavy) cream, using about 100 ml (4 fl oz, 7 tablespoons) cream for 1 litre (1¾ pints, 4⅓ cups) purée. Season with salt and pepper and serve very hot, preferably with roasted or braised white meat.

Brussels sprouts au gratin

Prepare some buttered Brussels sprouts. Butter a gratin dish, tip the sprouts into it, sprinkle with grated cheese and melted butter, and brown for about 10 minutes in a very hot oven.

Brussels sprouts Mornay

Heap some buttered Brussels sprouts in a buttered gratin dish, coat generously with Mornay sauce, sprinkle with grated cheese and melted butter, and brown for about 10 minutes in a very hot oven.

Brussels sprouts with butter or cream

Plunge the sprouts into boiling salted water and cook them quickly, uncovered. When they are still firm, remove and drain. Melt some butter in a shallow frying pan, using about 25 g (1 oz, 2 tablespoons) for 800 g (1¾ lb) sprouts, and brown the sprouts. Adjust the seasoning, cover and simmer until the sprouts are completely cooked.

If desired, the sprouts may be coated with double (heavy) cream, using 100 ml (4 fl oz, 7 tablespoons) for 800 g (1¾ lb) vegetables, before they are covered to finish cooking.

Purée of Brussels sprout soup

Trim 500 g (18 oz) Brussels sprouts and blanch them for 2 minutes in boiling water. Rinse in cold water and drain thoroughly, then sweat gently in 50 g (2 oz, ¼ cup) butter. Purée the cooked sprouts in a food processor or blender. Pour the purée into a saucepan and add 1.75 litres (3 pints, 7½ cups) chicken stock and 250 g (9 oz) floury potatoes, cut into quarters. Bring to the boil and cook for about 30 minutes. Rub through a sieve and add sufficient stock to obtain the desired consistency. Adjust the seasoning. Just before serving, beat in 50 g (2 oz, ¼ cup) butter, cut into small pieces.

Sautéed Brussels sprouts

Cook some sprouts in boiling water until tender, then drain thoroughly. Melt some butter in a frying pan and toss the sprouts lightly in it. Transfer them to a vegetable dish and sprinkle with chopped parsley.

They may also be served with noisette butter (moistened first with lemon juice), *à l'indienne* (accompanied by a curry sauce and boiled rice), *à la milanaise* (sprinkled with grated Parmesan, then moistened with noisette butter), or *à la polonaise*, as for cauliflower.

Buckwheat

Russian kasha

Crush 500 g (18 oz, 3¾ cups) fresh buckwheat and soak in sufficient warm water to make a thick paste. Season with salt and put it in a deep cake tin (pan) or charlotte mould (traditionally an earthenware pot is used). Bake in a preheated oven at 180°C (350°F, gas 4) for 2 hours. Remove the thick crust formed on the surface and pour the remaining soft paste into a dish. Add 65 g (2½ oz, 5 tablespoons) butter and mix well with a spatula. Spread the paste out on a greased surface, cover it with a board, then press it until it is about 1 cm (½ in) thick. Cut into shapes with a pastry (cookie) cutter and fry in clarified butter until golden brown. Serve with soup.

Russian kasha with Parmesan cheese

Prepare a *kasha* of buckwheat as described. Spread a thin layer of the soft paste over the bottom of a buttered gratin dish. Sprinkle with grated Parmesan cheese and a little melted butter, alternating the layers until all the ingredients are used up. Smooth the final layer of *kasha* carefully, then sprinkle with Parmesan cheese, top with melted butter and brown in a preheated oven at 230°C (450°F, gas 8). Serve melted butter separately.

Bulgur

Tabbouleh

Put 250 g (9 oz, 2½ cups) bulgur wheat into a bowl. Add plenty of cold water to cover and leave to soak for 20 minutes; drain thoroughly in a fine sieve. Place the bulgar in a large salad bowl. Add 500 g (18 oz, 3 cups) finely diced juicy tomatoes with their juice, 250 g (9 oz, 1½ cups) finely chopped onions, 2 tablespoons of both chopped fresh mint and parsley. Season with salt and pepper. Mix in 100 ml (4 fl oz, 7 tablespoons) olive (or a mixture of olive and some sesame) oil and the juice of 3 lemons. Leave in a cool place for 2–3 hours, stirring occasionally. Just before serving, garnish with 8 spring onions (scallions) and leaves of fresh mint.

Cabbage

Bigos

The Polish national dish, bigos is also known as 'hunter's stew'. It is made of alternate layers of sauerkraut and meat simmered for a long time. Large Polish boiling sausage is also cut up and added to the stew, which often includes wild mushrooms.

Rinse 4 kg (9 lb) sauerkraut and drain it well. Peel, core and dice 4 dessert apples, sprinkling the pieces with lemon juice, and add to the sauerkraut with

2 large chopped onions. Melt 4 tablespoons lard in a flameproof casserole and cover with a fairly thick layer of sauerkraut, then add a layer of diced meat. Continue filling the pot with alternate layers of meat and sauerkraut, finishing with a layer of sauerkraut and adding a little lard every now and then. Pour in enough stock to cover the sauerkraut. Cover the pot and cook in a preheated oven at 180°C (350°F, gas 4) for 2–3 hours. Make a white roux and add some of the cooking liquor. Pour this sauce over the *bigos* and cook for a further 30 minutes.

Braised cabbage

Prepare a cabbage: blanch, drain, cool in cold water and drain once again. Separate the leaves and discard the large ribs. Scrape and dice a carrot. Line a flameproof casserole with bacon rashers (slices) stripped of half their fat and add the diced carrot, then the cabbage, forming a heap. Season with salt and pepper and add a little grated nutmeg, an onion stuck with a clove and a bouquet garni. Pour in stock to two-thirds cover the cabbage and place a very thin strip of bacon on top. Cover the casserole and bring the stock to the boil over a ring. Then place the casserole in a preheated oven at 180°C (350°F, gas 4) and cook for about 1½ hours.

Cabbage charlotte with olives

Blanch a cabbage, then cook in water and put through a vegetable mill. To the resulting purée add 100 ml (4 fl oz, 7 tablespoons) water, 1 egg yolk and a little grated cheese. Stone (pit) and coarsely chop 30 black (ripe) olives and add them to the cabbage purée with a stiffly whisked egg white. Mix well. Butter a charlotte mould and sprinkle with dried breadcrumbs. Pour the mixture into the mould and cook in a preheated oven at 220°C (425°F, gas 7) for about 30 minutes.

Chinese cabbage à la pékinoise

Remove the outer leaves from a Chinese cabbage and slice it into 10 cm (4 in) strips. Cut some very thin slices of ham to the same length and finely slice 5 or 6 spring onions (scallions) and their stems. Heat 2 tablespoons oil in a shallow frying pan, add the cabbage and brown for 2–3 minutes. Arrange the pieces of cabbage in a steaming basket, add the sliced onion and a little fine salt, and steam for 30 minutes. Then insert the slices of ham between the pieces of cabbage and steam for a further 4–5 minutes. Serve the cabbage and ham together.

Fried eggs à l'alsacienne (with sauerkraut)

Fry some eggs in goose fat, then arrange them on a bed of braised sauerkraut, alternating them with half-slices of ham. Surround the ingredients with a border of demi-glace sauce.

Green cabbage salad

Remove any withered outer leaves, cut the cabbage into four and cook for about 12 minutes in boiling salted water. Drain, cool and wipe. Cut the quarters into a julienne and season with a well-spiced vinaigrette. Sprinkle with chopped herbs or finely shredded spring onions (scallions).

Paupiettes of cabbage

Blanch a whole cabbage for 7–8 minutes in boiling salted water, then drain and cool it. Pull off the large outer leaves, removing the tougher ribs. Chop the leaves from the central heart and to them add an equal volume of forcemeat. Make paupiettes by rolling this mixture in the large leaves, using 1 tablespoon per leaf; tie them up with kitchen thread. Line a flameproof casserole with 100 g (4 oz) bacon, 150 g (5 oz, 1 cup) diced carrots and 150 g

(5 oz, 1 cup) finely diced onion. Put the cabbage paupiettes on top and barely cover with rich stock. Cover the pan, bring to the boil, then cook in a preheated oven at 200°C (400°F, gas 6) for 1¼ hours. Transfer to a serving dish and reduce the strained cooking liquor by half, then use to glaze the paupiettes. These paupiettes form a perfect garnish for braised meat.

Pickled red cabbage

Prepare the cabbage: cut it into quarters, remove and discard the large ribs, then cut it into strips. Place in a large basin, sprinkle with a generous tablespoon of fine salt and mix well. Cover and leave for at least 48 hours in a cool place, turning over the cabbage strips several times. Drain the cabbage and arrange it in layers in an earthenware jar, inserting between each layer 4–5 peppercorns, 3 small pieces of bay leaf and ½ garlic clove, chopped. Boil enough red wine vinegar to cover the cabbage, leave to cool, then pour it over the cabbage. Seal the jar and leave to marinate for at least 36 hours. The cabbage can be served in various hors d'oeuvre or as a condiment with cold beef or pork.

Red cabbage à la flamande

Remove any withered leaves, slice off the stump (core) at the base of the leaves and cut the cabbage into four sections, then into thin strips. Wash and dry. Melt 40 g (1½ oz, 3 tablespoons) butter in a saucepan, add the cabbage, sprinkle with salt and pepper, moisten with 1 tablespoon vinegar, then cover and cook over a gentle heat. Meanwhile, peel 3 or 4 tart apples, cut them into quarters, remove the cores and slice them finely. Add them to the cabbage after 1 hour of cooking, sprinkle with 1 tablespoon brown sugar, replace the lid and cook for a further 20 minutes. Serve the cabbage with boiled pork or boiled or braised beef.

Red cabbage à la limousine

Prepare the cabbage and cut it into thin strips. Melt 4 tablespoons lard (shortening) in a saucepan. Add the cabbage and about 20 large peeled sweet chestnuts. Add sufficient stock to barely cover the vegetables. Season with salt and pepper, cover the pan and leave to cook gently for about 1½ hours. Serve to accompany roast pork or pork chops.

Red cabbage salad

Select a very fresh and tender red cabbage (break off a large leaf to test it), remove the large outer leaves, cut the cabbage into four and remove the white centre. Slice the quarters into fine strips, about 5 mm (¼ in) wide, blanch them for 5 minutes in boiling water, then cool and wipe them. Place in a salad bowl, sprinkle with 200 ml (7 fl oz, ¾ cup) boiling red wine vinegar, mix, cover and leave to marinate for 5–6 hours. Drain the cabbage and season it with salt, pepper and oil. Unblanched red cabbage can be used for a very crisp salad: shred the wedges finely. Add 2 tablespoons of soft brown sugar with the vinegar if liked.

Sauerkraut

Remove the core and any green or damaged outer leaves from some white cabbages. Using a knife with a broad blade or a special shredder or food processor, cut the cabbages into very fine strips. Wash and drain thoroughly. Line the bottom of an earthenware crock with large cabbage leaves or vine leaves and arrange the shredded cabbage in layers, covering each layer with coarse salt, and sprinkling with juniper berries or other flavourings, if liked. Continue until the crock is two-thirds full. Put a handful of coarse salt on the final layer. Cover with a cloth to help exclude air, then with a wooden lid that fits down inside the crock. Place a heavy weight on this lid. By the next day, the weight should have forced out sufficient liquid (water drawn out of the cabbage by the salt) to cover the lid. Make sure that there is always enough liquid to keep the weighted lid covered. Keep in a cool place, skimming off scum or foam.

After at least three weeks, when no more scum or foam forms above the cabbage, the sauerkraut is ready to eat. Each time some sauerkraut is taken out, ladle off the covering liquid, replace the cloth, the lid and the weight, and add fresh water to cover.

Sauerkraut is best eaten fresh and should be pale in colour and crunchy. It should not be kept too long; eventually it turns yellow and acquires a more pronounced flavour.

Sauerkraut à l'alsacienne

Thoroughly wash 2 kg (4½ lb) raw sauerkraut in cold water, then squeeze and disentangle it with your fingers. Peel 2 or 3 carrots and cut into small cubes. Peel 2 large onions and stick a clove in each.

Coat the bottom and sides of a large flameproof casserole with goose fat or lard. Pile in half the sauerkraut add add the carrots, onions, 2 peeled garlic cloves, 1 teaspoon ground pepper, 1 tablespoon juniper berries and a bouquet garni. Add the rest of the sauerkraut, a raw knuckle of ham and 1 glass of dry white Alsace wine and top up with water. Season lightly with salt, cover the casserole and bring to the boil. Then transfer the casserole to a preheated oven at 190°C (375 °F, gas 5) and cook for 1 hour. Remove from the oven, add a medium-sized smoked shoulder of pork and 575–800 g (1¼–1¾ lb) smoked belly (salt pork). Cover, bring to the boil on the hob (stove top), then cook in the oven for a further 1½ hours.

Meanwhile, peel 1.25 kg (2¾ lb) potatoes. After 1½ hours, remove the pork belly from the casserole and add the potatoes. Leave to cook for a further

30 minutes. During this time, poach 6–8 Strasbourg sausages in barely simmering water. When the sauerkraut is cooked, remove and discard the bouquet garni and the cloves and return the pork belly for 10 minutes to reheat it. Arrange the sauerkraut in a large dish and garnish with the potatoes, sausages and meat cut into slices.

Sauerkraut au gras for garnish

Follow the recipe above for sauerkraut *à l'alsacienne*, but replace the water with unskimmed stock and do not add meat. Cook gently for 3 hours. It is served as a garnish for poultry or meat.

Sauerkraut salad à l'allemande

Thoroughly wash 1 kg (2¼ lb) raw sauerkraut, squeeze and disentangle it with your fingers. Place it in a saucepan along with 2–3 large whole onions, salt and pepper, then cover with either stock or water to which 1 tablespoon cooking oil has been added. Cook over a gentle heat for about 2½ hours, then drain and leave to cool. Dice the onions and return them to the sauerkraut. Press the sauerkraut, season with vinaigrette and pile into a deep dish. Garnish with quarters of hard-boiled (hard-cooked) eggs and cubes of cooked beetroot (red beet).

Sichuan-style Chinese cabbage

Clean a Chinese cabbage and cut it into pieces about 3 cm (1¼ in) long. Wash, blanch, cool and drain. Heat 3 tablespoons oil in a frying pan. Chop a large garlic clove and lightly brown it in the oil. Add the cabbage, a little Sichuan pepper and some salt; stir well and leave to cook for 1 minute. Then add 1 teaspoon marc brandy and 1 teaspoon caster (superfine) sugar and stir well for 1 minute. Adjust the seasoning and serve very hot.

Soft-boiled or poached eggs à l'alsacienne

Cook the eggs. Put a layer of braised sauerkraut on a dish and place the boiled or poached eggs on it, alternating them with large strips of bacon which have been cooked in their own fat. Coat with a demi-glace sauce.

Sou-fassum

A whole cabbage stuffed with a forcemeat of Swiss chard, bacon, onions, rice and sausagemeat, typical of Nice, in France. Traditionally, it is wrapped in a net, known as a *fassumier*, and cooked in the stock of a mutton pot-au-feu.

Trim a large green cabbage, blanch for 8 minutes in boiling salted water, then cool and drain. Detach the large leaves, remove their ribs and spread them out flat on a net or a piece of muslin (cheesecloth), soaked and wrung out. Chop the remainder of the cabbage. Make the forcemeat by mixing 250 g (9 oz) blanched chopped Swiss chard leaves; 200 g (7 oz, 1 cup) lean bacon, diced and browned; 100 g (4 oz, ⅔ cup) chopped onions, fried in butter; 2 large tomatoes, peeled, seeded and crushed; 100 g (4 oz, ⅔ cup) blanched rice; 800 g (1¾ lb, 3 cups) sausagemeat and 1 crushed garlic clove.

Layer the forcemeat and chopped cabbage on the leaves, then fold them around the stuffing in a neat ball. Tie up the net or muslin, plunge the cabbage into a mutton pot-au-feu (or other) stock and simmer for about 3½ hours. Drain the cabbage, unwrap and arrange on a round dish. Pour over a few tablespoons of stock and serve hot.

Stuffed cabbage

Blanch a whole cabbage in salted boiling water for 7–8 minutes. Cool it in cold water, drain and remove the stump (core). Moisten a piece of fine cloth or muslin (cheesecloth), wring it out and lay it on the working surface. On top of the cloth, lay four lengths of kitchen thread to form a star shape. Place the cabbage in the centre of the crossed threads and open out the larger leaves one by one. Remove the central heart, chop and mix with an equal volume of fine well-seasoned pork forcemeat. Fill the centre of the cabbage with the mixture, then fold back the large leaves to recreate the original shape. On top, place two very thin strips of fat bacon in a cross and secure them by knotting the threads over them. Wrap the cabbage in the cloth and tie it up.

Line a flameproof casserole with 100 g (4 oz) bacon, 150 g (5 oz, 1 cup) diced carrots and 150 g (5 oz, 1 cup) finely diced onion. Put the cabbage on top and barely cover it with rich stock. Cover, bring to the boil, then cook in a preheated oven at 200°C (400°F, gas 6) for 1½ hours. Drain the cabbage, unwrap it and remove the strips of fat bacon. (Alternatively, the cabbage may be prepared and cooked in a net, and without the strips of bacon.) Serve the cabbage in a deep dish, keeping it hot, and coat with the cooking juices, reduced by half.

Cardoons

To prepare

Clean the base of the cardoon, cutting off the hard stems. Remove the tender stalks, one by one, and cut into 7.5 cm (3 in) slices; sprinkle with lemon juice. Cut the heart into four and plunge the stalks and heart into boiling water. Bring back to the boil, cover and leave to simmer very gently until tender.

Buttered cardoons

Braise some blanched cardoons in butter for 20 minutes. Arrange in a vegetable dish and sprinkle with roughly chopped mint or parsley.

Cardoon purée

Prepare some buttered cardoons and reduce to a purée by pressing through a sieve or using a food processor or blender. If desired, a third of its volume of potato purée or a few tablespoons of thick béchamel sauce may be added. Add butter to serve.

Cardoon salad

Cut some cooked cardoons into thick matchsticks. Add some well-seasoned vinaigrette and sprinkle with chervil and roughly chopped parsley.

Cardoons à la lyonnaise

Clean some cardoons, cut them up and blanch them in white vegetable stock. Braise gently in butter. Add a few spoonfuls of lyonnaise sauce and simmer for about 10 minutes. Arrange the cardoons in a dish and serve very hot.

Cardoons in béchamel sauce

Drain the blanched cardoons and arrange on a flameproof dish. Add butter, cover and leave to simmer for 15 minutes. Now add some béchamel sauce and simmer for another 5 minutes. Serve in a vegetable dish.

Cardoons Mornay

Drain the cooked cardoons and arrange on a buttered gratin dish. Cover with Mornay sauce and sprinkle with grated Parmesan cheese and melted butter. Brown in a preheated oven at 240°C (475°F, gas 9).

Cardoons with herbs

Braise some blanched cardoons in butter for 10 minutes. Add several tablespoons of sauce with fines herbes and simmer for 10 minutes.

Fried cardoons

Drain cooked cardoons and marinate for 30 minutes in a mixture of olive oil, lemon juice and chopped parsley. Then dip the cardoons in batter and deep-fry in hot oil. Drain and season with salt.

Carrots

Carrot flan

Bake a pastry flan case blind and fill with a lightly sweetened carrot purée. Cover with slices of glazed carrot, pouring over their cooking juices, and place in a preheated oven at 240°C (475°F, gas 9) for a few minutes.

Carrot purée

Cook 500 g (18 oz) sliced new carrots in salted water to which 1 teaspoon granulated sugar and 1 tablespoon butter has been added. When the carrots are cooked, drain and make into a purée by pressing them through a fine sieve or using a blender. Heat the purée, adding a few spoonfuls of the carrots' cooking liquid if it is too thick. At the last moment, add 50 g (2 oz, ¼ cup) fresh butter. Mix well and arrange on a vegetable dish. Carrot purée can also be made using the carrots from a pot-au-feu.

Carrot purée with cream

Heat 4 tablespoons double (heavy) cream and add to some carrot purée.

Carrot salad with orange

Put 500 g (18 oz, 3¾ cups) grated carrots into a salad bowl. Remove the peel and pith from 4 oranges, separate the segments from the membrane and dice the flesh finely. Thinly slice 2 large mild onions and break up the slices into rings. Pour some lemon vinaigrette over the diced carrots just before serving, then add the diced orange to the salad bowl. Toss the carrot and orange and garnish with the onion rings.

Carrots à la forestière

Braise some carrots in butter, then add half their volume of mushrooms, also braised in butter. Adjust the seasoning and sprinkle with parsley.

Carrots with cream

Cut some old carrots into segments and hollow out the centres. Cook in salted water, and before they become soft, drain, cover with boiling double (heavy) cream and reduce by two-thirds. Arrange in a dish and serve very hot.

Carrots with raisins

Cut some new carrots into slices and fry in melted butter. Lightly sprinkle with flour, then add just enough water to cover them and 1 tablespoon brandy. Cover. Halfway through cooking (after about 15 minutes), add a handful of raisins. Finish cooking with the lid on over a gentle heat.

Crécy soup

Scrape 500 g (18 oz) very tender carrots, slice thinly and cook them with 50 g (2 oz, ¼ cup) butter in a covered pan. Add 1 tablespoon shredded onion, a pinch of salt and ½ teaspoon sugar. When the vegetables are soft, add 1 litre (1¾ pints, 4⅓ cups) beef or chicken consommé, bring to the boil and add 100 g (4 oz, ½ cup) rice. Cook slowly with the lid on for about 20 minutes, then put it through a blender and strain. Add a few more spoonfuls of consommé, heat and add 25 g (1 oz, 2 tablespoons) butter. Adjust the seasoning. Serve with small croûtons fried in butter.

Glazed carrots

Clean some new, preferably fat, carrots, leaving medium-sized ones whole, but cutting large ones into halves or quarters. Place in a frying pan large enough to hold them all without overlapping. Cover with cold water. For every 500 ml (17 fl oz, 2 cups) water add 25 g (1 oz, 2 tablespoons) sugar, 50 g (2 oz, ¼ cup) butter and ½ teaspoon salt. (When old carrots are used, hollow out the centres, scald them and drain, then cook with sugar and butter.) Bring to the boil over a high heat. When the water is boiling briskly, lower the heat, cover the pan and leave to simmer until the liquid has almost completely evaporated. The carrots should now be cooked. Shake the pan so that the carrots are coated with the syrupy liquid.

Glazed carrots may be served with béchamel sauce (add a few spoonfuls of the sauce at the last moment), butter, cream (cover with boiling cream and reduce by two-thirds), herbs (sprinkle with chopped parsley or chervil) or meat juices (add a few spoonfuls of roast veal or poultry cooking juices).

Grated carrots with currants

Steep some dried currants in barely tepid lemon juice, then add them to grated raw carrots mixed with well-seasoned olive oil vinaigrette.

Royale of carrots à la Crécy

Cook 75 g (3 oz) carrots in butter over a low heat, adding salt and a pinch of sugar. Stir in 2 tablespoons béchamel sauce and the same amount of cream, and press through a sieve. Bind the mixture with 4 egg yolks, pour into dariole moulds and cook in a bain marie in a preheated oven at 200°C (400°F, gas 6) for 30 minutes.

Tajine of carrots

Put 1 kg (2¼ lb) sliced carrots into a tajine or saucepan. Add 5 tablespoons olive oil, then add 450 g (1 lb) finely sliced onions, a bouquet of coriander (cilantro), the same amount of parsley, 2 chopped garlic cloves, 1 teaspoon ground ginger, a pinch each of ground cumin, paprika and saffron powder, 2 turns of the pepper mill and a large pinch of salt. Mix, cover and cook over a very low heat for 1½ hours (using a heat diffuser). Just before serving, add 150 g (5 oz, 1 cup) black (ripe) olives and sprinkle with lemon juice.

Vichy carrots

Peel 800 g (1¾ lb) young carrots and cut into thin rounds. Place in a sauté pan and just cover with water, adding 1 teaspoon salt and a generous pinch of sugar per 500 ml (17 fl oz, 2 cups) water. Cook gently until all the liquid is absorbed. Serve the carrots in a vegetable dish, sprinkled with small pieces of butter and chopped parsley.

Cauliflower

Cauliflower à la polonaise

Divide a cauliflower into large florets and cook in boiling salted water until just cooked (the cauliflower should stay slightly firm). Reshape it in a round serving dish, sprinkle with 2–3 chopped hard-boiled (hard-cooked) eggs and chopped parsley, and keep in a warm place. Crumble 75 g (3 oz, about 3 slices) stale bread in 75 g (3 oz, ⅓ cup) melted butter in a frying pan. Fry until golden and sprinkle over the cauliflower; serve immediately.

Cauliflower and tomato pickle

Divide 2 medium-sized cauliflowers into florets and arrange them in layers in a terrine with 675 g (1½ lb) firm tomatoes (quartered), 4 coarsely chopped onions and a chopped cucumber. Sprinkle each layer with an equal quantity of salt – a total of about 200 g (7 oz, 1 cup). Cover with cold water, place a sheet of foil over the top and leave in a cool place for 24 hours.

The next day put the vegetables into a strainer and rinse them under running water to remove the excess salt. Drain and place in a large saucepan. Sprinkle with 1 teaspoon mustard powder, 1 teaspoon ground ginger and 1 teaspoon black pepper and add 250 g (9 oz, 1½ cups, firmly packed) brown sugar. Pour in 750 ml (1¼ pints, 3¼ cups) white wine vinegar and bring to the boil over a medium heat, stirring frequently. Simmer for 15–20 minutes, stirring, until the vegetables are just beginning to soften but are still firm.

Remove the pan from the heat, put the vegetables in clean jars and completely cover with vinegar. The proportions given will make 3 kg (6½ lb) pickle. The jars should be stored in a cool, dry place away from the light.

Cauliflower au gratin

Divide the heart into florets and cook them in salted water or steam. Remove, drain and toss them in butter. Transfer to a buttered gratin dish, coat with Mornay sauce, sprinkle with grated Gruyère cheese and melted butter, and brown for about 10 minutes in a preheated oven at 230°C (450°F, gas 8).

Croûtes du Barry

Prepare some individual croûtes and top with cauliflower florets cooked gently in butter. Coat with Mornay sauce, sprinkle with grated cheese and brown in a preheated oven at 240°C (475°F, gas 9).

Du Barry cream soup

Steam a small fresh cauliflower until it breaks up easily. Put it through a food processor and pour it into a large saucepan. Prepare 500 ml (17 fl oz, 2 cups) white sauce by adding 600 ml (1 pint, 2½ cups) milk to a white roux of 25 g (1 oz, 2 tablespoons) butter and 40 g (1½ oz, 6 tablespoons) plain (all-purpose) flour. Mix this sauce with the cauliflower and simmer gently for 12–18 minutes. Press through a sieve if necessary. Dilute with a few tablespoons of white stock or milk. Heat and adjust the seasoning. Add 200 ml (7 fl oz, ½ cup) single (light) cream and stir while heating.

Du Barry salad

Steam some very small white cauliflower florets for about 4 minutes in a pressure cooker or about 12 minutes in an ordinary saucepan. Drain and cool completely, and heap them in a salad bowl. Garnish with radishes and small sprigs of watercress. Pour some well-seasoned vinaigrette with added lemon over the salad and sprinkle with chopped herbs. Toss the salad just before serving.

Du Barry soup

Cook a cauliflower in salted water, then press it through a sieve (or purée in a blender). Mix with it a quarter of its weight of potato purée, then add enough consommé or milk to obtain a creamy consistency. Finally, add some single (light) cream – about 150 ml (¼ pint, ⅔ cup) for 5 portions. Adjust the seasoning, and sprinkle with chopped parsley. Butter may also be added.

Omelette du Barry

Steam some very small florets of cauliflower. Take them out while they are still a little crisp and fry them in butter. Pour on eggs, beaten with salt, pepper and chopped chervil, and cook like a large pancake.

Sautéed cauliflower

Divide the heart into florets and steam them until they are still slightly firm and do not disintegrate. Heat some butter in a frying pan or sauté pan and lightly brown the florets. Arrange them in a dish and moisten with the cooking butter. Cauliflower may also be sautéed in olive oil with chopped garlic.

Celeriac (celery root)

To prepare

Peel like a potato, rinse and sprinkle with lemon juice. To cook, cut into pieces and blanch for 5 minutes in boiling salted water. To serve as a vegetable, celeriac may be braised, cooked in its juices or prepared as julienne and braised. It can also be prepared as a purée (like cardoons) and as a cream soup. Steamed in slices, it retains all its flavour. Celeriac can be preserved, especially grated and seasoned with vinegar, in pickles, etc.

Celeriac croquettes

Peel a celeriac root, cut it into pieces and blanch. Then cook in salted water for about 30 minutes. Add the same weight of peeled potatoes, cut into cubes, and simmer until cooked. Drain the vegetables and dry, either in the oven or in a saucepan. Pass them through a vegetable mill and mix the resulting purée with egg yolks – 4 per 1 kg (2¼ lb) of purée – and chopped parsley. Divide the paste obtained into little balls, flatten them out and coat in batter. Plunge the croquettes into boiling oil or fat and leave to turn golden, then remove and drain on paper towels. Serve the croquettes with roast beef, veal, pork, leg of lamb or leg of venison.

Celeriac en rémoulade

Peel a large celeriac root, grate it coarsely and blanch for 2 minutes in boiling salted water. Drain and refresh with cold water then dry thoroughly. Transfer to a vegetable dish, add rémoulade sauce and, if desired, sprinkle with chopped parsley.

Celeriac julienne

Peel a celeriac root and cut into thick strips. Blanch for 3 minutes in boiling salted water, then refresh in cold water and drain. Put the strips into a pan with a knob of butter and a little sugar, to taste. Cover and sweat for about 15 minutes. Adjust the seasoning and sprinkle with finely chopped herbs. Use to garnish roast meats, fried meats and braised fish, such as cod.

Celeriac velouté soup

Prepare a white roux with 40 g (1½ oz, 3 tablespoons) butter and 40 g (1½ oz, 6 tablespoons) flour. Moisten with a generous 750 ml (1¼ pints, 3¼ cups) chicken consommé. Blanch 300 g (11 oz) sliced celeriac, and simmer in 40 g (1½ oz, 3 tablespoons) butter for about 20 minutes. Add to the consommé, bring to the boil and cook until the celeriac breaks up. Reduce to a purée in a food processor. Dilute with a little consommé to obtain the desired consistency and heat. Off the heat, thicken the soup with a mixture of 3 egg yolks beaten with 100 ml (4 fl oz, 7 tablespoons) double (heavy) cream. Finally, whisk in 75 g (3 oz, 6 tablespoons) butter. Reheat but do not boil.

Doria salad

Dress shredded celeriac (celery root) with rémoulade sauce and pile it in a deep salad bowl. Cover with thin slices of white truffle. Surround with a border of cooked green asparagus tips and thin strips of cooked beetroot (red beet) that has been seasoned with vinaigrette. Sprinkle with sieved hard-boiled (hard-cooked) egg yolk and chopped parsley.

Gougères with celeriac, celery and cream of caviar

Fit a piping (pastry) bag with a large, fluted nozzle. Prepare choux paste using 100 ml (4 fl oz, ½ cup) water and omitting the sugar. Beat 50 g (2 oz, ½ cup) grated Gruyère cheese into the paste. Pipe 4 rings 10 cm (4 in) in diameter and bake in a preheated oven at 240°C (475°F, gas 9). Slice in half horizontally and cool on a wire rack.

Coarsely chop some frisée; season with salt, pepper and lemon juice. Cut celery and celeriac (celery root) into matchsticks. Mix the frisée, celery and celeriac with 200 ml (7 fl oz, 1 cup) whipped whipping cream and 25 g (1 oz, 1 generous tablespoon) caviar, working very gently with two forks in order not to damage the caviar.

Arrange a circle of lamb's lettuce around the edge of each plate and place the gougère bases in the middle. Carefully spoon the cream mixture on to the bases and cover with the gougère tops. Serve freshly filled, garnished with diced tomato.

Ragoût of celeriac

Peel a celeriac root and cut it into small oval-shaped pieces. Blanch these for 5 minutes in boiling water, then place in a flameproof casserole with butter, salt and pepper and let it stew gently, with the lid on, for about 30 minutes. Bind with cream sauce, sprinkle with coarsely chopped parsley and serve as a garnish to roast or braised white meat.

Salade à d'Albignac

Heap some shredded celeriac, dressed with mayonnaise, in a salad bowl or on a platter. Sprinkle the top of the salad with thinly sliced black truffle and around the edge arrange the following: thin slices of poached chicken breast dressed with lemon vinaigrette, prawns (shrimp) dipped in tomato ketchup, slices of white truffle dipped in olive oil seasoned with salt and pepper, tiny lettuce hearts, and quarters of hard-boiled (hard-cooked) eggs dressed with vinaigrette.

Stuffed celeriac à la paysanne

Cut some small celeriac roots in half and blanch them. Scoop out the pulp, leaving a lining at least 1 cm (½ in) thick. Dice the pulp and add an equal volume of both carrots and onions softened in butter. Season with salt and pepper. Fill the half celeriacs with this mixture and place on a buttered ovenproof dish. Sprinkle with grated Gruyère cheese and small knobs of butter. Pour 3 tablespoons stock into the dish and cook in a preheated oven at 220°C (425°F, gas 7) until browned.

Celery

Braised celery

Drain some blanched celery sticks on a cloth. Tie them in bunches of two or three, and place them in a buttered flameproof casserole lined with bacon rinds or chopped bacon, chopped onions and sliced carrots. Add sufficient stock to cover the vegetables and seasoning to taste. Bring to the boil over the heat, then cover and transfer to a preheated oven at 180°C (350°F, gas 4) to cook for 1½ hours.

Celery can be prepared *au maigre* by omitting the bacon rinds and replacing the stock with water.

Celery à la milanaise

Cut the sticks from a head of celery into strips, chop them into small pieces, and cook them *au blanc* or blanch for 10 minutes. Drain thoroughly and place half of them in a buttered ovenproof dish. Sprinkle with grated Parmesan cheese, top with the remaining celery and sprinkle with more Parmesan cheese. Pour melted butter over the top and brown in a preheated oven at 240°C (475°F, gas 9). Just before serving, pour a few spoonfuls of noisette butter over the top.

Celery-flavoured consommé

Use beef or chicken consommé. Finely chop the inner sticks of a head of celery and add to the other ingredients when clarifying the consommé.

Celery in butter

Blanch and drain the sticks and place them in a well-buttered pan. Add salt and pepper. Moisten with several spoonfuls of white stock or water, cover and cook for about 45 minutes.

Celery sauce

Trim and slice the tender sticks and hearts from two bunches of celery. Place in a saucepan with a bouquet garni and an onion studded with cloves. Add sufficient stock just to cover the contents, cover and heat until simmering. Simmer until the celery is tender. Purée the celery with its cooking juices and return it to the rinsed pan. Add 200 ml (7 fl oz, ¾ cup) cream sauce, and reduce until the required consistency is achieved. Adjust the seasoning and sprinkle with very finely chopped parsley. This sauce can accompany boiled or braised poultry.

Celery with béchamel sauce

Braise the celery and arrange in a buttered dish. Sweat for 10 minutes. Cover with béchamel sauce and simmer for a few minutes.

Celery with cream

Blanch the celery and cut each stick in half lengthways. Arrange in a buttered flameproof casserole and season with salt and pepper. Cover with light stock and bring to the boil. Cover the casserole and transfer to a preheated oven at 180°C (350°F, gas 4) to cook for about 1 hour.

Drain the celery and bend the pieces in half, arranging them in a vegetable dish. To make the sauce, skim any butter off the cooking liquid, reduce, and add 3 tablespoons béchamel sauce. Moisten with 200 ml (7 fl oz, ¾ cup) double (heavy) cream and reduce by half. Add 1 tablespoon butter, mix, sieve and pour the sauce over the celery.

Cream of celery soup

Chop 2 celery hearts. Blanch, then cook them in a covered pan in 50 g (2 oz, 4 tablespoons) butter until tender. Prepare 500 ml (17 fl oz, 2 cups) white sauce by adding 600 ml (1 pint, 2½ cups) milk to a white roux of 25 g (1 oz, 2 tablespoons) butter and 40 g (1½ oz, 6 tablespoons) plain (all-purpose) flour. Mix this sauce with the celery and simmer gently for 12–18 minutes. Purée in a food processor or blender, then press through a sieve if necessary. Dilute with a few tablespoons of white stock or milk. Return to the heat then taste and adjust the seasoning. Add 200 ml (7 fl oz, ¾ cup) single (light) cream, stirring as you warm it through.

Purée of celery soup

Scrub 500 g (18 oz) celery sticks. Chop the celery or the same weight of blanched peeled celeriac and sweat in 50 g (2 oz, ¼ cup) butter. Purée the cooked celery in a food processor or blender. Pour the purée into a saucepan and add 1.75 litres (3 pints, 7½ cups) chicken stock and 250 g (9 oz) floury potatoes, cut into quarters. Bring to the boil and cook for about 30 minutes.

Rub through a sieve and add sufficient stock to obtain the desired consistency. Adjust the seasoning. Just before serving, beat in 50 g (2 oz, ¼ cup) butter, cut into small pieces.

Royale of celery

Cook 75 g (3 oz, ¾ cup) finely sliced celery sticks in butter; add 1 tablespoon béchamel sauce and 2 tablespoons consommé. Bind the mixture with 4 egg yolks, pour into dariole moulds and cook in a bain marie in a preheated oven at 200°C (400°F, gas 6) for 30 minutes.

Chestnuts

Boiled chestnuts

Place some peeled chestnuts in a saucepan and cover with cold water. Season with salt and pepper and add some chopped celery. Bring to the boil and simmer gently for 35–45 minutes. Drain well and serve with butter.

Braised chestnuts

Peel some chestnuts and spread them evenly over the bottom of a large greased casserole. Place a bouquet garni and a celery stick in the centre, season with salt and pepper and add enough stock just to cover them. Cover the casserole and cook in a preheated oven at 220°C (425°F, gas 7) for about 45 minutes (do not stir the chestnuts during cooking in case they break). Serve with braised or roast meat.

Chestnut purée

Boil some peeled chestnuts, drain them, press them through a sieve and place the purée in a saucepan. Add 150 ml (¼ pint, ⅔ cup) double (heavy) cream per 1 kg (2¼ lb) chestnuts and reheat, stirring constantly. Then add 50 g (2 oz, ¼ cup) butter and adjust the seasoning. If the purée is too thick, add a little of the strained cooking liquid. Chestnut purée can be used to make soup or a savoury soufflé.

Chestnut stuffing

Boil and peel 450 g (1 lb) chestnuts, then coarsely chop them. Finely chop 1 large onion, 1 celery stick and 1 garlic clove, and sweat with 2 crumbled bay leaves in a covered pan in 50 g (2 oz, ¼ cup) butter for about 30 minutes, until thoroughly softened but not browned. Stir in the grated zest of 1 lemon, 2 tablespoons lemon juice and 4 tablespoons brandy or sherry. Remove from the heat. Discard the bay leaves, then add 2 tablespoons thyme leaves, 1 tablespoon chopped tarragon and a handful of parsley, chopped. Stir in the chestnuts and season with salt, pepper and freshly grated nutmeg.

Consommé Nesselrode

Prepare some game consommé and make some small savoury choux buns. Mix some chestnut purée with one-third of its weight of Soubise purée and use the mixture to fill half of the choux. Fill the remainder with a very dry mushroom duxelles. Garnish the consommé with the choux buns.

Omelette à la châtelaine

Add 150 g (5 oz, ⅔ cup) finely sliced onions, softened in butter, to 500 g (18 oz, 3 cups) braised and coarsely crumbled chestnuts. Fill an omelette with this mixture and surround it with a thin line of cream sauce.

Purée of chestnut soup

Peel 575 g (1¼ lb) chestnuts and cook in a saucepan with 1.5 litres (2¾ pints, 6½ cups) stock or consommé until they begin to disintegrate. Peel 200 g (7 oz) celeriac, cut it into slices and blanch for 2 minutes in boiling water. Drain and pat dry. Sweat in 25 g (1 oz, 2 tablespoons) butter with 1 tablespoon finely chopped onion. Add the celeriac to the cooked chestnuts and cook together for a further 10 minutes. Put through a blender or food processor. Dilute with a little stock or boiled milk and whisk in 50 g (2 oz, ¼ cup) butter cut into small pieces. Serve with small croûtons fried in butter.

Roast chestnuts

Using a sharp pointed knife, cut a circular incision around the chestnuts through the husk and the inner skin. Roast in a pan over hot embers, shaking them often. Chestnuts can also be roasted in a very hot oven. In this case, add a little water to the pan.

Soft-boiled or poached eggs à la châtelaine

Prepare some shortcrust pastry tartlets and bake blind. Prepare some chestnut purée and add a quarter of its volume of Soubise purée. Season well. Fill the bottom of the tartlets with this mixture, place 1 soft-boiled (soft-cooked) or poached egg in each of them and coat with a chicken velouté sauce. Serve very hot.

Stewed chestnuts

Peel the chestnuts and place them in a buttered sauté pan. Cover them either with clear white stock or with water. Add a pinch of salt, 1 teaspoon caster (superfine) sugar and a chopped celery stick. Bring to the boil, cover and cook gently for about 45 minutes.

Chick peas

Chick peas à la catalane

Soak 500 g (18 oz, 3 cups) chick peas in cold water for at least 12 hours, changing the water several times. Drain them and place in a pan with a carrot, an onion, 2 celery sticks and the white part of a leek, all thinly sliced. Add a piece of smoked bacon weighing about 250 g (9 oz) and a bouquet garni and cover with 2 litres (3½ pints, 9 cups) cold water. Bring to the boil, skim, add salt and pepper, reduce the heat and add 3–4 tablespoons oil.

Simmer gently for 2–3 hours, depending on the quality of the chick peas. Then add a piece of strong *chorizo* and cook for a further 30 minutes. Remove the bouquet garni, the bacon and the *chorizo* and drain the chick peas. Then put the chick peas into a saucepan together with 200 ml (7 fl oz, ¾ cup) tomato sauce spiced with garlic. Cut the *chorizo* into slices, slice the bacon and add them to the chick peas. Simmer for 15 minutes, pour into a deep dish and serve piping hot.

Hummus

Soak 175 g (6 oz, 1 cup) chick peas overnight. Drain and bring to the boil in fresh water (not salted), cover and simmer for 2–2½ hours, until the chick peas are completely tender. Drain and purée in a food processor with 2 chopped garlic cloves until coarse, not completely smooth. Add 100 ml (4 fl oz, 7 tablespoons) tahini and 60 ml (2 fl oz, ¼ cup) freshly squeezed lemon juice, then process again, gradually adding 60 ml (2 fl oz, ¼ cup) olive oil. Stir in seasoning to taste with plenty of chopped parsley.

If a food processor is not available, the chick peas can be mashed and the garlic crushed, then the remaining ingredients can be beaten in by hand. The hummus can be seasoned with ground roasted cumin seeds or ground roasted coriander seeds.

Socca

A flour made from chick peas in the Nice region of France. A thick porridge is made from it, which can be cooked au gratin, used to fill a tart, or sliced (when cold), fried in olive oil and served with sugar. The latter is a popular delicacy, which is sold in the streets.

Mix 125 g (4½ oz, 1 cup) chick pea flour with 250 ml (8 fl oz, 1 cup) water, salt, pepper and 1 tablespoon olive oil. Whisk vigorously. Pour into 2 large buttered gratin dishes. Cook in a preheated oven at 240°C (475°F, gas 9) for 20 minutes. Prick the bubbles that have formed on the surface of the socca, then grill (broil) until golden under a preheated grill (broiler).

Chicory (endive)

Braised chicory

Trim and wash 1 kg (2¼ lb) chicory (endive) and place in a flameproof casserole with 25 g (1 oz, 2 tablespoons) butter, a pinch of salt, the juice of a quarter of a lemon, and 3 tablespoons water. Bring quickly to the boil without a lid, then leave to boil over a medium heat for 35 minutes.

Chicory can also be braised very gently in 50 g (2 oz, 4 tablespoons) butter, with a little salt and lemon juice, but without water, for 45 minutes.

Chicory à la Mornay

Braise some chicory (endive) heads, drain them carefully, and stir 300 ml (½ pint, 1¼ cups) Mornay sauce into the cooking juices. Coat an ovenproof dish with this sauce and arrange the chicory heads in the dish. Cover the chicory with more Mornay sauce, sprinkle with grated Parmesan cheese and then lightly with melted butter, and brown in a preheated very hot oven at 240°C (475°F, gas 9).

Chicory au gratin

Braise some chicory heads and drain them thoroughly. Arrange them in a gratin dish that has been buttered and sprinkled with grated cheese (Comté, Gruyère, Parmesan or even dried Edam). Sprinkle the chicory with more grated cheese and melted butter, then brown in a preheated oven at 240°C (475°F, gas 9).

Chicory fritots

Braise some chicory heads, keeping them fairly firm, then drain thoroughly and leave to cool. Cut them into quarters and steep for 1 hour in olive oil containing some lemon juice and pepper. Drain, dip in batter and deep-fry in very hot oil (180°C, 350°F). When the fritters have turned golden, lift them out of the oil, drain on paper towels, sprinkle with fine salt and serve with fried parsley.

Chicory purée

Braise some chicory until very soft, then rub through a sieve or use a blender to obtain a purée. Butter or cream can be added (reduce the cream a little first), as can white sauce – use 300 ml (½ pint, 1¼ cups) sauce per 1 kg (2¼ lb) purée. The purée can be browned in a hot oven if desired.

Chicory salad à la flamande

Separate the chicory into leaves and divide them in half. Sprinkle lightly with lemon juice to prevent discoloration. Add some diced cooked beetroot (red beet) and garnish with orange segments. Season with a mustard vinaigrette and sprinkle with chopped hard-boiled (hard-cooked) egg yolk and chives.

Chicory soufflé

Prepare 250 g (9 oz) braised or stewed chicory (endive), dry it over the heat and rub through a sieve. Stir in 150 ml (¼ pint, ⅔ cup) béchamel sauce and 40 g (1½ oz, ⅓ cup) grated Parmesan cheese if desired. Sprinkle with nutmeg, add 3 fairly large egg yolks and fold in 3 egg whites whisked fairly stiffly. Preheat the oven for 15 minutes at 220°C (425°F, gas 7). Butter a soufflé mould 20 cm (8 in) in diameter and coat with flour. Pour in the mixture and bake in the preheated oven at 200°C (400°F, gas 6) for 25 minutes, without opening the door, until well risen and a deep golden-brown on top.

Chicory with ham

Braise some chicory heads. Prepare some very thick white sauce (enough for 2–4 tablespoons per head) and add 50 g (2 oz, ½ cup) grated Gruyère cheese per 250 ml (8 fl oz, 1 cup) sauce. Drain the chicory heads, wrap each in a slice of Paris ham and arrange side by side in a buttered gratin dish. Cover with the hot white sauce, sprinkle with grated Gruyère cheese and dot with butter. Brown in a preheated oven at 240°C (475°F, gas 9).

Chicory with noisette butter

Braise some chicory heads, drain them and put them in a serving dish. Add 20 g (¾ oz, 1½ tablespoons) butter to the cooking juices and reduce until they turn brown. Sprinkle the chicory with the noisette butter.

Chiffonnade of chicory with cream

Wash and dry the chicory (endive) and remove the small bitter cone situated at the root. Cut the leaves into thin strips 1 cm (½ in) wide. Melt some butter in a shallow frying pan and add the chicory – use 40–50 g (1½–2 oz, 3–4 tablespoons) butter for each 1 kg (2¼ lb) chicory. Stir and add ½ teaspoon sugar, 2 tablespoons lemon juice, and salt and pepper. Cover the pan and cook gently for 30–35 minutes. Stir in 100–150 ml (4–5 fl oz, ½–⅔ cup) double (heavy) cream and heat quickly. Serve very hot.

Courgettes (zucchini) & marrows (summer squash)

Courgette flowers with truffles

Chop 500 g (18 oz) button mushrooms and sprinkle them with the juice of ½ lemon. Melt 25 g (1 oz, 2 tablespoons) butter in a frying pan and add 1 tablespoon chopped shallots. As soon as the butter begins to sizzle, add the mushrooms, season with salt, stir and cook for 3–4 minutes. Drain in a fine colander over a small saucepan and reserve the liquid. Return the mushrooms to the pan and dry over a high heat, then reduce the heat to the minimum setting or turn it off. Pour 5 tablespoons single (light) cream into a mixing bowl, add 2 egg yolks and stir the mixture with a whisk. Add to the mushrooms, stirring, and cook very gently for 2 minutes. Do not overheat or boil the mixture as it will curdle. Check the seasoning and cool.

Drain 6 black truffles (each 15 g, ½ oz) and add their juice to that of the mushrooms. Taking great care not to damage them, wipe clean 6 courgette (zucchini) flowers without washing them. Open up the petals and put 2 teaspoons of the mushroom mixture inside each flower. Put 1 truffle in the middle of each flower and close up the petals again. Place the flowers in the top part of a couscous pan or steamer and cover with foil. Trim and wash 500 g (18 oz) tender spinach or lamb's lettuce (corn salad), and set aside.

Reduce the mushroom juice until only 3 tablespoons remains. Whisk in 250 g (9 oz, 1 cup) butter cut into small pieces. Season with salt and pepper and transfer to a bain marie.

Steam the flowers for 15 minutes. Arrange the spinach or lamb's lettuce on a dish and place the courgette flowers on it. Pour the butter sauce over the courgette flowers. Sprinkle with chervil and serve.

Courgette omelette

Slice some courgettes (zucchini) into thin rounds and sauté them in butter in a frying pan. Beat some eggs with chopped parsley, salt and pepper, pour them into the pan over the courgettes and cook the omelette on both sides like a thick pancake.

Courgette purée

Peel and slice the courgettes (zucchini), place them in a saucepan and just cover them with water. Add some salt and 3–4 garlic cloves and cook them, covered, for about 15 minutes. If the resulting purée is very watery, dry it carefully on the heat without allowing it to stick to the bottom of the pan. Add some butter. Pour the purée into a vegetable dish and sprinkle with chopped herbs, or spread it in a greased gratin dish, top with grated Gruyère cheese and butter, and brown in the oven.

Courgettes à la créole

Peel the courgettes (zucchini) and remove the seeds. Dice the flesh and cook in a little lard (shortening) until golden brown. Add salt, cover, and cook them over a very gentle heat, stirring from time to time. When completely softened (after 20–25 minutes), mash with a fork, and continue to cook, stirring continuously until the pulp is golden brown. Adjust the seasoning.

Courgette salad

Peel the courgettes (zucchini) and cut the flesh into fine strips. Toss with a little well-seasoned vinaigrette and sprinkle with a mixture of chopped chervil and tarragon. Serve at once.

Courgette salad with lime

Lightly peel and coarsely grate the courgettes (zucchini). Toss with a little lime juice and the grated zest of ½–1 lime. Add a generous sprinkling of snipped chives and a little chopped fresh coriander leaves (cilantro). Season to taste, toss well and serve at once.

Courgettes à la mentonnaise

Cut the courgettes (zucchini) in half lengthways. Make an incision around the pulp, 1 cm (½ in) from the edge, and several smaller incisions in the centre of the pulp. Season the courgettes with salt and put them upside down on paper towels to remove the excess moisture. Dry, then sauté gently in olive oil until they are golden brown. Drain, remove the pulp from the centre without damaging the skin, and chop it.

Blanch some spinach in boiling water, then drain, cool, chop and cook it in butter in a covered pan. Mix the courgette pulp with an equal amount of cooked spinach and fill the courgette halves with this mixture. Sprinkle with

1 tablespoon grated Parmesan cheese and add a little garlic and some chopped parsley. Sprinkle with breadcrumbs and olive oil and brown in the oven.

Courgettes à la niçoise

Partially peel the courgettes (zucchini), slice them thinly and sauté them in oil with an equal quantity of peeled tomatoes. Add some parsley and garlic, and season with salt and pepper.

Courgettes à la provençale

Do not peel the courgettes (zucchini). Cut them into long thick slices, sprinkle them with salt and leave for 15 minutes. Then pat them dry, coat them with flour and sauté them in oil in a frying pan. Brush a gratin dish with oil, cover the bottom with rice cooked in meat stock, then add some of the courgette slices. Sauté some slices of tomato and onion in oil and add chopped parsley and garlic. Place the onion and tomato slices in the gratin dish on the courgettes and cover with the remaining courgettes. Sprinkle with grated cheese and brown in a preheated oven at 230°C (450°F, gas 8).

Glazed courgettes

Cut the courgettes (zucchini) into small uniform olive-shaped pieces. Blanch them lightly in boiling salted water and drain them. Place them in a sauté pan with 2 tablespoons butter, a pinch of salt and a small amount of sugar. Cover the courgettes with cold water, bring to the boil and cook, covered, over a low heat until the liquid has almost completely evaporated. Sauté the courgettes in this reduced sauce.

Glazed courgettes may be used as a garnish for poached fish or roast, fried or sautéed white meats.

Sautéed courgettes

Slice the courgettes (zucchini) and toss them with a little flour. Season with salt and sauté in oil or butter. Sprinkle with freshly ground black pepper and a squeeze of lemon juice. Serve immediately.

Stuffed courgettes

Cut the courgettes (zucchini) in half lengthways and hollow out. Prepare the stuffing: cook some rice and drain. Mix with minced (ground) lamb, chopped onion and fennel softened in butter, crushed garlic and seasoning.

Fill the courgette halves with the stuffing and place them close together in a greased ovenproof dish. Cover and cook in a preheated oven at 180°C (350°F, gas 4) for about 1 hour or until the filling is cooked and the courgettes are tender. Uncover the dish for the final 20 minutes. Serve the courgettes coated with tomato sauce.

Marrow au gratin

Peel a large marrow (summer squash) and cut it into several medium-sized pieces. Blanch them in boiling salted water for 4–5 minutes, drain and pat them dry. Place them in a greased gratin dish on a layer of grated cheese. Pour some melted butter over the top and brown in a preheated medium oven.

Marrow au gratin may also be prepared with alternate layers of marrow and sliced onions (softened in butter) or with rice cooked in meat stock.

Marrow flower fritters

Pick very fresh marrow (summer squash) flowers and wash them only if really necessary. Pat them dry, dip them in a light batter and deep-fry them in hot fat at 180°C (350°F) until golden brown. Drain the fritters, sprinkle with salt and serve very hot as an hors d'oeuvre.

Scrambled eggs à l'arlésienne

Halve some courgettes (zucchini), remove most of the pulp and cut into dice. Cook the empty cases lightly in olive oil and also sauté the diced flesh in oil. Prepare a concentrated garlic-flavoured tomato fondue. Make the scrambled eggs and add the diced courgettes and the tomato fondue (1 tablespoon per 2 eggs). Fill the courgette shells with the mixture and arrange them in an oiled gratin dish. Sprinkle with grated Parmesan cheese and a little olive oil and brown quickly in a preheated oven at 240°C (475°F, gas 9).

Cucumbers & gherkins

Buttered cucumber

Place blanched segments of cucumber in a sauté pan with some butter – allow 50 g (2 oz, ¼ cup) per 1 kg (2¼ lb) of cucumber; add salt, pepper, and 2 tablespoons water. Begin by boiling fast, then cover and simmer very gently for about 30 minutes. Just before serving, add a fresh piece of butter, stir, pour into a vegetable dish and sprinkle with chopped herbs. Buttered cucumber can be served with poultry and white fish.

Cold cucumber soup

Cut a large cucumber into small pieces. Peel 12 small new onions and cut into quarters. Chop these vegetables in a food processor and put them into a blender with the same quantity of cottage cheese and some salt and pepper: the resultant purée should be well seasoned. Place in the refrigerator until ready to serve. Then dilute the purée with iced water to obtain the consistency of a fairly thick soup and sprinkle with chopped chives or parsley.

Cucumber salad

Cut the cucumbers into semicircular slices. Add a well-seasoned vinaigrette generously flavoured with herbs (parsley, chervil, chives) or coarsely chopped fresh mint leaves. This salad can be served as an hors d'oeuvre or to accompany cold white meat or fish.

Cucumber salad with yogurt

Peel a large cucumber, split lengthways, and remove the seeds. Cut the flesh into very thin half-slices, dust with 1 teaspoon fine salt and leave for 30 minutes in a colander for the cucumber to lose some of its water. Rinse under the cold tap, wipe well and mix with 3 tablespoons yogurt sauce.

Cucumber stuffed with crab

Halve and hollow out 3 medium-sized cucumbers. Sprinkle with fine salt and leave to sweat for about 1 hour. Mash 250 g (9 oz, 1 cup) crabmeat (fresh or canned) and dice some fennel finely (enough for 3 tablespoons). Also dice very finely 150 g (5 oz) cooked ham. Make some mayonnaise with 1 egg yolk, 2 teaspoons mustard and 250 ml (8 fl oz, 1 cup) oil; add salt, pepper and 1 tablespoon each wine vinegar and tomato ketchup. Mix the mayonnaise, crabmeat, fennel and ham and season. Drain the cucumber halves thoroughly and fill with the stuffing. Keep in a cool place; when ready to serve, sprinkle the cucumbers with chopped herbs and arrange on lettuce leaves.

Instead of mayonnaise, double (heavy) cream flavoured with tomato ketchup, lemon juice and cayenne can be used, and shelled prawns (peeled shrimp) can be substituted for the crabmeat.

Cucumbers with cream

Cut the cucumber flesh into segments and blanch. Grease a sauté pan, add the pieces of cucumber with some salt and pepper, cover and cook very gently for about 10 minutes; then add some heated double (heavy) cream – allow 200 ml (7 fl oz, ¾ cup) per 1 kg (2¼ lb) cucumber – and continue cooking uncovered. The cucumber can also, after salting and draining, be cooked au gratin or served with Mornay sauce.

Gherkins à la russe

Boil some salted water with caster (superfine) sugar, using 1 tablespoon salt and 1 teaspoon sugar per 1 litre (1¾ pints, 4⅓ cups) water. Allow to cool completely. Wash some large fresh gherkins in warm water and cool them in cold water. Drain and pat dry. Layer them in a jar, separating each layer with a few fragments of fennel sprigs and, if available, a few fresh blackcurrant leaves (taken from the ends of the twigs). Press down well. Fill the jars with salted water (it should completely cover the gherkins) and leave to marinate in a cool place for at least 24 hours before serving. When preserving these gherkins, they can be sterilized, but they become softer in the process.

Gherkins pickled in vinegar (prepared cold)

Prepare and marinate the gherkins with salt as in the previous recipe. Then wash them in vinegared water, wipe them dry one by one and place them in jars. Add peeled white pickling onions, some fragments of bay leaf, sprigs of thyme and tarragon (which have been scalded, cooled and dried), 2–3 cloves, 1–2 small garlic cloves, 1 small chilli, a few black peppercorns and a few coriander seeds. Cover with white vinegar, seal the jars and store in a cool place. These gherkins can be eaten after 5–6 weeks, but they will improve with time (up to a year).

Gherkins pickled in vinegar (prepared hot)

Rub the gherkins with a rough cloth, then place them in a terrine. Add some coarse salt, stir and leave for 24 hours. Remove the gherkins and dry them one by one. Place them in a terrine and cover with boiled white wine vinegar. Marinate for about 12 hours. Strain off the vinegar and add 500 ml (17 fl oz, 2 cups) fresh vinegar to each 3 litres (5 pints, 13 cups) boiled vinegar, bring to the boil and, while still boiling, pour over the gherkins. Repeat the process the next day, then leave to cool completely. Scald some jars with boiling water and let them dry. Lay the gherkins in them in layers, adding seasoning every 2 layers (fragments of bay leaf, sprigs of thyme and tarragon, which have been scalded, cooled and dried, cloves and 1–2 chillies per jar). Cover with vinegar, cover the jars and store in a cool place.

Savoury orange and cucumber salad

Remove all the peel and pith from some oranges and slice them into rounds about 5 mm (¼ in) thick. Remove the seeds. Peel and finely slice some cucumber, sprinkle the slices with salt and leave them to drain. Rinse the slices in cold water and dry them. Arrange the slices of orange and cucumber alternately in a round glass dish. Dress with a well-seasoned vinaigrette.

Stuffed cucumber

Peel 2 medium even-shaped cucumbers, split them in half lengthways and remove the seeds and a little of the flesh. Prepare an *à gratin* forcemeat. Grease a gratin dish or, better still, line it with pieces of pork rind with the fat removed. Cover with a layer of finely chopped carrots and onions and sprinkle with a little chopped parsley. Fill the cucumber halves with the stuffing and arrange them in the dish. Add beef or chicken stock until it comes two-thirds of the way up the cucumber boats.

Bring to boiling point on the hob (stove top), then transfer to a preheated oven at 220°C (425°F, gas 7) and cook for 35 minutes. Cover with foil as soon as the top of the stuffing starts to dry out. Arrange the cucumbers on a serving dish and keep warm. Reduce the cooking liquid to 200 ml (7 fl oz, ¾ cup), thicken with beurre manié, pour over the cucumber and serve very hot.

Stuffed cucumber à la russe

Finely slice a cucumber and cut each slice into quarters. Cut 3 other cucumbers into boat shapes. Mash the contents of a can of tuna or salmon, roughly chop 6 small (pearl) onions and mix together the fish, onions, and quartered cucumber slices with 300 g (11 oz, 1⅓ cups) cottage cheese (well drained). Season with salt and pepper. Fill the cucumber boats with this mixture and put in a cool place. When ready to serve, sprinkle with 1 sieved hard-boiled (hard-cooked) egg and chopped herbs.

Tzatiki

Peel 1 cucumber (English cucumber) and cut it in half lengthways. Scoop out and discard the seeds from the middle, then coarsely grate the remainder of the vegetable. Place the grated cucumber in a sieve and sprinkle it lightly with salt. Leave to drain over a bowl for about 30 minutes. Squeeze the excess liquid from the cucumber, then place it in a bowl. Add 1 crushed garlic clove and a squeeze of lemon juice. Stir in 300 ml (½ pint, 1¼ cups) Greek yogurt. Finely chop the leaves from 2–3 sprigs of mint and add them to the tzatziki. Season with a little cayenne pepper and chill for about 1 hour before serving. Offer warm crusty bread with the tzatziki.

Custard marrow

To prepare

The custard marrow, also known as *chayote* in France, *christophine* or *brionne* in the West Indies and *chouchoute* in Madagascar and Polynesia, keeps for a long time. Before completely ripe, it may be consumed raw in salads, peeled, cored and finely sliced. It is especially common in Caribbean cookery. Not fully ripe until it starts to germinate, the gourd is peeled and puréed for making *acras* (savoury fritters) and very fine gratins.

Custard marrows à la martiniquaise

Press some boiled custard marrows in a cloth to extract the maximum amount of water and mix this pulp with bread soaked in milk. Brown some peeled and finely sliced spring onions (scallions) in butter, then blend with the mixture of bread and custard marrow. Season and spread out in a gratin dish, smoothing the top. Moisten with olive oil, sprinkle with fresh breadcrumbs and reheat in the oven.

Custard marrows au blanc

Divide the custard marrows into quarters and cut into large lozenge shapes. Cook in a blanc, keeping them slightly firm, or blanch for 5 minutes in salted water. Drain, dry and arrange them flat in a shallow frying pan in which 3 tablespoons white consommé or water have been heated. Cover and cook very gently. When cooked, arrange in a serving dish and pour over the buttery pan juice; alternatively, serve with béchamel sauce, cream, au gratin, in a salad, with a well-seasoned vinaigrette, with Mornay or tomato sauce.

Custard marrows braised in gravy

Divide the custard marrows into quarters and cut into lozenge shapes; blanch for 5 minutes in salted water and drain. Cover a shallow frying pan with bacon rinds, carrots and sliced onions, and put the custard marrows on top. Season with salt and pepper and cover with clarified stock. Cook quite gently, first covered, then uncovered. When the liquid is three-quarters reduced, add some meat juice and leave to simmer for a few minutes. Drain the custard marrows and keep them hot in the serving dish. Strain the pan juice, add butter and pour it over the custard marrows. Sprinkle with chopped parsley.

Endive (chicory)

Braised endive

Prepare the endive (chicory) as for endive *au gratin*. Make a white roux, using 40 g (1½ oz, 3 tablespoons) butter and 40 g (1½ oz, 6 tablespoons) plain (all-purpose) flour for every 500 g (18 oz) endive; season with salt, pepper, a little sugar and some grated nutmeg, then add 600 ml (1 pint, 2½ cups) stock. Add the chopped endive and cook briefly on the hob (stove top) in a flameproof casserole. Then cover the casserole and cook in a preheated oven at 180°C (350°F, gas 4) for about 1½ hours. Veal gravy may be added.

Endive au gratin

Remove the hard or dark green leaves from the heads of curly endive. Cut off the remaining leaves at the beginning of the stump and rinse them well in water. Drain and blanch for 10 minutes in plenty of boiling salted water. Cool, drain, chop finely and then mix with 4–5 tablespoons béchamel sauce per 450 g (1 lb) endive. Arrange the endive on a buttered gratin dish and sprinkle with 75 g (3 oz, ¾ cup) grated Gruyère cheese and 2 tablespoons melted butter. Brown in a preheated oven at 240°C (475°F, gas 9).

Endive salad with bacon

Cut 250 g (9 oz) smoked bacon for each head of curly endive into very fine strips and brown them in butter in a frying pan. Clean the endive, rinse it and dry it as thoroughly as possible. Season with a well-flavoured vinaigrette and then scatter the sizzling-hot bacon strips over the top. Tiny fried garlic-flavoured croûtons are usually added. Serve immediately.

Stewed endive

Prepare the endive as for braising, and place it in a saucepan with 50 g (2 oz, ¼ cup) butter for each 450 g (1 lb) endive. Season, add 500–600 ml (17–20 fl oz, 2–2½ cups) water, cover and cook in a preheated oven at 180°C (350°F, gas 4) for 1½ hours. When cooked, the endive may be tossed in butter, reduced cream or béchamel sauce just before serving.

Fennel

Braised fennel

Trim, halve and core fennel bulbs. Put them in an ovenproof dish. Sauté 2 diced bacon rashers (slices), 1 chopped onion and 1 diced carrot in a little olive oil until slightly softened, then sprinkle over the fennel. Moisten with a few tablespoons of chicken stock or dry white wine (or a mixture of both). Season to taste. Cover and cook in a preheated oven at 180°C (350°F, gas 4) for about 1 hour or until tender. Turn the fennel halfway through cooking and add a little extra stock or wine, if necessary, to keep the vegetables moist.

Fennel salad

Hard-boil (hard-cook) 2 eggs and shell them. Boil 100 g (4 oz, ¾ cup) long-grain rice. Leave to cool. Peel 12 small pickling (baby) onions. Clean 1 large bulb of fennel and slice it finely. Cut 4 small tomatoes into quarters. Add a little well-seasoned vinaigrette to the rice and put into a salad bowl. Place all the other ingredients on top of the rice, together with some black olives. Sprinkle with chopped herbs and serve with anchovy sauce.

Fennel sauce

Prepare 250 ml (8 fl oz, 1 cup) English butter sauce and add 1 tablespoon chopped blanched fennel. Serve with boiled or grilled (broiled) fish.

Fern

To prepare

The young shoots or fronds (also called 'violin scrolls') are harvested in Quebec and New Brunswick in early spring. They are shaken to remove the fine reddish dust covering them, then blanched for a few minutes. The shoots are either eaten cold or reheated in butter and sprinkled with lemon juice. They are a good accompaniment for meat and fish.

Fiddlehead fern and Matane prawn salad

Cook 575 g (1¼ lb) fiddlehead ferns for 3 minutes in boiling water. Drain well and set aside. Prepare a vierge sauce, made with 250 ml (8 fl oz, 1 cup) extra-virgin olive oil, the juice of 2 lemons, salt and pepper.

Brown 1 chopped onion in 100 ml (4 fl oz, 7 tablespoons) extra-virgin olive oil. Add 6 ripe tomatoes, peeled, seeded and crushed. Cook for 5 minutes over a high heat, stirring, then add 3 tablespoons sherry vinegar. Cook for 3 minutes to reduce then season to taste. Add 2 tablespoons snipped chives. Spoon the tomato mixture on to serving plates and top with fiddlehead ferns. Add 100 g (4 oz) peeled, cooked Matane prawns (shelled Matane shrimp). Garnish with unpeeled prawns (unshelled shrimp). Serve immediately with the vierge sauce.

Garlic

Aïgo boulido

This is the Provençal name for a soup made from boiled water (hence its name, which may also be spelled *bouïdo* or *bullido*) and garlic. It is one of the oldest culinary traditions of this region, where they have the saying *l'aïgo boulido suavo lo vito* (garlic soup saves one's life).

Bring 1 litre (1¾ pints, 4⅓ cups) water to the boil in a saucepan. Season with ½ teaspoon salt and 6 crushed garlic cloves. Boil for about 10 minutes, then add a small sprig of sage, preferably fresh, one quarter of a bay leaf and a small sprig of thyme to the soup. Immediately remove the pan from the heat and leave to infuse for several minutes. Remove the herbs and discard. Blend 1 egg yolk with a little of the cooled soup, then stir it back into the soup to thicken it. To serve, pour the soup over slices of bread which have been sprinkled with olive oil.

Aïgo boulido with poached eggs

Poach some eggs in aïgo boulido stock. Place a slice of bread in each hot soup plate and top this with a poached egg. Ladle the soup over and sprinkle with chopped parsley to serve.

If preferred, to make a more substantial dish, 2 chopped and seeded tomatoes, a small sprig of fennel, a pinch of saffron threads, a piece of dried orange zest and 4 sliced cooked and peeled potatoes may be added to the basic aïgo boulido stock. In this case, serve the poached eggs separately on the potatoes and pour the flavoured soup over the slices of bread sprinkled with chopped parsley.

Aillade sauce

Peel 4 garlic cloves, crush or finely chop them and place in a bowl with salt and pepper. Gradually blend in 2 tablespoons olive oil, stirring well. Mix in 2–3 teaspoons vinegar, a few sprigs of chopped parsley and, if desired, 2 teaspoons chopped shallots and chives.

Aïoli

Peel 4 large garlic cloves (split them in two and remove the germ if necessary). Pound the garlic with 1 egg yolk in a mortar or blender. Add salt and pepper and, while pounding or blending, very gradually add 250 ml (8 fl oz, 1 cup) olive oil, as for a mayonnaise. The sauce is ready when it is thick and creamy

Aïoli without eggs

Cook a whole head of garlic, unpeeled, in a hot oven for about 30 minutes. Peel the cloves and mash to a purée. Add salt and pepper, and thicken like a mayonnaise by working in 150 ml (¼ pint, ⅔ cup) olive oil and 150 ml (¼ pint, ⅔ cup) groundnut (peanut) oil.

Garlic butter with cooked garlic

Peel 8 large garlic cloves and plunge in boiling salted water. Boil for 7–8 minutes, dry and purée. Work into 250 g (8 oz) butter softened by creaming or in a food processor. Garlic butter is used to complete some sauces, and adds the final touch to garnishes for cold hors d'oeuvres.

Garlic butter with raw garlic

Crush 2–4 garlic cloves and add to 250 g (8 oz) butter softened by creaming or in a food processor. Mix well. A little finely chopped parsley and grated lemon zest can be added to complement the raw garlic.

Garlic oil

Blanch and crush garlic cloves, add olive oil and press through a sieve. Alternatively, add grated garlic to olive oil and press through a muslin cloth (cheesecloth). Garlic oil is used to season salads and raw vegetables.

Garlic purée

Blanch some garlic cloves, then gently sweat them in butter. Add a few spoonfuls of thick béchamel sauce and either press through a sieve or liquidize in a blender. Garlic purée is used in sauces and stuffings.

Garlic stuffing

Crush the yolks of hard-boiled (hard-cooked) eggs in a mortar with an equal quantity of blanched garlic cloves. Add fresh butter (half the volume of ingredients in the mortar), season with salt and pepper and press through a sieve or crush in a blender. Chopped herbs may also be added. This stuffing is used to garnish cold hors d'oeuvres and to spread on canapés.

Garlic toast

Cut some slices of bread 5 mm (¼ in) thick and grill (broil) them lightly. Spread them with garlic purée and sprinkle with a thin layer of breadcrumbs and a little olive oil. Brown quickly in a hot oven and serve hot with a salad.

Roast garlic

Remove any loose outer layers of papery covering from a large head of garlic and trim off the stalk at the top. Brush with a little oil and wrap in foil. Prepare 1 head for 2 portions. Cook in a preheated oven at 200°C (400°F, gas 6) for 30–40 minutes. Use a sharp knife to slice the head of garlic horizontally in half. Serve with salt, olive oil and warm crusty bread.

Jerusalem artichokes

Jerusalem artichoke and hazelnut salad

Peel the required quantity of Jerusalem artichokes and cook them for about 10 minutes in salted white wine. Drain and slice. Put the slices into a salad bowl and season with oil, mustard and lemon juice. Chop lightly toasted hazelnuts and scatter them over the artichokes.

Jerusalem artichoke pie with foie gras and truffle

Peel and finely cut 575 g (1¼ lb) pink Jerusalem artichokes into slices 3 mm (⅛ in) thick. Cook in stock for 5 minutes, then drain. Slice 50 g (2 oz) truffles very finely. Cut very thin slices across the width of a lobe of foie gras. Season with salt and pepper, and add some nutmeg. Line the bottom and sides of a well-buttered medium-sized soufflé mould with the slices of Jerusalem artichoke. Place a thin layer of truffle on top, then a layer of foie gras. Repeat the layering until all the ingredients are used up and cover with foil. Press down with a smaller mould. Cook in a bain marie in a preheated oven at 180°C (350°F, gas 4) for 20 minutes. Unmould on to a serving dish and pour over a warm vinaigrette made with walnut oil and sherry vinegar, flavoured with chervil or flat-leafed parsley.

Jerusalem artichokes à l'anglaise

Peel some Jerusalem artichokes, cut into quarters, and trim to egg shapes if they are large. Blanch for 5 minutes in boiling water, then dry them. Cook gently in butter in a covered pan for about 30 minutes. Stir in a few tablespoons of light béchamel sauce or double (heavy) cream and simmer for about 10 minutes. Serve as a garnish for veal, for example, sprinkled with chopped chervil and tarragon.

Salad of Jerusalem artichokes

Prepare like a potato salad, using small new Jerusalem artichokes, cooked in water for 20 minutes, peeled and cut into uniform pieces. Dress with a sunflower oil vinaigrette seasoned with shallot and sprinkle with parsley.

Leeks

Boiled leeks

Trim and clean some young leeks, keeping only the white parts. Cut these all to the same length, split them, wash well and tie together in bunches. Cook for about 10 minutes in boiling salted water until just tender (they must not fall to pieces). Untie them, drain thoroughly on a cloth or paper towels, and arrange them in a warm dish. Garnish with chopped parsley and serve hot melted butter separately.

Alternatively, coat with melted butter seasoned and flavoured with lemon juice, or with reduced and seasoned cream.

Braised leeks

Trim and wash 12 leeks, keeping only the white parts. Cut into slices and place in a casserole with 50 g (2 oz, ¼ cup) butter, salt and pepper, and 5–6 tablespoons water or meat stock. Braise for about 40 minutes. Arrange the leeks in a vegetable dish and pour the braising liquid, enriched with an extra 15 g (½ oz, 1 tablespoon) butter over them.

Cream of leek soup

Shred and blanch 500 g (18 oz) leeks, then cook them in 40–50 g (1½–2 oz, 3–4 tablespoons) butter in a covered pan. Prepare 750 ml (1¼ pints, 3¼ cups) white sauce by adding 900 ml (1½ pints, 1 quart) milk to a white roux of 25 g (1 oz, 2 tablespoons) butter and 40 g (1½ oz, 6 tablespoons) plain (all-purpose) flour. Mix this sauce with the leeks, them simmer gently for 12–18 minutes. Purée in a food processor or blender, then press through a sieve if necessary. Dilute with a few tablespoons of white stock or milk. Heat and adjust the seasoning. Add 200 ml (7 fl oz, ¾ cup) single (light) cream and stir while heating.

Leek flamiche

Make 500 g (1 lb 2 oz) shortcrust pastry (basic pie dough). Roll out two-thirds of the dough to line a 28 cm (11 in) pie plate. Cut and thinly slice 1 kg (2¼ lb) leeks (the white parts only) and slowly cook them in butter. Add 3 egg yolks and adjust the seasoning. Spread the mixture over the pastry on the pie plate. Roll out the remaining dough large enough to cover the top of the dish. Dampen and pinch the edges together to seal and mark a criss-cross pattern on the top with the tip of a knife. Glaze with beaten egg. Make a slit in the centre and bake in a preheated oven at 200°C (400°F, gas 6) until the pastry is golden brown.

Leek flan with cheese

Butter a 25 cm (10 in) flan ring (pie pan) and line it with 350 g (12 oz) shortcrust pastry (basic pie dough). Prick the base and bake blind in a preheated oven at 200°C (400°F, gas 6) for 12 minutes. Allow to cool. Clean, trim and slice 800 g (1¾ lb) leeks (the white part only) and braise them gently for about 14 minutes in 40 g (1½ oz, 3 tablespoons) butter. Strain. Make 400 ml (14 fl oz, 1¾ cups) Mornay sauce and allow to cool. Completely cover the base of the flan with half the sauce. Spread the leeks on top and cover with the remainder of the sauce. Sprinkle with 40 g (1½ oz, ⅓ cup) grated Parmesan cheese and 25 g (1 oz, 2 tablespoons) knobs of butter and place in a preheated oven at 240°C (475°F, gas 9) until brown.

Leeks à la crème

Put the well-washed white parts of leeks into a buttered casserole. Add salt and pepper, cover and braise in butter for 15 minutes. Completely cover with crème fraîche, then continue to simmer, with the lid on, for 30 minutes. Arrange the leeks in a vegetable dish, add a few tablespoons of crème fraîche to the pan juices and pour over the leeks.

Leeks à la vinaigrette

Use the white part of the leeks only, wash well and cook in boiling salted water. Drain on a cloth to remove any surplus liquid and arrange in a dish. Season with vinaigrette, containing mustard if liked. Sprinkle with chopped parsley and chervil or sieved hard-boiled (hard-cooked) egg yolk.

Leeks au gratin

Trim the leeks and use only the white parts. Wash them well, blanch for 5 minutes in plenty of boiling salted water, drain them, then cook slowly in butter. Arrange the cooked leeks in an ovenproof dish, sprinkle with grated cheese (preferably Parmesan) and melted butter, and place in a preheated oven at 240°C (475°F, gas 9) until brown.

Leeks with béchamel sauce

Blanch the white parts of some trimmed washed leeks for 5 minutes in boiling salted water. Drain thoroughly and braise in butter. Prepare a béchamel sauce that is not too thick. Arrange the leeks in a long dish, cover with the sauce and serve hot.

Porée of Charente

Chop the whites of 1.5 kg (3¼ lb) leeks and soften them in 100 g (4 oz, ½ cup) slightly salted butter in a frying pan. Add 200 ml (7 fl oz, ¾ cup) fish stock, 200 g (7 oz, ¾ cup) crème fraîche, a pinch of coarse salt and the same of pepper. Arrange 6 fillets of turbot or John Dory, 6 pieces of monkfish, 6 scallops and 6 langoustine tails on top. Cover and poach for 8 minutes. Serve the fish on the bed of leeks. Thicken the liquid with 2 egg yolks and pour it over the fish. Garnish with chervil.

Terrine of leeks and fresh goat's cheese

Wash and tie into a bundle 1.25 kg (2¾ lb) leeks and cook in boiling salted water. Cut off the green part so that the white part is the same length as the terrine. Cool quickly in ice-cold water and drain for 2 hours under a press. Wash and trim 200 g (7 oz) tomatoes and cut into small cubes. Season with olive oil and chopped chives and chervil. Heat 500 ml (17 fl oz, 2 cups) chicken, ham or vegetable stock and dissolve 10 sheets of soaked leaf gelatine in it. Allow to cool.

Line the terrine with cling film (plastic wrap). Pour a little jelly over the bottom and line the sides with leeks, alternating green and white. Put a first layer of tomatoes with 5 small fresh goat's cheeses in the middle. Continue with a layer of jelly, a layer of tomatoes and then fill the mould with the remaining leeks and the jelly. Press to remove excess liquid. Place in the refrigerator to chill for 14 hours. Unmould the terrine on a board and cut into slices. Pour some vinaigrette on top. Sprinkle with some fresh diced tomato, sprigs of chervil and chopped chives.

Vichyssoise

Slice 250 g (9 oz) leeks (white part only) and cut 250 g (9 oz) peeled potatoes into quarters. Soften the leeks in 50 g (2 oz, ¼ cup) butter in a covered saucepan or casserole without allowing them to brown. Then add the potatoes, stir and pour in 1.75 litres (3 pints, 7½ cups) water. Season with salt and pepper and add a small bouquet garni. Bring to the boil and cook for 30–40 minutes. Purée the potatoes and leeks in a food processor or blender and return to the pan. Blend in at least 200 ml (7 fl oz, ¾ cup) crème fraîche and return just to the boil, stirring frequently. Allow the soup to cool and chill in the refrigerator for at least 1 hour. Serve sprinkled with chopped chives in consommé cups.

Lentils

Green or brown lentil purée

Pick over the lentils and place them in a large saucepan, cover with plenty of cold water, bring to the boil, then skim. Add salt, pepper, a bouquet garni, a large onion stuck with 2 cloves and a small diced carrot. Cover and simmer gently for 30–45 minutes (the cooking time will depend on the type and freshness of the lentils). Remove the bouquet garni and the onion. Reduce the lentils to a purée in a food processor or blender while still hot, then heat the purée through gently, beating in a knob of butter. If desired, add a little stock, water, boiled milk or cream before beating in the butter.

Hot lentil salad

Cook green or brown lentils in boiling water for 30–35 minutes, until tender but still whole. Cut thick bacon rashers (slices) into strips and brown the strips in a little butter. Allow about 100 g (4 oz) bacon for 350 g (12 oz, 1½ cups) lentils. Prepare a vinaigrette and add to it 1 tablespoon red wine. Drain the lentils and place them in a warm dish. Add the pork, dress with the vinaigrette and sprinkle with plenty of chopped parsley. Mix the salad and serve hot or cold. A little finely chopped mild onion or a chopped bunch of spring onions (scallions) can be added, and the vinaigrette can be flavoured with a crushed garlic clove.

Red lentil purée

Allow 450 ml (¾ pint, 2 cups) water for 225 g (8 oz, 1 cup) lentils. Add 1 finely chopped onion, 1 finely diced carrot and 1 bay leaf, bring to the boil, reduce the heat to the lowest setting and cover the pan tightly. Cook gently for 20–30 minutes, or until the water has been absorbed and the lentils are tender. Purée in a food processor or beat well, then press through a sieve, if required. Season and enrich with butter or cream.

Lettuce

Braised lettuce au gratin

Braise the lettuces in meat stock or water and arrange in an ovenproof dish. Cover with Mornay sauce, sprinkle with grated cheese, top with melted butter and cook in a preheated oven at 220°C (425°F, gas 7) until brown.

Chiffonnade of cooked lettuce

Wash and dry some lettuce leaves, discarding the coarser leaves. Roll up several leaves and cut each roll into very thin slices, then shake them out into strips. Melt some butter in a shallow frying pan and add the lettuce *chiffonnade* and some salt – use 40 g (1½ oz, 3 tablespoons) butter per 500 g (18 oz) lettuce leaves. Cook gently without a lid until all the juice from the lettuce has evaporated. Add 2 tablespoons double (heavy) cream and reheat.

Chiffonnade of raw lettuce

Wash and dry some lettuce leaves, discarding the coarser leaves. Roll up several leaves and cut each roll into very thin slices, then shake them out into strips. Toss in vinaigrette if it is to be used as a garnish for meat, fish or cold shellfish. It may also be mixed with green walnuts, a julienne of ham, meat or cold chicken and Emmental cheese, and then sprinkled with vinaigrette and chopped herbs.

Creamed lettuce with spring onion soufflés

Clean and trim 4 lettuces, blanch them in salted water and leave to cool. Press them dry in a cloth, then roll up, several leaves at a time, and slice very finely.

Melt 25 g (1 oz, 2 tablespoons) butter in a large saucepan. Peel and finely chop 1 onion and add to the butter. Add the lettuce chiffonade and sweat for 4–5 minutes. Pour in 1 litre (1¾ pints, 4⅓ cups) chicken stock. Cook for 5 minutes then pass through a blender and put to one side. Peel 30 small spring onions (scallions), keeping only the white part. Chop very finely and place in a saucepan. Add 2 tablespoons water and cook uncovered for 20 minutes. Purée the spring onions in a food processor or blender and then thicken 300 g (11 oz, 1½ cups) of the purée with 1 teaspoon cornflour (cornstarch) and 3 egg yolks. Season with salt. Whisk 5 egg whites and 25 g (1 oz, 3 tablespoons) albumen powder or powdered egg white until they form stiff peaks and carefully fold into the purée. Fill 6 buttered ramekins or ovenproof moulds with this mixture. Cook for 12 minutes in a preheated oven at 180°C (350°F, gas 4).

Reheat the creamed lettuce, add 100 ml (4 fl oz, 7 tablespoons) single (light) cream and 50 g (2 oz, ¼ cup) butter. Heat through without boiling and check the seasoning. Pour the creamed lettuce into bowls. Unmould the soufflés and place in the bowls. Add a slice of grilled, smoked streaky bacon to each soufflé.

Lamb's lettuce mixed salad

Peel and chop 200 g (7 oz, 1 cup) cooked beetroot (beet). Trim, wash and slice into rings 200 g (7 oz) chicory (endive). Wash 250 g (9 oz) lamb's lettuce (corn salad) and pat dry. Peel, core and thinly slice an eating apple, then sprinkle with lemon juice to prevent discoloration. Place all these ingredients in a salad bowl. Prepare a vinaigrette, seasoning it with mustard, pour on to the salad and mix together well. A small handful of coarsely chopped walnuts can be added to the salad, or a little Roquefort cheese can be mixed into the vinaigrette.

Lamb's lettuce salad with bacon

Cut 150 g (5 oz) thick rindless streaky (slab) bacon rashers (slices) into pieces. Trim, peel and wash 400 g (14 oz) lamb's lettuce (corn salad). Arrange in a salad bowl. Brown the bacon pieces in a little butter and add to the salad. Sprinkle with vinaigrette.

Lettuce à la crème

Braise the lettuces in stock or water. Divide each lettuce in two, folding each in half, and place in a buttered pan. Moisten with cream and simmer until the cream has reduced by half. Transfer to a dish and garnish with croûtons.

Lettuce à l'italienne

Braise some lettuce hearts, then drain them well and arrange them in a buttered gratin dish. Moisten with Italian sauce, using 1 tablespoon per lettuce. Cover the pan and simmer over a gentle heat for about 20 minutes. Place the lettuce hearts in a ring and arrange some sautéed veal around the outside. If desired, the lettuces can be sprinkled with a little lemon juice.

Lettuce salad

Prepare a lettuce chiffonnade, incorporating a julienne of unsmoked ham, breast of chicken, and either Gruyère or Emmental cheese. Dress with a vinaigrette made with walnut oil and sprinkle with chopped herbs.

Reine Pédauque salad

Mix together 200 ml (7 fl oz, ¾ cup) double (heavy) cream, 2 tablespoons oil, 1 tablespoon mustard, 2 tablespoons lemon juice, ½ teaspoon paprika and a little salt. Pour this mixture over a border of 12 lettuce-heart quarters arranged around a shallow dish. Garnish the centre with shredded lettuce dressed with vinaigrette and sprinkled with fresh stoned (pitted) cherries. Place a slice of peeled orange, pith removed, on each lettuce-heart quarter.

Stuffed lettuce

Trim the lettuces, blanch for 5 minutes, cool under running water and blot dry. Halve each lettuce without cutting through the base. Season them inside. Fill each lettuce with a generous tablespoon of fine forcemeat mixed with mushroom duxelles. Tie each lettuce together and braise in stock or water.

Stuffed lettuce can be served on its own with fried croûtons, or it may be used as a garnish for roast or sautéed meat.

Maize

American salad

Line individual salad bowls with lettuce leaves. For each serving, mix together 1 tablespoon diced pineapple, 2 tablespoons sweetcorn, either canned or cooked in boiling water, 1 tablespoon shredded poached chicken breast, and 1 tablespoon peeled, seeded and diced cucumber. Dress with 2 tablespoons vinaigrette flavoured with tomato ketchup and pile in the bowls. Garnish each bowl with quarters of hard-boiled (hard-cooked) egg and tomato.

Attereaux à la piémontaise

Attereau, the name for a skewer, is a term for ingredients coated in bread-crumbs and fried. Prepare some polenta: boil 1 litre (1¾ pints, 4⅓ cups) water with 1–2 teaspoons salt (or to taste), then add 250 g (9 oz, 2 cups) cornmeal and mix thoroughly. Cook for 25–30 minutes, stirring continuously with a wooden spoon. Then add 50–65 g (2–2½ oz, 4–5 tablespoons) butter and season with salt and pepper. Spread it over a lightly oiled square baking sheet and allow to cool completely. Cut into 4 cm (1½ in) squares and thread on to skewers. Coat in breadcrumbs and deep-fry in hot oil at 175–180°C (347–356°F) until brown. Drain on paper towels and arrange on a dish. Garnish with fried parsley and serve with a well-reduced tomato sauce.

Corn fritters

Make a smooth batter using 100 g (4 oz, 1 cup) plain (all-purpose) flour, 2 eggs and 100 ml (4 fl oz, 7 tablespoons) water. Add 225 g (8 oz, 1 cup) thawed frozen or drained canned sweetcorn. Stir well, adding seasoning to taste and a little nutmeg. Shallow fry spoonfuls of the sweetcorn in batter in a mixture of sunflower oil and butter until golden underneath and set. Turn and cook the second sides until golden. Serve with deep-fried breadcrumb-coated chicken and fried bananas as American Maryland chicken.

Fresh corn with béchamel sauce

Choose fresh cobs with tender grains. Leave only one layer of leaves on and cook in boiling salted water for about 15 minutes (be careful to keep the water on the boil). Drain the cobs and remove the leaves. Scrape the kernels from the cobs and serve with a light béchamel sauce.

Parmesan polenta

Boil 1 litre (1¾ pints, 4⅓ cups) water with 1–2 teaspoons salt (or to taste), then add 250 g (9 oz, 2 cups) cornmeal and mix together thoroughly. Cook for 25–30 minutes, stirring continuously with a wooden spoon. Then add

50–65 g (2–2½ oz, 4–5 tablespoons) butter and 75 g (3 oz, ¾ cup) grated Parmesan cheese. Pour the porridge on to a damp plate, spreading it out in an even layer, and leave to cool completely. Cut into squares or diamond shapes and fry in butter until golden. Arrange on a serving dish and sprinkle with grated Parmesan cheese and noisette butter.

Polenta gratin

Dice 2 boneless chicken breasts. Chop 2 onions and 75 g (3 oz, ½ cup) olives very finely. Season with salt, pepper and chopped fresh coriander (cilantro) and fry until golden. Remove from the pan. Brown 2 chopped onions and add 2 tomatoes, peeled, seeded and crushed, then remove. Brown 250 g (9 oz, 1¾ cups) cooked polenta (cornmeal), cut into squares, in the olive oil. Return the onions and tomatoes, shaking the pan to mix them with the polenta. In a roasting tin (pan), put a layer of chicken, then a layer of polenta. Continue this layering process until all the ingredients have been used up. Gratiné in a preheated oven at 240°C (475°F, gas 9) for 5 minutes and serve very hot.

Mushrooms

Baked ceps

Wipe 4 perfect cep caps. Make a cross-shaped cut on top of each and place in an ovenproof dish or roasting tin (pan). Season lightly with salt and pepper and add a drop of olive oil. Put in a preheated oven at 240°C (475°F, gas 9) for 5 minutes. Turn the ceps, season again and bake for a further 3 minutes. Arrange the ceps with their undersides facing upwards and garnish each with a very thin slice of lightly cooked foie gras or diced, lightly grilled Parma ham. Serve with a red chicory salad, in a dressing of sherry vinegar and olive oil.

Bouchées with mushrooms

Make smaller cases using a 6 cm (2½ in) diameter pastry (cookie) cutter. Fill with morel (or button) mushrooms in cream or in a cream sauce.

Canapés with mushrooms

Prepare a dry well-browned duxelles of mushrooms and add béchamel sauce (1 part to 3 parts duxelles). Spread this on lightly toasted slices of bread and sprinkle with fresh breadcrumbs and a little melted butter. Brown in a preheated oven at 230°C (450°F, gas 8).

Cep omelette

Brown 200 g (7 oz, 2 cups) sliced cep mushrooms in butter or oil and add them, with some chopped parsley, to 8 eggs, beating them all together. Cook the omelette. Garnish with a line of chopped ceps sautéed in butter or oil.

Any edible mushrooms can be used to flavour this omelette.

Ceps à la bordelaise

Trim the ceps; cut them into thin slices if they are very large, halve them if of medium size, or leave them whole if they are small. Put them in a shallow frying pan with oil and lemon juice, leave to cook slowly with the lid on for 5 minutes, then drain. Heat some oil in another frying pan, place the ceps in it and sprinkle with salt and pepper. Lightly brown them, then drain. Sprinkle with chopped parsley and serve very hot.

In Paris, ceps *à la bordelaise* are lightly fried and served with chopped shallots, fried bread and chopped parsley.

Ceps à la hongroise

Trim and wash 500 g (18 oz) ceps. Cut them into thin slices if they are large; leave them whole if they are small. Cook them slowly in butter with 2 tablespoons chopped onion, salt, pepper and 1 teaspoon paprika. Then add sufficient crème fraîche to cover the contents of the pan and reduce. Finally, sprinkle with chopped parsley if desired.

Ceps à la mode béarnaise

Trim and wash some large ceps and put them in the oven to release the excess juices. Stud them with garlic, sprinkle with salt and pepper, coat with oil and grill (broil) them. Mix some breadcrumbs, chopped garlic and parsley and brown this mixture in a frying pan with oil. Scatter the grilled ceps on top and serve immediately.

Ceps à la provençale

Prepare as for ceps *à la bordelaise*, but use olive oil and fry for longer. When the ceps are cooked, sprinkle them with finely chopped garlic as well as the chopped parsley.

Ceps au gratin

Trim the ceps, separating the caps from the stalks; season with salt and pepper, then coat with melted butter or oil. Arrange the caps in a buttered or oiled gratin dish with their tops downwards. Chop the stalks and add 1 chopped shallot for every 200 g (7 oz, 2 cups) stalks, together with some parsley; brown in oil and season with salt and pepper. Finally, add 1 tablespoon fresh breadcrumbs for every 200 g (7 oz, 2 cups) stalks and mix all the ingredients together. Fill the caps with this mixture, sprinkle with some more fresh breadcrumbs, moisten with oil or melted butter, and brown in a preheated oven at 240°C (475°F, gas 9) or under a hot grill (broiler).

Ceps en terrine

Trim and wash 800 g (1¾ lb) ceps and separate the caps from the stalks. Chop the stalks together with 3–4 garlic cloves, 3–4 shallots and a small bunch of parsley and brown everything in a shallow frying pan in 3 tablespoons olive oil. Add salt and pepper. Place the caps in a separate covered frying pan with 2 tablespoons olive oil and some salt, and heat gently until they have discharged their juices. Drain them. Line the bottom and sides of an ovenproof earthenware dish with very thin rashers (slices) of smoked streaky bacon. In it, place a layer of the caps, then the chopped mixture, then a second layer of caps. Cover with more smoked rashers, put the lid on the dish, place in a preheated oven at 200°C (400°F, gas 6) and cook for just under an hour.

Cream of mushroom soup

Clean 675 g (1½ lb) mushrooms, putting 100 g (4 oz) aside. Cook the remaining mushrooms in 40–50 g (1½–2 oz, 3–4 tablespoons) butter. Prepare 750 ml (1¼ pints, 3¼ cups) white sauce by adding 900 ml (1½ pints, 1 quart) milk to a white roux of 25 g (1 oz, 2 tablespoons) butter and 40 g

(1½ oz, 2 tablespoons) plain (all-purpose) flour. Mix this sauce with the lightly cooked mushrooms and simmer gently for 12–18 minutes. Purée in a food processor, then press through a sieve if necessary. Dilute with a few tablespoons of white stock or milk. Heat and adjust the seasoning. Finely shred the reserved mushrooms and sprinkle with lemon juice. Add to the soup with 200 ml (7 fl oz, ¾ cup) single (light) cream and stir while heating.

Croquettes Montrouge

Prepare a dry mushroom duxelles and add half its volume of chopped ham and a third of its volume of bread soaked in milk and then squeezed. Add some chopped parsley and 2 egg yolks for each 250 g (9 oz) of mixture, mix well and season to taste. Shape the preparation into balls the size of tangerines. Flatten them slightly, coat with egg and breadcrumbs, and deep fry in oil at 190°C (375°F). Drain on paper towels and sprinkle with salt.

Croustades Montrouge

Line some tartlet moulds with shortcrust pastry and bake blind. Fill them with a thick purée of creamed mushrooms. Sprinkle fresh breadcrumbs evenly over the purée and moisten with a little melted butter, then brown in a preheated oven at 240°C (475°F, gas 9).

Escalopes of foie gras Montrouge

Prepare a thick mushroom purée. Slice some foie gras and prepare an equal number of slices of bread of the same size. Fry the bread in butter. Sauté the foie gras in clarified butter and put each slice on a slice of fried bread. Arrange in a ring on a flat dish with the mushroom purée in the centre and keep warm. Deglaze the foie gras pan with Madeira and a little stock, boil down to reduce and thicken with a little arrowroot. Pour the sauce over the foie gras.

Flan Brillat-Savarin

Make a flan case (pie shell) of fine savoury pastry and bake blind. While still warm, fill with very creamy scrambled eggs with truffles. Heat some sliced truffles in clarified butter, season with salt and pepper, and arrange on the eggs. Sprinkle with grated Parmesan cheese and melted butter. Brown well.

Grilled ceps

Thoroughly clean and trim some fresh ceps. Cut shallow slits into the caps and marinate the ceps for at least 30 minutes in a mixture of olive oil, lemon juice, chopped garlic, chopped parsley, a pinch of cayenne, salt and pepper. Drain the ceps and grill (broil) them. Sprinkle with chopped parsley and serve very hot. Alternatively, the ceps may be moistened with melted butter or simply washed and wiped, sprinkled with salt and pepper, quickly grilled and basted with oil or melted butter at the time of serving.

Grilled saffron milk caps à la Lucifer

Blanch the caps from 575 g (1¼ lb) young saffron milk caps for 3 minutes, drain and blot dry.

Prepare 200 ml (7 fl oz, ¾ cup) devilled sauce, boil down to reduce, then add 1 teaspoon paprika, 300 ml (½ pint, 1¼ cups) brown sauce and 2 tablespoons tomato purée (paste). Stir, cook over a moderate heat and add salt. Add 1 tablespoon Worcestershire sauce and a generous pinch of cayenne. Strain through a sieve, return to the pan and keep hot in a bain marie.

Chop a small bunch of parsley and a little fennel. Brush the mushroom caps with olive oil and grill (broil) for 4 minutes. Then rub them with garlic and arrange them on a dish. Sprinkle them generously with the chopped parsley and fennel, together with about 100 g (4 oz, 1 cup) grated Parmesan cheese and some salt. Whisk the hot sauce and pour it over the mushrooms.

Hazelnut and Caesar's mushroom soup

The Caesar's mushroom is an edible wild mushroom with an orange-yellow cap, known as the royal agaric or the 'king of mushrooms' because of the fineness of its flesh and its scent.

Clean, peel and finely dice 675 g (1½ lb) Caesar's mushrooms, then wash and shred 6 round lettuces. Season the lettuce with salt and pepper and 1½ tablespoons caster (superfine) sugar. Heat 75 g (3 oz, 6 tablespoons) butter in a saucepan until it begins to turn brown, then put in the lettuce and the mushrooms; cook over a low heat, with the pan covered, for 30 minutes. Add a knuckle of veal, 1 litre (1¾ pints, 4⅓ cups) milk and 6 tablespoons rice which has been boiled for 1 minute. Salt lightly and mix in 1 tablespoon fairy-ring mushrooms (*Marasmius oreades*) or wood blewits (*Lepista nuda*) in dried or powdered form. Cook over a moderate heat for 2 hours.

Take out the knuckle and rub the soup through a fine sieve. Return it to a low heat. Pound a handful of shelled and skinned hazelnuts and mix them with 75 g (3 oz, 6 tablespoons) butter. Press this paste through a fine sieve into a hot soup tureen; add 3 egg yolks and 120 ml (4½ fl oz, ½ cup) double (heavy) cream. Pour on the soup, beating vigorously.

Leafy truffle salad

Prepare a vinaigrette by whisking together salt, 2½ teaspoons aged wine vinegar and 2½ teaspoons sherry vinegar, 5 tablespoons groundnut (peanut) oil, pepper and 1 tablespoon truffle juice.

Wash and trim 20 g (¾ oz) curly endive (frisée), 20 g (¾ oz) oak leaf lettuce, 20 g (¾ oz) lollo rosso, 20 g (¾ oz) red chicory (endive), 20 g (¾ oz) Batavia lettuce, 20 g (¾ oz) Nice mesclun, 20 g (¾ oz) lamb's lettuce (corn salad), 20 g (¾ oz) rocket (arugula), 10 g (⅓ oz) watercress, 7 g (¼ oz) marjoram, 10 g (⅓ oz) chervil, 10 g (⅓ oz) flat-leafed parsley, 7 g (¼ oz) sage,

10 g (⅓ oz) dill, 10 g (⅓ oz) tarragon, 4 small mint leaves and 4 small celery leaves. Place the herbs and salad leaves, except for the celery and mint, in a large salad bowl and toss. Add 10g (⅓ oz) chopped truffle, toss again, then add the prepared vinaigrette. Toss gently again to coat all the leaves. Arrange the salad in a pile on each of 4 plates. Sprinkle each with a little more chopped truffle and garnish with a celery leaf and a mint leaf. Sprinkle a few drops of aged wine vinegar on top and serve.

Marinated ceps

Trim and wash 800 g (1¾ lb) ceps and cut them into thin slices. Fry them in deep hot oil for 2 minutes, then cool them under cold water and wipe off the excess. To prepare the marinade, heat a mixture of 200 ml (7 fl oz, ¾ cup) olive oil, 3 tablespoons wine vinegar, 1 tablespoon chopped fennel, 2 teaspoons lemon peel, a bay leaf cut into four, 2 small sprigs of thyme, salt and freshly ground pepper. Bring this mixture to the boil and leave to boil for 5 minutes. Place the ceps in an earthenware dish and cover with the boiling marinade, strained through a sieve. Add 2 large garlic cloves and 1 tablespoon chopped parsley. Stir, then cover and leave to stand in a cool place for at least 24 hours before serving.

Morels à la crème

Clean 250 g (9 oz) morels. Wash them briskly in cold water and dry them thoroughly. Leave them whole if they are small, cut them up if they are large. Put the morels in a shallow frying pan with 15 g (½ oz, 1 tablespoon) butter, 1 teaspoon lemon juice, 1 teaspoon chopped shallots, salt and pepper. Braise for 5 minutes, then cover with double (heavy) cream and reduce until the sauce has thickened. Just before serving, add 1 tablespoon cream and some chopped parsley.

Morels in herb sauce

Put into a saucepan a pinch of rosemary, sage, thyme and basil, a quarter of a bay leaf, a clove, a little pepper and a little grated nutmeg. Add a shredded onion and a ladleful of good consommé and simmer for a few minutes, then strain through muslin (cheesecloth). Add about 30 cleaned morels to the strained liquid and bring to the boil, pour in some thick allemande sauce and reduce. Just before serving, add a little chicken stock, a little butter, some lemon juice and 1 tablespoon chopped chervil.

Mushroom barquettes

Prepare some scrambled eggs and a mushroom duxelles. Spread a layer of scrambled eggs and a layer of mushrooms in each cooked barquette. Fry some breadcrumbs and sprinkle over the barquettes. Bake for a few minutes in a preheated oven at 200°C (400°F, gas 6) just to warm the barquettes through.

Mushroom blanc

Bring 6 tablespoons water with 40 g (1½ oz, 3 tablespoons) butter, the juice of ½ lemon and 1 scant tablespoon salt to the boil. Add 300 g (11 oz, 3½ cups) mushrooms and boil for 6 minutes. Drain and retain the cooking stock to flavour a white sauce, fish stock or marinade.

Mushroom crêpes

Prepare some savoury crêpe batter and leave it to stand. Meanwhile, prepare a duxelles with 500 g (18 oz, 6 cups) mushrooms, 1 or 2 shallots, a small garlic clove, 20 g (¾ oz, 1½ tablespoons) butter, salt and pepper, and 300 ml (½ pint, 1¼ cups) béchamel sauce.

Make 12 crêpes, cooking each one as follows: melt a knob of butter in a frying pan and pour a small quantity of batter into the pan, tilting it in all directions to spread a thin film of batter. Cook over a moderate heat until the crêpe slides when the pan is shaken. Then turn the crêpe over and cook the other side for about 2 minutes. Place a tablespoon of the mixed béchamel sauce and duxelles on each crêpe and roll it up. Arrange the crêpes close together on a lightly buttered ovenproof dish and sprinkle them with 50 g (2 oz, ½ cup) grated cheese. Top with 25 g (1 oz, 2 tablespoons) melted butter and either brown them under the grill (broiler) or reheat them in a preheated oven at 230°C (450°F, gas 8). Serve very hot.

The sauce may be replaced by 6 tablespoons double (heavy) cream.

Mushroom croquettes

Clean and dice some mushrooms, sprinkle with lemon juice and sauté them briskly either in oil or in butter. Add some chopped shallot and parsley, a little thyme, or bay leaf, a chopped garlic clove, salt and pepper. Bind this salpicon with a thick béchamel sauce and leave to cool. Chill. Divide the mixture into equal portions and roll them into cylinders. Dip the cylinders in batter, plunge into very hot oil and brown. Drain and dry on paper towels. Serve very hot (possibly with a tomato sauce), either as an entrée or as a vegetable.

Mushroom croûtes

Cut some round pieces of bread, 4–5 cm (1½–2 in) in diameter and 2 cm (¾ in) thick, from a stale loaf. Use a round cutter with a diameter smaller than that of the croûtes to press lightly on each croûte to mark the lid. Fry the croûtes in butter or oil. When they are golden, drain and remove the central circles for lids, then hollow out.

Fill them with mushrooms (preferably field mushrooms) *à la crème*. Sprinkle with breadcrumbs and brown in a preheated oven at 220°C (425°F, gas 7) or under the grill (broiler). Serve hot.

Mushroom duxelles

Clean and trim 250 g (9 oz, 3 cups) button mushrooms and chop them finely, together with 1 onion and 1 large shallot. Melt a large knob of butter in a frying pan, add the chopped vegetables, salt and pepper and a little grated nutmeg (unless the duxelles is to accompany fish). Cook over a brisk heat until the vegetables are brown and the water from the mushrooms has evaporated. If the duxelles is for use as a garnish, add 1 tablespoon cream.

Mushroom essence

Clean and dice about 450 g (1 lb) open-cap cultivated mushrooms, then place them in a saucepan and season with salt. Add a little white wine and water. Bring to the boil, stirring, then reduce the heat and cover the pan tightly. Cook for about 20 minutes, until the mushrooms are greatly reduced. Strain the liquor through a sieve, pressing or squeezing the mushrooms dry. Boil the liquor to reduce it to a full-flavoured essence.

Mushroom fritters

Wash some small, fresh button mushrooms. Pat dry and coat with flour. Dip in batter, deep-fry in hot oil and serve with a highly seasoned tomato sauce.

Mushroom purée

Prepare 200 ml (7 fl oz, ¾ cup) béchamel sauce. Add to it 6 tablespoons double (heavy) cream and stir over a brisk heat until reduced by a third. Chop 500 g (18 oz, 6 cups) mushrooms. Press through a sieve or blend in a food processor. Place the resulting purée in a frying pan and stir over a brisk heat until the vegetable juice has completely evaporated. Add the béchamel, a pinch of salt, a little white pepper and a dash of grated nutmeg. Stir again over the heat for several minutes. Off the heat, blend in 50 g (2 oz, ¼ cup) butter.

Mushroom salad

Clean some very fresh mushrooms. Slice them finely and sprinkle with lemon juice to prevent them from turning brown. They may be served with either a very highly seasoned vinaigrette dressing with added lemon juice and chopped herbs or with a mixture of cream, vinegar or lemon juice, salt, pepper and chopped chives. Keep in a cool place until ready to serve.

Mushrooms à la hongroise

Clean and wash some mushrooms and cut off the stalks. If the mushrooms are very small, leave them whole; if they are larger, cut them in quarters and dip them in lemon juice. Gently sauté them in butter without letting them colour. Pour off the butter from the sauté pan and replace it with cream, lemon juice, paprika, salt and pepper. Reduce by half, sprinkle with chopped parsley and serve very hot.

Mushrooms à l'anglaise

Choose good-quality cultivated mushrooms. Trim, wash and remove the stalks. Season the caps with salt and pepper. Butter small round lightly toasted pieces of bread. Place a mushroom, hollow side up, on each slice, garnished with a little maître d'hôtel butter. Arrange the toast in a gratin dish, cover and bake in a preheated oven at 180°C (350°F, gas 4) for 12–15 minutes.

Mushrooms à la poulette

Clean some mushrooms by rinsing them under water several times and draining well; then stew them in butter, without letting them colour. Add just enough poulette sauce to bind the mushrooms; check and adjust the seasoning if necessary. Serve the mushrooms sprinkled with chopped herbs in a warmed vegetable dish.

Mushrooms cooked in butter

Cut some raw cultivated mushrooms into thin slices. Season with salt and pepper, sauté in butter in a frying pan over a brisk heat and serve in a vegetable dish, possibly with chopped herbs or thinly sliced onions softened in butter, *à la lyonnaise*.

Mushrooms cooked in cream

Sauté the mushrooms in butter, cover them with boiling double (heavy) cream and simmer for 8–10 minutes, until reduced. This preparation may be used as a filling for flans or vol-au-vent.

Mushroom soufflés

Add 4 egg yolks to 400 ml (14 fl oz, 1¾ cups) mushroom purée, followed by 4 stiffly whisked egg whites. Butter some small ramekins and divide the mixture between them. Place them in a preheated oven at 190°C (375°F, gas 5) and cook for about 20 minutes without opening the oven door. The soufflés are cooked when they have filled the moulds and the tops have browned. Serve immediately.

Mushroom stuffing

Clean some mushrooms, remove the caps and set them aside to use as garnishes. Chop the stalks and toss them in very hot butter (or olive oil) with chopped shallots, salt, pepper and (optional) a dash of grated nutmeg. Then add some fresh breadcrumbs, chopped parsley, 1 egg (either whole or just the yolk), salt and pepper.

The stuffing may be used to fill mushroom caps or other vegetables, such as tomatoes, aubergines (eggplants), courgettes (zucchini) and cabbage, and also as a fish or meat stuffing.

Mushroom velouté soup

Prepare a white roux with 40 g (1½ oz, 3 tablespoons) butter and 40 g (1½ oz, 6 tablespoons) flour. Moisten with a generous 750 ml (1¼ pints, 3¼ cups) chicken consommé. Simmer 400 g (14 oz, 4½ cups) sliced cultivated mushrooms in 40 g (1½ oz, 3 tablespoons) butter for about 20 minutes. Add them to the consommé, bring to the boil and cook for 10 minutes. Reduce the mixture to a purée in a food processor or blender. Dilute with a little consommé to obtain the desired consistency and heat. Remove from the heat and thicken the soup with a mixture of 3 egg yolks beaten with 100 ml (4 fl oz, 7 tablespoons) double (heavy) cream. Finally, whisk in 75 g (3 oz, 6 tablespoons) butter. Reheat but do not boil.

Omelette with green clitocybes

Clitocybes are characterized by having gills that extend along the stalk and a drooping cap with a depression in the centre; the name comes from the Greek *klitos* (sloping) and *kubê* (head). The best for eating are the funnel-shaped clitocybe (pale-buff or yellow-ochre cap), the nebulous or *petit-gris* clitocybe (grey-brown), the geotropic or *tête-de-moine* clitocybe (yellow-ochre) and the sweet-smelling clitocybe (green). All must be picked when young and consumed fresh, with the stalks discarded. Their aniseed, bitter almond or mint flavour is sometimes fairly strong. They must be cooked thoroughly.

Choose 18 caps of aniseed-flavoured green clitocybes and clean them thoroughly. Brown the 6 choicest ones whole in butter with 1½ teaspoons chopped onions. Cook in a covered pan for 10 minutes over a gentle heat. Season with salt and pepper and keep warm. Cut the remaining 12 caps into thin strips and cook in butter for 5 minutes over a moderate heat. Remove and drain in a fine sieve.

Beat 8 eggs lightly, add salt and a little curry powder, and blend in 8 knobs of butter, then the drained julienne of mushrooms. Cook the omelette in very hot olive oil, constantly moving the frying pan over a brisk heat and lifting up the edges. Serve garnished with the 6 whole caps and accompanied with a green salad dressed in walnut oil containing ½ teaspoon anisette.

Oyster mushroom croûtes

Use a zester to pare the zest off 1 lemon in fine shreds. Mix the lemon zest with 1 finely chopped garlic clove and 1 teaspoon finely chopped fresh tarragon. Cut fairly thick slices off a baguette or ciabatta loaf at an angle, brush them with a little olive oil and bake in a preheated oven at 200°C (400°F, gas 6) for about 20 minutes or until lightly browned and crisp.

When the croûtes are almost ready, heat a large knob of butter with a good layer of olive oil in a large sauté pan. Add 1 teaspoon fennel seeds and allow them to sizzle gently for 1 minute. Trim and wipe small to medium oyster mushrooms; if using large mushrooms, cut them in half or quarters. Add the mushrooms to the pan. Sprinkle in the lemon zest, garlic and tarragon, then cook for about 3 minutes over medium heat, turning the mushrooms occasionally. Stir about 2 teaspoons Dijon mustard into the pan juices between the mushrooms. Sprinkle with salt and pepper and a generous quantity of chopped fresh dill, then toss lightly.

Spoon the oyster mushrooms on to the baked croûtes. Add wedges of lemon so that they can be squeezed over the mushrooms just before they are eaten. Serve at once.

Parasol mushrooms à la suprême

Prepare the caps of 1 kg (2¼ lb) young parasol mushrooms, without washing them. Make a white roux with 25 g (1 oz, 2 tablespoons) butter and 40 g (1½ oz, ⅓ cup) flour and then add 500 ml (17 fl oz, 2 cups) hot chicken stock.

Let it cook over a low heat for 15 minutes. Turn the heat up and thicken the sauce with 1 egg yolk mixed with 4 tablespoons double (heavy) cream. Season with salt and mild red paprika and keep warm in a bain marie. In a shallow frying pan, cook 65 g (2½ oz, ¼ cup) chopped onions seasoned with ½ teaspoon paprika in butter. When the onions start to turn pale golden, add the mushroom caps and sauté them briskly for 5 minutes, then season with salt, a little grated nutmeg and a bouquet garni to which sprigs of basil and tarragon have been added. Cover the pan and cook for 10 more minutes over a high heat. Drain the mushrooms and keep them hot in the pan with a little butter. Whisk the sauce and add to the mushrooms; check the seasoning. Serve piled up on small slices of white bread which have been fried golden brown in noisette butter.

Ragoût of mushrooms

Clean and slice 500 g (18 oz, 6 cups) large cultivated mushrooms, sauté them in butter or oil, then add a small glass of Madeira and some cream sauce. Reduce the sauce over a low heat until it is thick and creamy, sprinkle with coarsely chopped parsley and serve as a garnish for roast or braised white meat or for braised fish.

Ragoût of truffles

Peel 8 fresh 40 g (1½ oz) truffles, cut into quarters, and season with salt and pepper. Add 100 ml (4 fl oz, 7 tablespoons) dry Banyuls and marinate for 20 minutes at room temperature.

Reduce by half 200 ml (7 fl oz, ¾ cup) good full-bodied red wine in a flameproof casserole, lightly rubbed with garlic. Blend in 1 teaspoon flour mixed with 2 teaspoons butter, bring to the boil, then add the truffles and their wine marinade.

Cover with foil and put on the lid, bringing the edges of the foil over the top; cook in a preheated oven at 180°C (350°F, gas 4) for 10 minutes.

Cut some stale bread into 3–4 cm (1½ in) croûtons, dry them slightly in the oven, then rub with garlic and spread the soft side with goose or duck fat. Serve the truffle ragoût in its casserole, with the croûtons handed in a separate dish.

Salad of chanterelles with endive

Wash and drain 1 large endive (chicory) and 250 g (9 oz) chanterelles. Season the chanterelles with salt and pepper and sauté in butter for 2 minutes. Add 2 chopped shallots and 4 tablespoons chopped flat-leaf parsley and cook for 1 minute. Make a vinaigrette with 2 tablespoons wine vinegar, 6 tablespoons olive oil, 2 tablespoons groundnut (peanut) oil, 1 tablespoon walnut oil, salt and pepper. Toss half the dressing with the endive and the remainder with the warm chanterelles. Arrange the endive on plates and place the chanterelles on top. Sprinkle with chopped chives, parsley and chervil.

Sauté of Piedmont truffles

White or black truffles may be used for this recipe, which can be prepared at table in the following way. Finely slice the truffles. Place in a silver dish a few tablespoons of olive oil or butter and some good meat glaze, the size of an egg, cut into small pieces. Place the truffles on top with a little salt, white pepper and some grated nutmeg. Sprinkle with a few tablespoons of oil or a few pieces of fine butter. The silver dish, covered with its lid, is placed on a spirit heater in front of the host, who frequently stirs the truffles with a spoon, replacing the lid on the dish each time. About 8 minutes' cooking should be sufficient for the truffles. The host then squeezes in the juice of a lemon and serves his or her guests.

Scrambled eggs with ceps

Slice some cep mushrooms, season with salt and pepper, and sauté them in butter or oil with a little garlic. Make the scrambled eggs and add the ceps. Place in a serving dish with a generous tablespoon of fried ceps in the centre. Sprinkle with fried croûtons.

Other varieties of mushroom may be used: chanterelles, blewits, horn of plenty, or cultivated button mushrooms.

Soft-boiled (or poached) eggs brimont

Add some Madeira or cream to a chicken velouté and reduce. Fill a cooked, shallow puff pastry pie crust (shell) with mushrooms cooked in cream. Arrange the eggs in a ring on top. Fill the centre with small chicken croquettes. Coat with the reduced velouté sauce and garnish each egg with a slice of truffle.

Stuffed mushrooms

Choose large mushrooms of a similar size. Remove the stalks so that the cavities of the caps are fully exposed. Arrange the caps in a buttered or oiled dish and season with salt and pepper. Coat with oil or melted butter and place them in a preheated oven at 200°C (400°F, gas 6) for 5 minutes. Stuff each one with duxelles. Dust with fine breadcrumbs, sprinkle with olive oil and brown.

Mushrooms may be filled with different mixtures, such as chopped vegetables, forcemeat, mirepoix, salpicon or risotto.

Truffle-flavoured consommé

Use beef or chicken consommé. Add 40 g (1½ oz, ⅓ cup) fresh truffle peelings to the consommé 5 minutes before it has finished clarifying, and pour 1 tablespoon port or sherry into each soup dish.

Truffle salad

Clean some raw truffles and slice finely or cut into julienne strips. Make a vinaigrette with oil, vinegar, salt, pepper and lemon juice, but without herbs. (When fresh truffles are not available, preserved truffles can be used.)

The truffles may be mixed with sliced boiled potatoes (demi-deuil salad) or sliced artichoke hearts (impératrice salad).

Truffle sauce

Cook a very black fresh truffle in a mixture of half Madeira, half meat stock, with a little tomato purée (paste), for 10 minutes. Drain and cut into julienne strips. Cover the pan tightly and reduce the liquid to a few teaspoonfuls, then add 2 egg yolks and the julienne. Thicken with 200 g (7 oz, ¾ cup) clarified butter, as for a béarnaise sauce. Season with salt and pepper.

This sauce is served with poached fish, white meats and asparagus.

Truffles with champagne

Take 1.4 kg (3 lb) large well-rounded truffles, ideally ones that are of a good black colour. Rinse them in two or three lots of water. When they are well drained, place them in a saucepan lined with slices of bacon and cover with more bacon.

Coarsely dice 450 g (1 lb) desalted ham, and also the same quantity of fillets of veal and fresh pork. Cook in butter in a saucepan, adding finely sliced carrots and onions, sprigs of parsley, a few pieces of thyme, bay leaf, basil, half a garlic clove and 2 cloves; season with a little salt, white pepper, grated nutmeg and a dash of spices. When these ingredients begin to colour slightly, pour on 2 bottles of champagne (Ay is best); bring to the boil; skim and leave to simmer on a low heat without reducing. Then press through a sieve and pour it over the truffles.

Start cooking the truffles 1 hour before serving. Leave to boil gently for 45 minutes, then remove from the heat and keep very hot, without boiling. Just before serving, drain them and arrange them on a napkin folded on a silver dish; cover to keep them piping hot.

Truffle tourte à la périgourdine

Line a pie dish, 4–5 cm (1½–2 in) deep, with lining pastry and place on a baking sheet. Arrange on the bottom a layer of uncooked foie gras cut into large dice, seasoned with salt and pepper and sprinkled with *quatre épices* 'four spices' and Cognac, covering the pastry to within 1 cm (½ in) of the edge. Top with scrubbed and peeled whole truffles, seasoned with salt and pepper and sprinkled with *quatre épices* and Cognac. Place small slices of foie gras, seasoned with salt and pepper, on the truffles. Cover with a thin layer of pastry and seal the edges. Garnish the top with cut-out shapes of pastry and place a funnel in the centre. Brush with egg and bake in a preheated oven at 200°C (400°F, gas 6) for 40–45 minutes. Pour through the funnel a few tablespoons of reduced demi-glace sauce, flavoured with Madeira and truffle essence. The tourte is served hot or cold.

Okra

To prepare

When quickly fried in very hot oil, tender young okra retain their texture and do not become slimy, so stir-frying and deep-frying are useful methods. They can be cooked in butter or cream, braised with bacon, fried, puréed, or prepared with lime or rice. Okra are added to tajines, foutou and Caribbean ratatouille, and eaten with mutton in Egypt and chicken in the United States. When added early on in the cooking, the okra thicken the cooking liquor; added at the end, the young whole vegetables remain crisp.

Okra à la créole

Wash the okra carefully. If using dried vegetables, soak them in cold water for about 12 hours. Top and tail (stem and head) and put in a saucepan. Cover them amply with cold water and cook for 10–25 minutes, skimming from time to time. Drain and dry them. Peel and finely slice 150 g (5 oz) onions and cook in 2 tablespoons oil until soft. Add the okra and brown very gently. Scald, peel and seed 4 large tomatoes. Crush them and add to the okra with 2 crushed garlic cloves, salt, pepper, a little cayenne and powdered saffron. Cover and leave to cook very gently for at least 1 hour (more if using dried okra). Adjust the seasoning. Serve in a dish with a border of rice *à la créole*.

Onions & shallots

Bercy butter or shallot butter for meat

Poach 500 g (18 oz) diced beef marrow in salted water and drain. Cook 1 tablespoon chopped shallots in 1 tablespoon butter in a saucepan without browning. Add 200 ml (7 fl oz, ¾ cup) dry white wine and heat gently. Soften 200 g (7 oz, ¾ cup) butter and add to the pan, together with the marrow, 1 tablespoon chopped parsley, the juice of ½ lemon, salt and a generous pinch of milled pepper. This butter is poured on top of grilled (broiled) meat or fish and may also be served separately in a sauceboat.

Bercy sauce or shallot sauce for fish

Cook 1 tablespoon chopped shallots gently in 1 tablespoon butter without browning in a saucepan. Add 100 ml (4 fl oz, 7 tablespoons) white wine and 100 ml (4 fl oz, 7 tablespoons) fish stock. Reduce to half the volume. Add 200 ml (7 fl oz, ¾ cup) thin velouté sauce and boil vigorously for a few moments. Chop a small bunch of parsley. Remove the pan from the heat and add 50 g (2 oz, ¼ cup) softened butter; finally, add the chopped parsley and season with salt and pepper. This sauce is a suitable accompaniment to poached fish.

Fried onions

Peel some onions, slice them into rings 5 mm (¼ in) thick and separate the rings. Season with salt, dip in flour and fry in very hot oil. Drain them on paper towels and sprinkle with fine salt. They can also be marinated in oil and lemon juice for 30 minutes, then dipped in batter and fried.

Gratinée

This Parisian speciality is an onion soup topped with a gratin of bread and cheese. Finely slice 4 large onions. Heat 40 g (1½ oz, 3 tablespoons) butter and 4 tablespoons oil in a frying pan. Add the onions and stir until they are golden brown. Sprinkle with 25 g (1 oz, ¼ cup) plain (all-purpose) flour and stir until brown. Add 200 ml (7 fl oz, ¾ cup) dry white wine, reduce for a few minutes over a gentle heat, then pour in 1 litre (1¾ pints, 4⅓ cups) water or stock. Season with salt and pepper, add 2 small crushed cloves of garlic and a bouquet garni, then bring to the boil and cook very gently for 1 hour.

Meanwhile, in the oven dry some slices of bread cut from a long, thin French loaf. Mix 3 egg yolks with 6 tablespoons Madeira or port. Preheat the oven to 220°C (425°F, gas 7) and put a bain marie into it. When the onion soup is cooked, remove the bouquet garni, gradually add the mixture of egg yolks and Madeira, then divide the soup among 4 individual ovenproof soup bowls. Generously sprinkle the dried slices of bread with Gruyère and arrange on the surface of the soup. Place the soup bowls in the bain marie in the oven and cook until the top of the bread is well browned. Serve immediately.

Onion and honey tart

Peel and thinly slice 1 kg (2¼ lb) new onions. Cook in boiling water for 3 minutes and drain. Melt 25 g (1 oz, 2 tablespoons) butter in a thick-based saucepan, add the well-drained onions and cook without browning. Add 3 generous tablespoons mixed-flower honey, salt, 1 teaspoon ground cinnamon and a little pepper. Stir thoroughly and remove from the heat.

Line a flan tin (pie pan) with 300 g (11 oz) thinly rolled out shortcrust pastry (basic pie dough). Fill with the onions and bake in a preheated oven at 230°C (450°F, gas 8). When the tart is half-cooked, cover it with foil. Serve the tart warm either as an entrée or as a dessert.

Onion crêpes

Prepare some crêpes using batter for buckwheat crêpes or galettes. Fill each one with 1 tablespoon onion purée, roll it up and arrange in a lightly buttered ovenproof dish. Sprinkle with 50 g (2 oz, ½ cup) grated cheese. Top with 25 g (1 oz, 2 tablespoons) melted butter and either brown the crêpes under the grill (broiler) or reheat them in a preheated oven at 230°C (450°F, gas 8). Serve very hot.

Onion sauce

Cook 100 g (4 oz, ¾ cup) chopped onions in 300 ml (½ pint, 1¼ cups) milk seasoned with salt, pepper and nutmeg. As soon as the onions are cooked, strain and use the milk in which the onions were cooked to make a white sauce by stirring it into a roux made with 20 g (¾ oz, 1½ tablespoons) butter and 20 g (¾ oz, 3 tablespoons) plain (all-purpose) flour. Bring to the boil, add the chopped onions and cook gently for 8 minutes.

This traditional English sauce is poured over lamb or mutton, chicken, braised game or rabbit.

The onions can also be cooked in milk, then the liquid thickened with beurre manié, using the above proportions of butter and flour.

Onion soup

Finely chop 250 g (9 oz, 1½ cups) onions and fry them in butter without letting them get too brown. When they are almost ready, sprinkle with 25 g (1 oz, ¼ cup) plain (all-purpose) flour. Continue cooking for a minute or two, stirring the onions, then pour on 2 litres (3½ pints, 9 cups) white stock and flavour with 2 tablespoons port or Madeira. Continue to cook for a further 30 minutes. Put some slices of bread, which have been dried in the oven, into a soup tureen and pour the soup over them.

Onion tart

Line a buttered 28 cm (11 in) flan tin (tart pan) with 400 g (14 oz) shortcrust pastry and cook it blind. Meanwhile, prepare a Soubise purée with 1 kg (2¼ lb) onions. Spread this in the flan case, sprinkle with fresh breadcrumbs, dot with butter and brown it in a hot oven for about 15 minutes.

Périgord tourin

Lightly brown in goose fat, in a frying pan, 150 g (5 oz, 1 cup) finely chopped onion. Sprinkle with 1 tablespoon flour and add 2 crushed garlic cloves and a few tablespoons of boiling water. Stir to avoid lumps. Cook 2 large seeded tomatoes in 2 litres (3½ pints, 9 cups) stock. Drain, crush and return to the stock. Add the contents of the frying pan and boil for 45 minutes. Just before serving, blend in 2 egg yolks mixed with a few tablespoons of stock. Pour into a soup tureen over some thin slices of farmhouse bread.

Piémontaise sauce

Finely dice 2 large onions and brown in clarified butter. Strain, then cook in a good stock, skimming off all the fat. Blend in enough béchamel sauce to accompany an entrée, together with 225 g (8 oz, 2 cups) diced Piedmont truffles and 2 tablespoons pine nuts (kernels). After the sauce has boiled for a short while, add a little chicken glaze, a little garlic butter and the juice of 1 lemon. (The quantity of truffles can be reduced.)

Pissaladière

Prepare 675 g (1½ lb) bread dough, and work into it 4 tablespoons olive oil. Knead it by hand, roll it into a ball and leave to rise for 1 hour at room temperature. Soak 12 salted anchovies for a short while in cold water (or use 24 drained canned anchovy fillets).

Chop 1 kg (2¼ lb) onions and fry them gently until soft in a covered frying pan with 4–5 tablespoons olive oil, a pinch of salt, a little pepper, 3 crushed garlic cloves, 1 sprig of thyme and 1 bay leaf. Fillet the anchovies. Strain 1 tablespoon pickled capers, pound to a purée and add to the onions.

Flatten three-quarters of the dough to form a circle. Place on an oiled baking sheet and spread with the onion and caper mixture, leaving a rim around the edge. Roll up the anchovy fillets and press them into the onions, together with 20 or so small black (ripe) olives. Shape the rim of the dough to form a wide border that will retain the filling. Roll out the remainder of the dough and cut it into thin strips. Place these in a criss-cross pattern over the filling, pressing the ends into the border. Brush the dough with oil and cook in a pre-heated oven at 240°C (475°F, gas 9) for about 20 minutes.

The strips of dough may be replaced by anchovy fillets arranged in a criss-cross pattern if preferred.

Sage and onion sauce

Cook 2 large onions for 8 minutes in salted boiling water. Drain them and chop them. Put the chopped onion into a saucepan with 100 g (4 oz, 2 cups) fresh white breadcrumbs and 25 g (1 oz, 2 tablespoons) butter. Season with salt and pepper and add 1 tablespoon chopped fresh sage. Cook for 5 minutes, stirring constantly. Just before serving, add 3 tablespoons pan juices from the roast pork or goose that this sauce is served with.

Shallot butter

Peel 150 g (5 oz) shallots and chop finely. Blanch for 2–3 minutes in boiling water, blot and purée in a blender. Work into 150 g (5 oz, ⅔ cup) softened butter. Season with salt and pepper. This butter is served mainly with grilled (broiled) fish and meat.

Shallot sauce

Peel some shallots and chop them very finely. Add to a good wine vinegar and season with salt and pepper. This sauce is traditionally served with oysters or raw mussels.

Spanish onion chutney

Peel and slice 2 kg (4½ lb) Spanish onions or large mild onions. Tip them into a large saucepan along with 675 g (1½ lb, 3½ cups) brown sugar, 400 g (14 oz, 2½ cups) raisins or sultanas (golden raisins), 400 ml (14 fl oz, 1¾ cups) dry white wine, 400 ml (14 fl oz, 1¾ cups) white wine vinegar, 2 garlic cloves, 300 g (11 oz) crystallized (candied) ginger cut into pieces, a pinch of curry powder and 5 cloves. Boil for 1¾–2 hours, leave to cool completely, then pot.

Stuffed onions

Peel some large onions, taking care not to split the outer layer; cut them horizontally at the stalk end, leaving about three-quarters of their total height. Blanch them in salted water for 10 minutes, then refresh and drain them. Scoop out the insides, leaving a thickness all round of 2 layers.

Chop the scooped-out onion finely and mix it with some finely chopped pork, veal, beef, lamb or mutton. Season well. Stuff the onions with this mixture, put them in a buttered flameproof casserole and moisten with a few tablespoons of slightly thickened brown veal stock. Start the cooking, with the lid on, on the hob (stove top), then continue cooking in the oven, basting frequently to glaze the onions. A few minutes before they are cooked, sprinkle with breadcrumbs or Parmesan cheese, moisten with melted butter and brown the surface.

Onions can also be stuffed in the following ways:

• *à la catalane:* rice cooked in meat stock with sweet (bell) peppers fried in olive oil and chopped hard-boiled (hard-cooked) eggs.

- *à l'italienne:* rice cooked in meat stock with finely chopped onion, cooked lean ham and Parmesan cheese.
- *à la parisienne:* finely chopped onion mixed with a duxelles of mushrooms and chopped cooked lean ham.

Tourin des noces

Brown 1 large grated onion and 6 quartered tomatoes in lard or goose fat. Add 1.25 litres (2¼ pints, 5½ cups) hot water. Season well with salt and pepper. When the vegetables are cooked, rub them through a sieve. Add 1 tablespoon vermicelli and some small grilled (broiled) croûtons to the soup and boil for a few minutes more. Season with pepper and serve.

Palm hearts (hearts of palm)

To prepare

The terminal buds of certain palm trees, in particular the West Indian cabbage palm, which is also known as the 'coconut cabbage', 'glug-glug cabbage' or 'ti-coco cabbage'. The tender parts are eaten raw, thinly sliced in salad; the firmer parts are cooked and used to prepare *acras*, gratins or fillings for omelettes. The flavour is similar to that of artichoke. Canned palm hearts are also available.

Braised palm hearts

Rinse some palm hearts in water and wipe well. Melt some pork dripping (fatback) in a shallow frying pan. Cut some pieces of palm hearts about 5 cm (2 in) long, tie them together in bunches and lightly brown them in the fat over a gentle heat for 30 minutes. Add 1 teaspoon flour, blending it in, then mix in 1 tablespoon tomato purée (paste) and some very concentrated chicken stock. Bring to the boil, stirring and cook for several minutes, then simmer gently until the sauce is reduced. Serve with a little of the sauce.

Palm hearts in salad

Drain a can of palm hearts, refresh them in cold water, wipe them and cut them into round slices. Peel a cucumber, remove the seeds and cut the pulp into dice. Peel, seed and dice 4 ripe firm tomatoes. Using a melon baller, scoop out some small balls from the pulp of an avocado. Mix together 200 ml (7 fl oz, ¾ cup) double (heavy) cream, some chopped chives, 2 tablespoons vinegar and 1 tablespoon lemon juice. Season liberally with salt and pepper. Combine the other ingredients with the sauce. Garnish some individual dishes with a lettuce chiffonnade. Divide the preparation between them and chill until time to serve.

Palm hearts with prawns

Thoroughly drain some canned palm hearts, refresh them in cold water, then wipe and coarsely shred them. Prepare a light well-seasoned mayonnaise coloured either with tomato ketchup or with a very reduced strained tomato sauce. Peel some cooked prawns (shrimps). Scald some bean sprouts, refresh them in cold water and dry them. Mix all the ingredients together and put in a cool place. Line some individual dishes with a lettuce chiffonnade, divide the mixture among them and serve chilled.

Peas

To prepare

When buying peas, make sure that the pods are smooth and bright green. The peas should be shiny and not too large, tender but not floury. The sooner peas are eaten after picking, the better they taste. Peas can be boiled or cooked in butter (*à la française*), with lettuce and small onions. They can also be cooked with bacon (*à la bonne femme*) or carrots (*à la fermière*) or flavoured with mint. The cooking time is quite short for freshly picked peas, but longer for those picked a few days previously.

Shell the peas and cook them in boiling salted water in an uncovered saucepan. They should be tender without becoming mushy or losing their colour (10–20 minutes depending on size and freshness). Drain them thoroughly and serve with butter. The peas can be flavoured by cooking them with a sprig of fresh fennel or mint and serving them sprinkled with chopped fresh fennel or mint.

Ambassadeur soup

To 1.5 litres (2¾ pints, 6½ cups) Saint-Germain soup (page 149), add 3 table-spoons shredded sorrel or a mixture of sorrel and lettuce softened in butter, 1½ tablespoons rice cooked in consommé, and some sprigs of chervil.

Lamballe soup

Prepare 750 ml (1¼ pints, 3¼ cups) Saint-Germain purée (page 149). Add 750 ml (1¼ pints, 3¼ cups) consommé with tapioca cooked in it and mix well. Garnish with chervil leaves.

Peas à la bonne femme

Melt some butter in a frying pan and lightly brown 12 baby (pearl) onions and 125 g (4½ oz, ½ cup) diced lean bacon. Remove the onions and bacon from the pan, add 1 tablespoon flour to the hot butter and cook for a few minutes, stirring with a wooden spoon. Stir in 300 ml (½ pint, 1¼ cups) white consommé, boil for 5 minutes, then add 675 g (1½ lb, 4½ cups) fresh shelled peas. Add the onions and bacon together with a bouquet garni and cook, covered, for about 30 minutes.

Peas à la crème

Boil 800 g (1¾ lb, 5¼ cups) fresh peas, shelled, drain them and put them back in the saucepan. Dry out a little over a brisk heat, then add 150 ml (¼ pint, ⅔ cup) boiling crème fraîche and boil until reduced by half. Adjust the seasoning and add a large pinch of sugar. Just before serving, add 2 tablespoons crème fraîche, blend well and sprinkle with chopped herbs.

Peas à la fermière

Clean 500 g (18 oz) baby carrots and peel 12 baby (pearl) onions. Brown them in butter in a saucepan. When the carrots are brown but still firm, add 800 g (1¾ lb, 5¼ cups) fresh peas, shelled, a coarsely shredded lettuce and a bouquet garni composed of parsley and chervil. Season with salt and sugar, moisten with 2 tablespoons water, cover the pan and simmer gently for about 30 minutes. Remove the bouquet garni. Blend in 40 g (1½ oz, 3 tablespoons) butter just before serving.

Peas à la française

Place 800 g (1¾ lb, 5¼ cups) fresh peas, shelled, in a saucepan together with a lettuce shredded into fine strips, 12 new small (pearl) onions, a bouquet garni composed of parsley and chervil, 75 g (3 oz, 6 tablespoons) butter cut into small pieces, 1 teaspoon salt, 2 teaspoons caster (superfine) sugar and 4½ tablespoons cold water. Cover the pan, bring slowly to the boil and simmer gently for 30–40 minutes. When the peas are cooked, remove the bouquet garni and stir in 1 tablespoon fresh butter then transfer to a vegetable dish and serve.

Peas in butter

Cook the peas in boiling salted water, drain them, and put them back in the saucepan over a brisk heat, adding a pinch of sugar and 100 g (4 oz, ½ cup) fresh butter per 1 kg (2¼ lb, 6¾ cups) fresh peas, shelled. Serve hot, sprinkled with chopped herbs.

Peas with ham à la languedocienne

Cut a medium onion into quarters and brown in goose fat in a sauté pan with 125 g (4½ oz) lean unsmoked raw ham. Add 800 g (1¾ lb, 5¼ cups) fresh shelled peas and brown lightly. Sprinkle with 1 tablespoon flour and cook for a few minutes. Then add 300 ml (½ pint, 1¼ cups) water, season with salt and caster (superfine) sugar, add a small bouquet garni and bring to the boil. Reduce the heat to a simmer and cook, uncovered, for about 45 minutes. Remove the bouquet garni and serve hot.

Peas with mint

Cook the peas with a few mint leaves in boiling salted water, drain them, and put them back in the saucepan over a brisk heat, adding a pinch of sugar and 100 g (4 oz, ½ cup) fresh butter per 1 kg (2¼ lb, 6¾ cups) fresh peas, shelled. To serve, arrange the peas in a vegetable dish and sprinkle them with scalded chopped mint leaves.

Saint-Germain purée

Prepare in the same way as Saint-Germain soup, but add 100–150 ml (4–5 fl oz, ½–⅔ cup) double (heavy) cream to the sieved peas.

Saint-Germain soup

Shell 800 g (1¾ lb) fresh peas and put into a saucepan with a lettuce heart, 12 small new onions, a bouquet garni with chervil added, 50 g (2 oz, ¼ cup) butter, 1 teaspoon salt and 1 tablespoon granulated sugar. Add 250 ml (8 fl oz, 1 cup) cold water, bring to the boil and cook gently for 30–35 minutes. Remove the bouquet garni and rub the vegetables through an ordinary sieve, then a fine one. Add a little consommé or hot water to obtain the desired consistency of soup and heat through. Add 25 g (1 oz, 2 tablespoons) butter, beat well and sprinkle with chopped herbs. If desired, a few peas and croûtons can be added to garnish.

Split pea purée

Soak some split peas for 1½ hours in cold water, drain, then place them in a saucepan with 2 litres (3½ pints, 9 cups) fresh cold water per 500 g (18 oz, 2⅓ cups) peas. Add 1 carrot, 1 celery stick, the white part of 1 leek and 1 onion, all chopped as for a mirepoix. Then add 1 bouquet garni including the green part of the leek and, if possible, a knuckle of ham and some lettuce leaves. Bring slowly to the boil, skim and season with salt and pepper. Simmer gently with the lid on for about 2½ hours. Then remove the bouquet garni and the ham. Rub the peas through a fine sieve or reduce to a purée in a blender or food processor. Pour the purée into a heavy-based saucepan and heat, stirring continuously with a wooden spoon and slowly pouring in a little of the strained cooking liquid. Blend in some cream, remove from the heat, add a knob of butter and serve piping hot.

Split pea soup

Rub some cooked split peas through a fine sieve or reduce to a purée in a blender or food processor, together with the vegetables they were cooked with. Add equal amounts of the cooking liquid and milk (or use one-third of this volume of cream instead of milk and replace the cooking liquid with consommé). Stir well and adjust the seasoning. Sprinkle with chervil. Fry some croûtons in butter or oil and serve separately. The ham used for cooking the split peas may also be added after being finely diced.

Peppers (bell peppers)

Grilled pepper salad

Cut some green (bell) peppers in half, removing the stalks and the seeds. Oil them very lightly and cook in a very hot oven or under the grill (broiler), skin side up, until the skin blisters and blackens. Peel them and cut into strips. Make a vinaigrette with olive oil, very finely chopped garlic, chopped parsley, lemon juice and a very small quantity of vinegar. Sprinkle over the pepper strips while they are still warm, marinate at room temperature for at least 2 hours, then chill in the refrigerator. Serve as a cold hors d'oeuvre with toast spread with tapenade, shrimps, small octopuses in salad and so on.

Peppers à la piémontaise

Grill (broil) some peppers or cook in a very hot oven until the skins blister and blacken. Peel them, remove the seeds and cut into strips. Make a risotto *à la piémontaise* (page 180). Arrange alternate layers of peppers and risotto in a buttered gratin dish. Finish with a layer of peppers, sprinkle with grated Parmesan cheese and melted butter, and brown in a hot oven.

Peppers à l'orientale

Cut the stalk ends off 500 g (18 oz) green (bell) peppers and remove the seeds. Grill, peel and cut into large dice. Gently fry 100 g (4 oz, 1 cup) chopped onions in a saucepan, without allowing them to brown, then add the peppers, a pinch of powdered garlic, 150 ml (¼ pint, ⅔ cup) clear stock and pepper. Simmer for 30–35 minutes, then adjust the seasoning and serve very hot as a garnish for white meat or mutton.

Ragoût of sweet peppers à l'espagnole

Seed and peel 6 sweet (bell) peppers, and cut them into large strips. Fry 100 g (4 oz, ⅔ cup) finely sliced onions in some olive oil in a shallow frying pan. Add the strips of pepper, some salt, pink pepper, and a large crushed garlic clove. Stir in 1 tablespoon flour and add 300 ml (½ pint, 1¼ cups) beef stock and 2 tablespoons tomato purée (paste). Cook very gently, covered, for 35 minutes. Taste and adjust the seasoning. Serve in a vegetable dish sprinkled with chopped parsley.

Stuffed pepper fritters

Peel and seed some very small green (bell) peppers, as for stuffed peppers *à la turque*. Marinate for 1 hour in a mixture of olive oil, lemon juice and chopped garlic, seasoned with salt, pepper and a pinch of cayenne. Peel and chop equal quantities of onions and mushrooms. Gently fry them in butter, add an equal volume of well-reduced tomato sauce, then some chopped garlic and parsley. Cook this mixture until it has the consistency of a thick paste. Drain and dry the peppers and stuff them with the mixture. Dip them in a light fritter batter and fry in very hot fat (180°C, 350°F) until golden. Drain and serve with a well-reduced tomato sauce.

Stuffed peppers

Cut the stalk ends off 12 very small green (bell) peppers. Remove the seeds and blanch for 5 minutes in boiling salted water. Prepare a stuffing by coarsely chopping 2 handfuls of very fresh sorrel leaves, 4 peeled seeded tomatoes, 3 Spanish onions, 3 green peppers and a small sprig of fennel. Place in a saucepan with 2 tablespoons warm olive oil and cook gently, stirring, until soft but not brown. Strain to remove the liquid and mix with an equal volume of rice cooked in meat stock.

Stuff the peppers with this mixture. Pour a little oil in a deep frying pan and arrange the stuffed peppers in it, closely packed together. Half-fill the pan with thin tomato sauce to which lemon juice and 200 ml (7 fl oz, ¾ cup) olive oil have been added. Cook for about 25 minutes with the lid on. Arrange the peppers in a shallow dish together with their cooking liquid. Leave to cool then refrigerate for at least 1 hour. Serve as an hors d'oeuvre.

Stuffed peppers à la turque

Cut away a small circle around the stalks of some (bell) peppers and put them in a very hot oven or under the grill (broiler) until the skin has blistered and blackened. Peel, cut off the stalk ends and seed them. Blanch for 5 minutes in boiling water. Cool, drain and dry thoroughly. Mix equal quantities of rice cooked in meat stock and cooked coarsely chopped mutton. Add some crushed garlic, chopped parsley and well-reduced tomato sauce; a handful of raisins soaked for 1 hour in warm water may also be added. Slightly widen the opening in the peppers and stuff them with the rice-and-mutton mixture.

Asparagus mousse with orange butter
Recipe on page 23

Asparagus velouté soup
Recipe on page 25

Cabécou figs en coffret with bean salad
Recipe on page 39

Sauerkraut à l'alsacienne
Recipe on page 61

Gougères with celeriac, celery and cream of caviar
Recipe on page 75

Fiddlehead fern and Matane prawn salad
Recipe on page 101

Jerusalem artichoke pie with foie gras and truffle
Recipe on page 105

Salade gourmande
Recipe on page 229

Peel and chop some onions and fry them gently in olive oil in a casserole without allowing them to brown. Then add the stuffed peppers, packing them tightly together. Pour in a mixture of equal proportions of stock and tomato sauce to come a quarter of the way up the peppers. Adjust the seasoning. Bring to the boil, cover and cook in a preheated oven at 230°C (450°F, gas 8) for 30–35 minutes. Arrange the stuffed peppers in a serving dish and pour the cooking liquid over them.

Potatoes

Aligot

Smoothly mash 1 kg (2¼ lb) soft *potato fondantes* (cooked very slowly in butter in a covered pan), add 1–2 crushed garlic cloves, 1 tablespoon bacon fat and sufficient milk to make a purée. Turn the purée into a bain marie, add 575 g (1¼ lb) thinly sliced fresh Laguiole cheese and stir vigorously with a wooden spoon until the cheese is evenly blended into the potato. The aligot is cooked when a smooth flowing elastic purée is formed.

Allumette potatoes

Cut some potatoes into small matchsticks 5 mm (¼ in) thick, using a variety that does not disintegrate during cooking. Wash and dry them, then plunge them into very hot fat and cook without letting them change colour. Drain, then plunge them back into the hot fat once again and cook until just golden. Drain and serve.

Baked potatoes with garlic

Peel 1.5 kg (3¼ lb) potatoes, cut them into slices, wash and pat dry on paper towels. Heat a mixture of oil and butter in a flameproof casserole, then add 4 chopped garlic cloves and 3 thinly sliced onions. Fry gently, stirring until soft. Add the potatoes and mix well. Cover the casserole and cook in a preheated oven at 200°C (400°F, gas 6) for about 1 hour, until the potatoes are tender. Sprinkle with chives.

Baked stuffed potatoes

Peel some large potatoes, trim off the ends and carefully scoop out the inside to leave cylinder shapes. Blanch the potato cylinders, drain and pat dry. Season them with salt and pepper inside and out, fill them with the chosen stuffing, then arrange them closely packed together in a buttered flameproof dish. Half-cover them with clear stock. Bring to the boil, then cover and cook in a preheated oven at 200°C (400°F, gas 6) for 30–35 minutes.

Drain the potatoes and arrange in a buttered ovenproof dish. Sprinkle with breadcrumbs or grated cheese (or a mixture of both), pour melted butter over them and brown in a preheated oven at 230°C (450°F, gas 8). The cooking juice may be used as the base for a sauce to go with the potatoes.

• *potatoes stuffed with duxelles:* Fill the potatoes with a highly seasoned duxelles.

• *stuffed potatoes à la charcutière:* Fill the potatoes with sausagemeat mixed with plenty of chopped parsley and garlic and, if desired, chopped onion fried in butter.

• *stuffed potatoes à la provençale:* Mix equal amounts of canned tuna in oil and chopped hard-boiled (hard-cooked) egg yolks. Bind with well-reduced tomato fondue or a rich tomato sauce and adjust the seasoning; this stuffing must be highly spiced.

Chatouillard potatoes

Pare some potatoes in a spiral to obtain strips 3 mm (⅛ in) thick; wash, wipe and deep-fry in oil heated to only 160°C (325°F). Gradually increase the temperature until the strips rise to the surface – at about 170°C (338°F). Drain them and leave them to cool slightly. Just before serving, plunge them into the oil heated to 180°C (350°F); they must swell up. Drain on paper towels before serving.

Darphin potatoes

Peel 1 kg (2¼ lb) potatoes, rinse and soak in cold water for 1 hour; grate or cut into thin matchsticks and remove excess moisture with a cloth. Pour 250 ml (8 fl oz, 1 cup) oil into a flan tin (pie pan) or dish and heat in a preheated oven at 240°C (475°F, gas 9). Melt 50 g (2 oz) butter in a frying pan, add half the potatoes and sauté them for 5 minutes. Then transfer them to the flan tin and press down. Repeat with the remaining potatoes. Sprinkle with a little extra oil and cook in the oven for about 20 minutes. Turn out the potato cake and serve very hot.

Dauphine potatoes

Peel 1 kg (2¼ lb) floury potatoes, cut them into quarters and cook in boiling salted water until very soft. Drain thoroughly and mash to a purée. Prepare some choux paste using 500 ml (17 fl oz, 2 cups) water, 125 g (4½ oz, ½ cup) butter, 250 g (9 oz, 2¼ cups) plain (all-purpose) flour, 7 eggs and a pinch of grated nutmeg and season with salt and a grinding of pepper. Mix the dough with an equal volume of the potato purée. Heat oil for deep-frying to about 175°C (347°F) and drop the mixture into it a spoonful at a time. When the potato balls are puffed up and golden, drain on paper towels, dust with fine salt and serve very hot.

Deep-fried potatoes

Peel or scrub the potatoes, slice or cut into fingers for making British-style chips. Cut fine fingers for French fries. Rinse, then dry the potatoes thoroughly. Heat the oil for deep-frying to 180°C (350°F). This temperature will drop to 150°C (300°F) when the potatoes are added and the oil should be reheated to 180°C (350°F). Continue cooking, uncovered, until the potatoes turn golden. Shake the basket or rearrange the potatoes occasionally so that they cook evenly.

Thick and fine chips (French fries), known as *pont-neuf* potatoes in French, should be drained when they are tender before they have turned brown. Reheat the oil and then add the potatoes again and cook until crisp and brown. This double-frying process gives chips a crisp, light finish.

When potatoes are cut very finely into potato straws, they will cause only a small drop in the temperature of the fat and need to be immersed only once.

Demi-deuil salad

Boil 675 g (1½ lb) potatoes until tender. Drain, cool, peel and slice the cooked potatoes. Cut 75–100 g (3–4 oz) truffles into thin strips. Make a sauce using 3 tablespoons single (light) cream, 1 teaspoon mustard, salt and pepper.

In a large salad bowl make a bed of lettuce seasoned with a little vinaigrette. Place the potatoes mixed with the sauce on it, then sprinkle with the strips of truffle.

Duchess potato croustades

Spread duchess potato mixture in a 4–5 cm (1½–2 in) thick layer on an oiled baking sheet and leave to cool completely. Use a smooth round cutter to cut into shapes 7.5 cm (3 in) in diameter. Coat these croustades with egg and breadcrumbs. To mark the lid, make a circular incision in the top 1 cm (½ in) from the edge and 3–4 cm (1¼–1½ in) deep. Deep-fry in oil heated to 180°C (356°F) until golden. Drain and dry on paper towels. Remove the lid and hollow out the inside, leaving only a base and a wall, about 1 cm (½ in) thick. Fill the croustades according to the instructions given in the recipe.

Duchess potatoes

Cut 500 g (18 oz) peeled potatoes into thick slices or quarters. Boil them briskly in salted water. Drain, put in a warm oven for a few moments to evaporate excess moisture, and press through a sieve. Put the purée into a saucepan and dry off for a few moments on the hob (stovetop), turning with a wooden spoon. Add 50 g (2 oz, ¼ cup) butter and season with salt, pepper and a little grated nutmeg. Mix in 1 egg and 2 yolks.

This mixture is easier to pipe while hot: it may be piped for borders or into swirls on a greased baking sheet to be served as duchess potatoes proper. Brush the cooled potatoes with beaten egg and brown them in a hot oven.

Alternatively, spread the purée on a buttered baking sheet, leave until cold and shape as indicated in the recipe.

Flat omelette à la savoyarde

Slice 250 g (9 oz) potatoes and sauté them in 40 g (1½ oz, 3 tablespoons) butter. Season with salt and pepper. Beat 8 eggs seasoned with salt and pepper and add 100 g (4 oz, 1 cup) Gruyère cheese in thin shavings. Add the potatoes to this mixture and pour it into a large frying pan. Cook on both sides like a thick pancake.

Flemish salad

Cook some peeled potatoes in salted water and lightly blanch some large peeled onions. Cut the potatoes into slices and chop the onions coarsely.

Clean some chicory (endive) and cut the leaves lengthways and across. Place all the ingredients in a salad bowl and mix with a fairly well-seasoned vinaigrette. Arrange in a dome and garnish with fillets of salt herring cut into strips. Sprinkle with chopped parsley and chervil.

Fried duchess potatoes

Heat some oil for deep-frying to about 180°C (350°F). Put some cooled duchess potato mixture in a piping (pastry) bag with a plain nozzle about 2 cm (¾ in) in diameter and pipe the mixture into the hot oil, cutting it off into about 4 cm (1½ in) lengths. Cook until golden brown, drain on paper towels and serve very hot.

Instead of piping the mixture, it may be spread out on a buttered baking sheet, cooled and cut into even-sized rectangles. These can be rolled into cylinders and then deep-fried.

German salad

Coarsely chop 400 g (14 oz, 2⅓ cups) boiled potatoes and 200 g (7 oz, 1⅓ cups) tart eating apples and mix with 2 tablespoons mayonnaise. Place in a salad bowl; garnish with a shredded gherkin and 2 herring fillets. Sprinkle with chopped parsley. Garnish with slices of cooked beetroot (red beet) and onion. Pour over a mustard-flavoured vinaigrette just before serving.

Gratin dauphinois

Peel and thinly slice 1 kg (2¼ lb) potatoes and arrange them in a generously buttered dish. Mix 2 whole eggs with a little milk, add 1 teaspoon salt, then whisk together with 600 ml (1 pint, 2½ cups) warmed milk or cream. Pour this mixture over the potatoes and dot with knobs of butter. Cook in a preheated oven at 220°C (425°F, gas 7) for about 50 minutes, if necessary protecting the top of the dish with foil towards the end of the cooking period.

The bottom of the dish can be rubbed with garlic, and a little grated nutmeg may be added at the same time as the salt. Grated Gruyère may also be added: one layer on the bottom of the dish and another on the top.

Gratin of potatoes à la hongroise

Bake the potatoes in their skins in the oven or in hot embers. Cut them in half and scrape out the insides; rub this through a sieve. Peel and chop some onions (use half the weight of the sieved potato) and soften them in butter in a covered pan. Season with salt, pepper and a sprinkling of paprika, then mix with the sieved potato. Stuff the potato jackets with this mixture and put in a buttered ovenproof dish. Cover with breadcrumbs, moisten with melted butter and brown in a preheated oven at 240°C (475°F, gas 9).

Hashed potatoes

Boil some potatoes in salted water, drain and chop up roughly. Sauté them well in butter in a frying pan. Add salt and pepper. Press them well down into the form of a cake, leave to brown and then turn out on a warm dish. Chopped onions fried in butter may be added to these hashed and browned potatoes, which are typical of American cooking.

Lorette potatoes

Prepare a dauphine potato mixture and add grated Gruyère cheese, using 100 g (4 oz, 1 cup) for 675 g (1½ lb) potato mixture. Divide the mixture into portions of about 40 g (1½ oz, 3 tablespoons) and mould into crescent shapes, or use a piping (pastry) bag to make stick shapes or knobs. Allow to dry for 30 minutes in the refrigerator, then deep-fry until golden brown. Drain on paper towels.

Lyonnaise potatoes

Parboil some potatoes and slice them. Melt some butter in a frying pan and add the potatoes. When they start to turn golden brown, add some finely chopped onions that have been softened in butter; allow 4 tablespoons onion per 675 g (1½ lb) potatoes. Sauté the mixture well. Arrange in a vegetable dish and sprinkle with chopped parsley.

Macaire potatoes

Bake 4 large floury unpeeled potatoes in the oven. Cut in half and remove the pulp. Mash the potato pulp with butter until smooth, allowing 100 g (4 oz, ½ cup) butter per 1 kg (2¼ lb) potato. Season with salt and pepper. Heat some butter in a frying pan and add the mashed potato, spreading it out into a flat round cake. Cook until golden, then, with the aid of a plate, turn the potato cake over and cook the other side.

Mashed potatoes

Peel and quarter potatoes or cut them into chunks if they are large. Boil in salted water for about 15 minutes or until tender. Drain thoroughly, then return them to the pan. Heat, shaking the pan, for a few seconds to evaporate moisture. Then remove from the heat and add 75 g (3 oz, 6 tablespoons) butter to each 800 g (1¾ lb) potato. Mash, then add a little milk and beat the potatoes with a wooden spoon until smooth. Adjust the seasoning, adding freshly ground white pepper.

The mash may be flavoured with grated cheese 75 g (3 oz, ¾ cup) per 800 g (1¾ lb) mash or placed in a buttered dish, sprinkled with a little melted butter and browned in the oven or under the grill (broiler).

Alternatively, a potato ricer, mouli grater or vegetable mill may be used to make the mash instead of a hand masher.

Pommes Anna

Peel 1 kg (2¼ lb) potatoes and cut into thin even round slices. Wash, wipe and season with salt and pepper. Slightly brown 75 g (3 oz, 6 tablespoons) butter in a special casserole (or in a sauté pan) and arrange the potatoes in circular layers, making sure that they are evenly coated with butter, then compress them into a cake with a wooden spatula. Cover and cook in a hot oven for 25 minutes. Quickly turn the whole cake over on to a flat dish and slide it back into the casserole to brown the other side.

Pont-neuf potatoes

Peel some large waxy potatoes, wash them and cut into sticks 1 cm (½ in) thick and 7 cm (2¾ in) long. Wash well and dry thoroughly in a cloth then deep-fry in oil heated to 170°C (338°F) for 7–8 minutes, until the potatoes begin to colour, then drain on paper towels. Just before serving, fry the potatoes once more in the oil, reheated to 180°C (350°F), until golden. Drain and sprinkle with fine salt.

Port-Royal salad

Mix together slices of boiled potato, chopped cooked French (green) beans, and slices of peeled apple lightly sprinkled with lemon juice. Add some mayonnaise to this mixture. Heap up in a salad bowl, pour over some more mayonnaise and garnish with French beans in a star shape. Surround with small lettuce hearts and quarters of hard-boiled (hard-cooked) eggs.

Potage julienne Darblay

Prepare 1 litre (1¾ pints, 4⅓ cups) puréed potatoes and dilute with about 500 ml (17 fl oz, 2 cups) consommé. Add 4 tablespoons julienne of vegetables which have been gently cooked in butter. Mix 3 egg yolks with 100 ml

(4 fl oz, 7 tablespoons) double (heavy) cream and use this liaison to thicken the soup. Before serving, blend in about 50 g (2 oz, ¼ cup) butter and garnish the soup with chervil.

Potato and leek soup

Cut off the green part of 12 leeks and remove the withered leaves. Peel and quarter 4 large potatoes. Thinly slice the cleaned green parts of the leeks, place in a large saucepan and fry in 25 g (1 oz, 2 tablespoons) butter. Add 1.5 litres (2¾ pints, 6½ cups) boiling water, bring back to the boil, then add the potatoes. Season with salt and pepper and leave to cook gently with the lid on for about 1 hour. Put through a food processor or blender and pour into a soup tureen. Sprinkle with chopped parsley and serve with small slices of bread dried in the oven.

Potato and turnip purée

Peel 800 g (1¾ lb) turnips and 800 g (1¾ lb) potatoes. Cut them separately into cubes. Put 8 juniper berries, 4–5 slices fresh root ginger, 1 teaspoon rosemary leaves and 1 teaspoon black peppercorns in a small linen bag. Peel and chop 2 medium-sized onions. Peel and chop 2 garlic cloves. Heat 3 tablespoons goose fat or duck fat in a flameproof casserole. Add the diced turnips. Season lightly with salt and a pinch of sugar, then brown. Add the potatoes and sauté them, then stir in the chopped onion and garlic. Moisten with a little chicken stock and cook over a low heat until the stock has evaporated. Meanwhile, heat 1 tablespoon fat in a frying pan and fry 12 croûtons on both sides.

Remove the linen bag from the vegetables, purée the vegetables in a food processor and correct the seasoning. Sprinkle with a little roasting juice if desired and serve garnished with the croûtons.

Potato cocotte

Cut some peeled potatoes into finger shapes, then trim into oblongs 4–5 cm (1½–2 in) long (keep the trimmings for a soup). Wash and drain the potatoes, place in a saucepan, cover with cold, unsalted water and bring rapidly to the boil. Drain the potatoes.

Heat a knob of butter and a little oil in a sauté pan big enough to hold the potatoes in a single layer. As soon as the fat is hot, add the potatoes, seal them over a brisk heat, then sauté them gently for about 15 minutes. Cover and place them in a preheated oven at 200°C (400°F, gas 6) and continue cooking for about 10 minutes. Check the potatoes while cooking and remove from the oven as soon as they have browned. Drain and season them with fine salt. Serve in a vegetable dish or next to the meat to be garnished, sprinkled with chopped parsley.

Potato croquettes

Peel and quarter 1.5 kg (3¼ lb) floury potatoes and cook in a saucepan of salted boiling water until they are quite tender (about 20 minutes). Drain the potatoes and dry them out over a low heat. Press through a sieve or blend them to a purée, add about 50 g (2 oz, ¼ cup) butter and gradually work in 4 beaten egg yolks with a fork. Spread the purée in a buttered dish and leave to cool completely.

Work the purée into a ball, using floured hands, then roll the ball into a long narrow cylinder; cut it into sections about 6 cm (2½ in) long. Round these sections slightly. Roll them in flour, coat with a mixture of 2 eggs lightly beaten with 1 tablespoon oil, and cover with breadcrumbs. Deep-fry the croquettes in oil heated to 180°C (350°F) for about 3 minutes, until they turn golden. Drain on paper towels and serve very hot with roast or grilled (broiled) meat.

Potatoes à la berrichonne

Chop 2 onions. Cut 100 g (4 oz) streaky bacon into small strips. Brown the onions and bacon in a flameproof casserole, then add 1 kg (2¼ lb) very small potatoes and brown slightly. Pour in just enough stock to cover, add a bouquet garni and season with salt and pepper, then cover and cook gently for 20–25 minutes. Serve sprinkled with chopped parsley.

Potatoes à la boulangère

Prepare 800 g (1¾ lb) peeled potatoes, cut into slices and brown them in 40 g (1½ oz, 3 tablespoons) butter. Slice 400 g (14 oz) onions and brown in 20 g (¾ oz, 1½ tablespoons) butter. Arrange alternate layers of potatoes and onions in a buttered ovenproof dish. Season with a little salt and pepper, then cover completely with stock. Cook in a preheated oven at 200°C (400°F, gas 6) for about 25 minutes, then reduce the oven temperature to 180°C (350°F, gas 4) and leave to cook for a further 20 minutes. If required, add a little extra stock while the potatoes are cooking.

Potatoes à la crème

Boil some firm, unpeeled potatoes in salted water. Peel them immediately, cut into thick slices and arrange them in a lightly buttered casserole. Cover with crème fraîche, season with salt, pepper and nutmeg, and cook them in a preheated oven at 200°C (400°F, gas 6) until the cream has completely reduced and the potatoes are tender. Add a little extra cream just before serving and sprinkle with chopped herbs.

Potatoes à la Cussy

Cut off both ends of big yellow potatoes, and cut them with a special cutter (called a *colonne*) into cork-shaped chunks, about 2.5 cm (1 in) in diameter.

Cut them into slices 5 mm (¼ in) thick. Dry on a cloth to absorb all water. Put them into a big pan with 225 g (8 oz, 1 cup) hot clarified butter and cook gently so that they colour without sticking to the pan or drying up. In the meantime, slice 6–8 truffles, toss them in butter with 1 tablespoon Madeira and a walnut-sized piece of chicken aspic. When the potatoes are cooked and have acquired a fine golden colour, remove them from the heat. Add the truffles and the juice of ½ lemon and serve piping hot.

Potatoes à la landaise

Fry 100 g (4 oz, ⅔ cup) chopped onions and 150 g (5 oz, 1 cup) diced Bayonne ham in goose fat or lard. When both are browned, add 500 g (18 oz) potatoes cut into large dice. Season with salt and pepper, cover and cook, stirring from time to time. Just before serving, add 1 tablespoon chopped garlic and parsley.

Potatoes à la maître d'hôtel

Put some potatoes in a saucepan of cold salted water, bring to the boil and boil until cooked. Peel and cut into thin slices. Place in a sauté pan and cover with boiling milk or water. Add 40 g (1½ oz, 3 tablespoons) butter per 800 g (1¾ lb) potatoes. Season with salt and pepper. Cover the pan and boil until the liquid has reduced. Turn into a dish and sprinkle with chopped parsley.

Potatoes à la normande

Peel 800 g (1¾ lb) potatoes, slice them thinly, wash and dry them, and sprinkle with salt and pepper. Butter a flameproof casserole and put in half the potatoes. Clean and slice 3 large leeks and chop a small bunch of parsley. Spread the leeks and parsley over the potatoes in the casserole, then cover with the rest of the potatoes. Add sufficient meat or chicken stock to cover the potatoes and dot with 50 g (2 oz, ¼ cup) butter cut into small pieces. Cover the casserole, bring to the boil, then transfer to a preheated oven at 220°C (425°F, gas 7) and cook for about 45 minutes, or until the potatoes are tender.

Potatoes à la paysanne

Peel and slice 1 kg (2¼ lb) waxy potatoes. Braise 100 g (4 oz, 3 cups) chopped sorrel in 25 g (1 oz, 2 tablespoons) butter with a crushed garlic clove, 1 tablespoon chopped chervil and some salt and pepper. Put a layer of potatoes in a buttered sauté pan, then a layer of the cooked sorrel and top with the remaining potatoes. Sprinkle lightly with salt, add a generous quantity of pepper and pour in sufficient stock to just cover the contents of the pan. Sprinkle with 25 g (1 oz, 2 tablespoons) butter cut into small pieces. Cover the pan and bring to the boil. Then transfer to a preheated oven at 200°C (400°F, gas 6) and cook for 50–60 minutes.

Potatoes à la sarladaise

Peel and wash 1.5 kg (3¼ lb) potatoes. Cut in half lengthways, then cut each half into quarters. Heat 2 tablespoons goose fat in a flameproof casserole until it turns a beautiful rich brown colour. Add the potatoes and cook over a high heat, stirring often. Remove the excess fat. Season with salt and pepper. Crush 4 garlic cloves, whole but not peeled, and add to the potatoes. If in season, add the stalks of 2 fresh ceps, cut into quarters. Cover and cook in a preheated oven at 200°C (400°F, gas 6) for 40 minutes.

Potatoes au jus

Peel some potatoes and cut into quarters. Butter a flameproof casserole and arrange the potatoes in layers. Half-cover with meat glaze or stock. Season with salt and pepper. Cover and bring to the boil, then cook in a preheated oven at 200°C (400°F, gas 6) for about 40 minutes, adding a little stock if necessary (these potatoes must be very soft). Sprinkle with chopped parsley.

Potatoes émiellées

Sauté some thinly sliced peeled potatoes in butter in a heavy-based frying pan, together with some small pieces of bacon and a bay leaf. Cover the pan when the potatoes are half-cooked so that they remain soft. When they are brown and well cooked, bring the pan to the table, break 1 egg per person into it and stir together so that the eggs set quickly. Serve with a salad.

Potatoes en papillotes

Wash some large potatoes thoroughly under cold running water, but do not dry them. Wrap each potato in a piece of foil and cook for 40–45 minutes, either in a preheated oven at 230°C (450°F, gas 8) or in the hot ashes of a fire.

Potatoes Mère Carles

Peel some waxy potatoes and cut out of them 28 large cork shapes about 5 cm (2 in) long. Pack the potato shapes tightly in a sauté pan and completely cover with cold salted water. Bring to the boil to blanch the potatoes, then drain.

Brown 50 g (2 oz, ¼ cup) butter in a sauté pan, then add the drained potato shapes, season with pepper and cover. Leave to brown for about 20 minutes, stirring frequently. Remove from the heat and leave to cool.

Remove the rind from 14 rashers (slices) of smoked streaky bacon and cut each rasher in half. Roll each potato shape in a half-rasher of smoked bacon. Arrange these in a sauté pan and cook, uncovered, in a preheated oven at 180°C (350°F, gas 4) for 10 minutes. Drain the cooking fat from the sauté pan and replace with 25 g (1 oz, 2 tablespoons) fresh butter. Roll the potatoes in this butter before serving.

Potato mousseline

Bake some unpeeled potatoes in the oven, peel them and rub the pulp through a sieve. Stir this mash over the heat, adding 200 g (7 oz, ¾ cup) butter per 1 kg (2¼ lb) mash, then 4 egg yolks. Season with salt, white pepper and grated nutmeg. Remove from the heat and add 200 ml (7 fl oz, ¾ cup) whipped cream. Heap the mixture in a buttered ovenproof dish, sprinkle with melted butter and brown in a preheated oven at 230°C (450°F, gas 8).

Potatoes vendangeurs de bourgogne

Place in a cast-iron or copper terrine 175 g (6 oz) smoked streaky bacon rashers (slices) with the rinds removed, then 225 g (8 oz) thinly sliced raw potatoes. Sprinkle with grated Gruyère cheese. Then add 150 g (5 oz) slightly salted belly pork, blanched and thinly sliced, and cover with 225 g (8 oz) potatoes, 50 g (2 oz, ½ cup) grated Gruyère cheese, then a further 150 g (5 oz) slightly salted belly pork prepared in the same way. Finish with 225 g (8 oz) potatoes, 50 g (2 oz, ½ cup) grated Gruyère cheese and a further 175 g (6 oz) smoked streaky bacon rashers with the rinds removed. Season lightly with pepper, scatter with a few knobs of butter and cook in a preheated oven at 200°C (400°F, gas 6) for 1¼ hours or until cooked through. Unmould and serve piping hot.

Potatoes with bacon

Heat 25 g (1 oz, 2 tablespoons) butter or lard in a flameproof casserole and sauté in it 125 g (4½ oz, ⅔ cup) diced blanched bacon together with 10 small (pearl) onions. Drain and remove. Cut some potatoes into oval shapes or cubes and brown them in the casserole. Season with salt and pepper, replace the bacon and onions, cover and cook gently for about 15 minutes. Sprinkle with chopped parsley and, if desired, finely chopped garlic.

Potato fondantes

Peel some potatoes and trim them to the shape of small eggs. Fry gently in butter for 5 minutes, then drain. Add more butter, cover and finish cooking in a preheated oven at 200°C (400°F, gas 6). When cooked, remove from the oven, add 4 tablespoons white stock and leave until the potatoes have absorbed the stock. Serve in a vegetable dish, without parsley.

Alternatively, fry the potatoes in butter in a sauté pan. When cooked, remove the potatoes, wipe out the pan with paper towels, then add fresh butter – 100 g (4 oz, ½ cup) per 1 kg (2¼ lb) potatoes. Replace the potatoes, cover and keep warm over a very gentle heat or in a preheated oven at 150°C (300°F, gas 2) until all the butter is absorbed.

Potato galette

Bake 6 large floury (baking) potatoes in the oven for 45–60 minutes until soft. Cut them open and remove the flesh, then mix 400 g (14 oz, 3¾ cups) of this with 4 egg yolks, added one by one, and 1 teaspoon salt. Soften 150 g (5 oz, ⅔ cup) butter with a spatula and mix it in. Roll the potato dough into a ball and flatten it with the palm of the hand. Shape it into a ball again and repeat the operation twice more. Butter a baking sheet and flatten the dough to form a galette 4 cm (1½ in) thick. Trace a pattern on the top with the point of a knife, brush it with beaten egg, and bake in a preheated oven at 220°C (425°F, gas 7) until golden brown. If the galette is to be served as a dessert, add to the dough 125 g (4½ oz, ½ cup) sugar, orange-flower water and chopped blanched orange and lemon rind (zest).

Potato gnocchi

Cook 3 medium-sized potatoes in boiling salted water for about 20 minutes. Meanwhile grate 6–7 medium-sized peeled potatoes and squeeze them in a cloth to extract as much water as possible. Peel and mash the cooked potatoes, then mix them with the grated raw potatoes. Add 100–125 g (4–4½ oz, 1 cup) plain (all-purpose) flour, a little grated nutmeg, salt and pepper, then 2 eggs, one after the other. Mix thoroughly. Use 2 spoons to shape the paste into small, round portions. Drop them into a pan of boiling salted water and leave to simmer for 6–8 minutes. Drain the gnocchi and place on a cloth then put them in a buttered gratin dish and coat with 200 ml (7 fl oz, ¾ cup) crème fraîche and sprinkle with grated cheese. Brown in a very hot oven.

Potato nests

Peel some firm potatoes. Using a mandoline, cut them into very fine strips (matchsticks). Line the larger nest basket with an even layer of potato matchsticks, overlapping them slightly. Press them against the sides and trim them. Place the smaller basket inside the larger one so that the matchsticks are held in position. Deep-fry in hot oil at 180°C (350°F) for 5–6 minutes. Open the basket and the nest should come out quite cleanly.

Potato pancakes

Peel and wash some potatoes, pat them dry and grate coarsely. Drain on paper towels, then place in a bowl. Add salt and pepper, and for every 500 g (18 oz, 2½ cups) potatoes add 2 eggs beaten with 100 ml (4 fl oz, 7 tablespoons) milk and 1½ tablespoons melted butter. Mix thoroughly. Fry spoonfuls of the potato mixture in a buttered frying pan, distributing the potato evenly to make small, thick pancakes. When set and golden underneath, turn the pancakes and fry until golden on the second side. Keep cooked pancakes hot until the entire batch of batter is cooked. Serve in a warm dish.

A little grated cheese or grated garlic and chopped herbs can be added to this mixture. These pancakes may be served with coq au vin or roast meats.

Potato soufflé

Bind 400 g (14 oz, 1⅔ cups) mashed potato with 60 ml (2 fl oz, ¼ cup) double (heavy) cream. Add 3 egg yolks, then fold in 4 stiffly whisked egg whites. Preheat the oven for 15 minutes at 220°C (425°F, gas 7). Butter a soufflé mould 20 cm (8 in) in diameter and coat with flour. Pour in the mixture and bake in the preheated oven at 200°C (400°F, gas 6) for 30 minutes, without opening the door during cooking, until well risen and a deep golden-brown on top.

Chestnut, sweet potato or Jerusalem artichoke soufflés may also be made in this way. They can be flavoured with 75 g (3 oz, ¾ cup) grated Gruyère cheese or 50 g (2 oz, ½ cup) grated Parmesan cheese.

Potato subrics

Finely dice 500 g (18 oz) potatoes and blanch for 2 minutes in salted boiling water. Drain and wipe, then cook slowly in butter. Remove from the heat and bind them with 250 ml (8 fl oz, 1 cup) thick béchamel sauce. Add 3 egg yolks and 1 whole egg and season with salt, pepper and grated nutmeg, then leave to cool completely. Mould this mixture into small balls and cook in 40 g (1½ oz, 3 tablespoons) clarified butter in a frying pan until golden (about 3 minutes). Serve piping hot, with a cream sauce well seasoned with nutmeg.

Roast potatoes

Peel some potatoes and cut into fairly small, evenly sized pieces (leave them whole if they are small). Melt some butter or lard in a flameproof casserole – 100 g (4 oz, ½ cup) per 1 kg (2¼ lb) potatoes – then add the potatoes in a single layer. Roll the potatoes in the fat, season with salt, then cook at the top of a preheated oven at 190°C (375°F, gas 5) for 40 minutes or more, frequently basting with the fat until they turn golden and are cooked through.

Rösti

Peel and grate (or finely slice) 800 g (1¾ lb) potatoes which have been parboiled in their skins the night before. Add 1 teaspoon salt and, if liked, 100 g (4 oz, ½ cup) diced bacon. Melt 4 tablespoons lard in a frying pan and add the potatoes, turning them several times so that they become impregnated with the lard. Cook over a medium heat, stirring frequently. (If the potatoes seem a little dry, cover the pan; if they start to disintegrate, leave uncovered.) When they are cooked, draw together in the pan and raise the heat until a golden crust forms underneath. Turn this cake out on to a plate, crust upwards. It can be served with *longeoles* (coarse Savoy sausages).

Salad argenteuil

Cook some potatoes in their skins, dice them and dress with tarragon mayonnaise. Pile into a salad bowl and garnish with white asparagus tips seasoned with oil and lemon. Make a border with shredded lettuce and quartered hard-boiled (hard-cooked) eggs.

Santé soup

Prepare 1.5 litres (2¾ pints, 6½ cups) fairly thin potato and leek soup. Cook 4 tablespoons shredded sorrel in butter until soft. Mix together and thicken with 3 egg yolks blended with 100 ml (4 fl oz, 7 tablespoons) double (heavy) cream. Beat in 50 g (2 oz, ¼ cup) butter, cut into small pieces, and sprinkle with chervil. Serve with thin slices of French bread, dried out in the oven.

Sautéed cooked potatoes

Boil 15 unpeeled potatoes in salted water until almost tender. Drain and leave to cool, then peel and cut into slices. In a sauté pan heat a mixture of equal amounts of butter and oil; or use butter only: 50 g (2 oz, ¼ cup) per 800 g

(1¾ lb) potatoes. Brown the potatoes evenly for 12–15 minutes, first over a brisk heat, then over a gentle heat, uncovered, turning them often. Season with salt and pepper and sprinkle with chopped parsley.

Sautéed raw potatoes

Peel and cut 800 g (1¾ lb) waxy potatoes into slices or small cubes. Wash, pat dry and season with salt and pepper. Fry for 25 minutes in a frying pan in butter or oil – 50 g (2 oz, ¼ cup) butter or 4 tablespoons oil per 800 g (1¾ lb) potatoes – or in a mixture of equal amounts of butter and oil. Cover when brown, but toss frequently so that they cook evenly.

Soufflé potatoes

Peel some large waxy potatoes, wash and pat dry. Cut into slices 3 mm (⅛ in) thick. Wash and dry once again. Deep-fry in oil at 150°C (300°F) for about 8 minutes. Drain on paper towels and leave to cool. Reheat the oil to 180°C (350°F) and replace the potatoes in it. Cook until puffy and brown, then drain on paper towels. Serve in a very hot dish, sprinkled with salt.

Straw potatoes

Peel some large firm potatoes, cut them into very thin strips and leave them to soak in plenty of cold water for 15 minutes. Drain and wipe thoroughly, then deep-fry them in oil heated to 180–190°C (350–375°F) until they are golden (about 5 minutes). Drain them on paper towels, dust them with fine salt and serve them piping hot.

Stuffed baked potatoes

Bake some large potatoes in a preheated oven at 200°C (400°F, gas 6) for 1¼–1½ hours, until tender. Cut a slice off the top lengthways and scoop out the potato without breaking the skins. Press the pulp through a sieve and mix it with butter, a little milk or single (light) cream, salt and pepper. Fill the empty potato skins with the potato mixture, sprinkle with breadcrumbs or grated cheese (or a mixture of the two) and brown in the oven.

The sieved potato mixture can be enriched by using double (heavy) cream instead of milk or single cream. Fromage frais or yogurt can be used for a creamy, yet light, result. Grated Gruyère, Parmesan or mature (sharp) Cheddar cheese can be added. Chopped fresh parsley, dill, fennel or basil are good; snipped chives are excellent with other flavourings or on their own.

Stuffed baked potatoes à la cantalienne

Prepare some baked potatoes. Add an equal volume of braised chopped cabbage to the pulp and adjust the seasoning. Fill the potato skins with this mixture, sprinkle with grated cheese and a little melted butter or lard (shortening) and brown in a preheated oven at 230°C (450°F, gas 8).

Stuffed baked potatoes à la florentine

Cook some baked potatoes. Mash half of the potato pulp and mix with twice its volume of spinach cooked in butter and chopped. Fill the potato skins with this mixture. Cover with Mornay sauce, sprinkle with Parmesan cheese and brown in a preheated oven at 230°C (450°F, gas 8) or under the grill (broiler).

Stuffed baked potatoes chasseur

Prepare some baked potatoes. Mix the pulp with an equal volume of thinly sliced chicken livers and mushrooms sautéed in butter. Adjust the seasoning and add a small quantity of chopped herbs. Fill the potatoes with this mixture, sprinkle with breadcrumbs and then with melted butter, and brown in a preheated oven at 230°C (450°F, gas 8).

Stuffed baked potatoes with ham and mushrooms

Cook some baked potatoes. Keep the pulp. Prepare equal amounts of chopped cooked ham, chopped mushrooms lightly fried in butter and chopped onions fried in butter. Bind with a little béchamel sauce. Season, adding paprika if desired. Stuff the potatoes, sprinkle with breadcrumbs and melted butter and brown in a preheated oven at 230°C (450°F, gas 8).

Stuffed potatoes à la basquaise

Fry some diced red and green (bell) peppers in oil. Hollow out some large peeled potatoes, place in boiling water for 5 minutes then wipe dry. Dice some Bayonne ham and moisten it with a garlicky tomato sauce. Add the peppers. Fill the potatoes with the mixture. Oil a dish, add the potatoes and season. Sprinkle with oil or melted goose fat, cover and bake in a preheated oven at about 180°C (350°F, gas 4) for 30–40 minutes. When the potatoes are cooked, sprinkle with breadcrumbs and melted fat and brown under the grill (broiler).

Stuffed potatoes à la Maintenon

Bake some unpeeled floury potatoes and remove the pulp. Prepare a salpicon with chicken, cooked tongue and mushrooms, bound with a light Soubise purée. Fill the potato skins with this mixture, forming a dome shape. Sprinkle with grated cheese, breadcrumbs and melted butter. Brown in the oven.

Stuffed potatoes Soubise

Bake some firm unpeeled potatoes, then scoop out the pulp. Prepare a well-reduced Soubise purée. Add one quarter of its volume of double (heavy) cream and reduce until extremely thick. Beat into the potato pulp. Stuff the potato skins with this mixture, place in an ovenproof dish and sprinkle with breadcrumbs and small knobs of butter. Brown in a very hot oven.

Pumpkin

Pumpkin au jus

Peel a pumpkin and remove the seeds and surrounding fibres. Cut the pulp into slices and blanch in boiling salted water for about 10 minutes. Drain thoroughly and put into a frying pan with some veal stock. Cover and simmer gently for about 20 minutes. Serve sprinkled with chopped parsley.

Pumpkin gratin à la provençale

Peel a fine ripe pumpkin and remove the seeds and their surrounding fibres. Cut the pulp into small dice and blanch for 10 minutes in boiling salted water; refresh in cold water and drain. Peel some onions (a quarter of the weight of the pumpkin), chop and sweat them gently for 5–6 minutes in butter. Rub a gratin dish with garlic and butter; arrange a layer of pumpkin pieces, then the onions, then the rest of the pumpkin, in the dish. Sprinkle with grated cheese and olive oil and brown in a preheated oven at 220°C (425°F, gas 7).

Pumpkin purée

Sweat the pulp of a pumpkin in butter and reduce to a purée. Cook some potatoes (one-third of the weight of the pumpkin) in boiling salted water and reduce to a purée. Mix the two purées, add a little boiling milk, and stir thoroughly. Remove from the heat and beat in some butter.

Pumpkin soup

Peel and seed a pumpkin to obtain 800 g (1¾ lb) pulp. Cut the pulp into small pieces and place in a saucepan with 50 g (2 oz, ¼ cup) butter and 8 tablespoons water. Add salt, cover the pan and sweat for about 20 minutes. Purée the pulp, pour into the rinsed-out saucepan and add 1 litre (1¾ pints, 4⅓ cups) stock or consommé. Bring to the boil, taste and adjust the seasoning and whisk in 50 g (2 oz, ¼ cup) butter cut into small pieces. Serve with small croûtons fried in butter.

Alternatively, the purée can be diluted with 1 litre (1¾ pints, 4⅓ cups) boiling milk and sweetened to taste. Thicken with 2 tablespoons ground rice blended with a little milk.

Sautéed pumpkin with spices

Melt 50 g (2 oz, 1 cup) salted butter in a frying pan and add 1 tablespoon clear honey and 4 crescent-shaped pieces of fresh pumpkin, each weighing about 200 g (7 oz). Fry until golden. When they have finished cooking, sprinkle with 1 teaspoon allspice, 1 teaspoon curry powder, the chopped zest of 1 unwaxed mandarin, 2 teaspoons freshly chopped mint leaves, the juice of ½ lemon and good-quality salt. Serve hot with chicken or sweetbreads.

Radish

Black radish as an hors d'oeuvre

Peel a black radish and slice it very thinly; soak the slices in a bowl with a small handful of table salt for an hour. Wash thoroughly, dry well and serve in an hors d'oeuvre dish accompanied by rye bread or wholemeal (whole wheat) bread with fresh or slightly salted butter.

Pink radishes à l'américaine

Wash the radishes and cut all the leaves to the same length. Wash and then split the radishes in four from tip to leaf end without cutting through the bases; put them in a bowl of water and ice cubes. When they open out like flowers, drain and serve in an hors d'oeuvre dish, with butter and salt.

Radish-leaf soup

Cut off the leaves from a bunch of fresh radishes and cook them gently in butter in a saucepan. Pour in some chicken stock. Add 3 peeled potatoes, salt and pepper. Cook over a low heat for 25 minutes, then pass the soup through a vegetable mill. Add 2 tablespoons crème fraîche, mix, then adjust the seasoning. Sprinkle with coarsely chopped chervil. This soup can be served with baked croûtons.

Rice

Rice à la créole

Thoroughly wash 500 g (18 oz, 2½ cups) long-grain rice and pour it into a sauté pan. Add salt and enough water to come 2 cm (¾ in) above the level of the rice. Bring to the boil and continue to boil rapidly with the pan uncovered. When the water has boiled down to the same level as the rice, cover the pan and cook very gently until the rice is completely dry (this will take about 45 minutes). The second part of the cooking process may be carried out in a cool oven.

Rice croustades

Cook some rice in stock – meat or poultry – with the fat in the stock or with added butter or olive oil. Bind with egg yolks – 5 yolks per 500 g (18 oz, 3 cups) rice or semolina. Spread out in a layer 4–5 cm (1½–2 in) thick and leave to cool completely. Use a smooth round cutter to cut into shapes 7.5 cm (3 in) in diameter. Coat these croustades with egg and breadcrumbs. To mark the lid, make a circular incision in the top 1 cm (½ in) from the edge and 3–4 cm (1¼–1½ in) deep. Deep-fry in oil heated to 180°C (356°F) until golden. Drain and dry on paper towels. Remove the lid and hollow out the inside, leaving only a base and a wall, about 1 cm (½ in) thick. Fill the croustades as required.

Rice pilaf

Sweat some very finely chopped onions in butter without browning. Add the unwashed rice and stir until it becomes transparent. Add 1½ times its volume in boiling water. Season with salt and add a bouquet garni. Put some greaseproof (wax) paper over the rice and cover with a lid. Cook for 16–18 minutes in a preheated oven at 200°C (400°F, gas 6). Remove from the oven and allow to stand for 15 minutes. Add butter and fork the grains.

Risotto à la milanaise

Heat 40 g (1½ oz, 3 tablespoons) butter or 4 tablespoons olive oil in a saucepan and cook 100 g (4 oz, ¾ cup) chopped onions very gently, without browning. Then add 250 g (9 oz, 1¼ cups) rice and stir until the grains become transparent. Add twice the volume of stock, a ladleful at a time, stirring with a wooden spoon and waiting until all the liquid has been absorbed before adding more. Adjust the seasoning, add a small bouquet garni, then add 200 ml (7 fl oz, ¾ cup) thick tomato fondue, 500 g (18 oz) pickled ox (beef) tongue, ham and mushrooms (in equal proportions, all chopped), and a little white truffle. Keep hot, if necessary, without allowing the rice to cook further.

Risotto à la piémontaise

Heat 40 g (1½ oz, 3 tablespoons) butter or 4 tablespoons olive oil in a saucepan and cook 100 g (4 oz, ¾ cup) chopped onions very gently, without browning. Then add 250 g (9 oz, 1¼ cups) rice and stir until the grains become transparent. Add twice the volume of stock, a ladleful at a time, stirring with a wooden spoon and waiting until all the liquid has been absorbed before adding more. Adjust the seasoning, add a small bouquet garni, then add 75 g (3 oz, ¾ cup) grated Parmesan cheese and 25 g (1 oz, 2 tablespoons) butter. Some saffron may also be added. Keep hot, if necessary, without allowing the rice to cook further.

Spring risotto

Clean, then cook separately in some oil and a little water 2 small purple artichokes, cut into quarters, 200 g (7 oz, 2⅓ cups) mushrooms, chopped and seasoned with oil and a few drops of lemon juice, and 2 small onions with their root stems intact, and 2 tablespoons sugar and a little salt. Blanch 1 bunch green asparagus, then fry lightly in butter. Now gently reheat all the vegetables together, except for the asparagus, so that their flavours blend. Gently sauté 500 g (18 oz, 2½ cups) rice in a little oil in a casserole, then bring 1.5 litres (2¾ pints, 6½ cups) stock to the boil and pour 1 ladle on to the rice, stirring until the liquid is completely absorbed. Continue like this until the rice is cooked. After 15 minutes, add the vegetables, except for the asparagus. Remove the rice from the heat, add 50 g (2 oz, ¼ cup) butter and 25 g (1 oz, ¼ cup) grated Parmesan cheese and stir well. Garnish with asparagus tips.

Salsify

To prepare

Scrape or peel the salsify with a potato peeler, cut it into chunks 7.5 cm (3 in) long, and put them as they are prepared into water with a little lemon juice or vinegar added to prevent discoloration. Cook in boiling vegetable stock, covered, at a steady gentle simmer for 1–1½ hours, according to the quality of the vegetable, then drain and pat dry before final preparations for serving. (Alternatively, cut the salsify into pieces and cook the pieces with the skin on. It will then be easier to peel the vegetable after cooking.) If the salsify is not to be used immediately, it can be stored in its cooking liquid in the refrigerator for 1–2 days, but it will lose some of its nutritional value.

Battered salsify fritters

Cut some cooked salsify into short lengths. Dry, dip in flour and then in batter. Deep fry in hot oil and serve with fried parsley. These fritters make a particularly good accompaniment to roast beet, pork or veal.

Buttered salsify

Cook the salsify. Just before serving, make some noisette butter. Drain the salsify thoroughly while it is still very hot, quickly pat dry, then place on a heated dish and pour the noisette butter over it.

Salsify à la polonaise

Cook the salsify in white stock, drain and dry, then stew in butter for about 10 minutes. Arrange in a deep dish and sprinkle with chopped hard-boiled (hard-cooked) egg yolks and parsley. Fry some fresh breadcrumbs in noisette butter – 25 g (1 oz, ½ cup) breadcrumbs to 100 g (4 oz, ½ cup) butter – and pour over the salsify.

Salsify au gratin

Wash, scrape or peel, and roughly chop 1 kg (2¼ lb) salsify. Plunge into water with lemon juice added, then cook for 1 hour, or until tender, in salted white stock. Drain and dry. Cook 2 chopped shallots in butter until soft. Pour over 500 ml (17 fl oz, 2 cups) double (heavy) cream and reduce. Add the salsify and a little stock. Season with salt and pepper and pour into a gratin dish. Sprinkle with grated Gruyère cheese and breadcrumbs and brown in a preheated oven at 220°C (425°F, gas 7) for 20 minutes.

Salsify fritters

Cook 1 kg (2¼ lb) salsify, drain and purée. Add 100 g (4 oz, ½ cup) butter and season with salt and pepper. Roll the purée into little balls, coat them in flour and deep-fry in hot oil at 180°C (350°F) until golden all over. Remove with a slotted spoon and drain on paper towels. Arrange on a warmed dish and garnish with fried parsley.

Salsify in stock

Wash, peel and cook the salsify, then drain and dry. Pour over some slightly thickened white veal stock or meat gravy. Cook in a preheated oven at 180°C (350°F, gas 4) for 15–20 minutes.

Salsify Mornay

Cook some salsify then drain it and dry on paper towels. Pour a layer of Mornay sauce into a gratin dish and arrange the cooked salsify on top of it.

Coat the salsify with another layer of Mornay sauce and sprinkle with some grated Parmesan cheese. Pour over some melted butter and brown in a preheated oven at 230°C (450°F, gas 8).

Salsify omelette with Brussels sprouts

Cook some salsify in white wine then cut it into dice. Braise the dice in butter and bind with some reduced velouté sauce. Reduce some demi-glace sauce and stir in some butter. Fill an omelette with the salsify mixture and serve it with noisette potatoes and Brussels sprouts sautéed in butter. Pour the demi-glace sauce around the omelette.

Salsify salad with anchovies

Cook some salsify in white stock, drain thoroughly and dry. Mix in some light, well-seasoned mayonnaise and chopped, drained, canned anchovy fillets (or whole filleted anchovies that have been soaked to desalt them). Sprinkle with chopped herbs.

Salsify sautéed à la provençale

Cook some salsify in white stock, drain, dry and sauté in olive oil. Just before serving, add a little chopped garlic and parsley or some tomato sauce.

Salsify with béchamel sauce

Cook, drain and dry 800 g (1¾ lb) salsify. Arrange the salsify in a buttered ovenproof casserole and cover with a layer of fairly thin béchamel sauce, made with 25 g (1 oz, 2 tablespoons) butter, 25 g (1 oz, ¼ cup) plain (all-purpose) flour and 450 ml (¾ pint, 2 cups) milk. Place the casserole in a preheated oven at 190°C (375°F, gas 5) and cook for 20 minutes, then pour over 2–3 tablespoons cream and reheat.

Salsify with mayonnaise

Cook the salsify and leave to cool, then drain thoroughly and dry. Add some well-seasoned mayonnaise or vinaigrette. Sprinkle with chopped herbs and serve with a cold white meat dish, such as rabbit in aspic.

Sautéed salsify

Cook some salsify in white stock, drain, dry and fry in butter. Sprinkle with salt, pepper and chopped herbs just before serving.

Sorrel

Chiffonnade of sorrel

Pick over the sorrel leaves and remove the hard stalks. Wash and dry the leaves and shred them finely. Melt some butter in a saucepan without letting it colour – allow 25 g (1 oz, 2 tablespoons) butter for 200 g (7 oz, 3½ cups) leaves. Add the sorrel, three-quarters cover the pan with a lid and let it cook gently until all the vegetable liquid has disappeared. The chiffonnade can be used as it is as a garnish; it can also be mixed with double (heavy) cream and reduced. A 'mixed' chiffonnade is a combination of sorrel and lettuce.

Germiny soup

Wash 300 g (11 oz) sorrel, finely shred into a chiffonnade and soften in butter. Add 1.5 litres (2¾ pints, 6½ cups) beef or chicken consommé. Mix 4–6 egg yolks with 300–500 ml (10–17 fl oz, 1¼–2 cups) single (light) cream. Use this to thicken the soup until the consommé coats the spatula. Do not allow the soup to boil. Add 1 tablespoon chervil leaves and serve with slices of French bread, dried in the oven.

Longchamp soup

Cut some sorrel into fine strips and soften it in butter in a covered saucepan. When well braised, add 4 tablespoons sorrel to 1 litre (1¾ pints, 4⅓ cups) puréed fresh peas. Cook some vermicelli in 500 ml (17 fl oz, 2 cups) stock and stir into the soup. Heat up the soup and sprinkle with parsley.

Preserved sorrel

Pick over the sorrel and remove the hard stalks. Wash and dry it, shred it finely and cook it in butter until it is completely dry. Pack it into a wide-mouthed jar. When it is quite cold, seal the jar and sterilize it. The sorrel can also be packed into containers and frozen. It is advisable to prepare only small quantities at a time.

Sorrel omelette

Prepare 4 tablespoons finely shredded sorrel. Cook gently in butter or bind with cream, and beat it into 8 eggs. Cook the omelette. It may be served surrounded with a ribbon of cream sauce.

Sorrel purée

Pick over the sorrel and remove the hard stalks. Wash and dry it. Put the leaves into a large saucepan and pour in boiling water, allowing 1 litre (1¾ pints, 4⅓ cups) water per 1 kg (2¼ lb) sorrel. Bring to the boil, cook for 4–5 minutes, then remove from the heat and drain in a sieve. In a flameproof casserole, make a white roux using 65 g (2½ oz, 5 tablespoons) butter and

40 g (1½ oz, 6 tablespoons) plain (all-purpose) flour. Add the sorrel and mix well together. Pour in 500 ml (17 fl oz, 2 cups) white stock and add salt and a pinch of sugar.

Cover the casserole, bring to the boil on top of the stove, then transfer it to a preheated oven at 180°C (350°F, gas 4) and cook for 1½ hours. Purée the sorrel in a food processor or blender and return it to the hob (stove top) to reheat. Bind it with 3 whole eggs beaten with 100 ml (4 fl oz, 7 tablespoons) double (heavy) cream. Finally add 100 g (4 oz, ½ cup) butter, in pieces.

Sorrel sauce

Cook 2 chopped shallots in 4½ tablespoons dry vermouth, then reduce by half. Add 175 ml (6 fl oz, ¾ cup) double (heavy) cream and reduce again until the sauce is thick and smooth. Add 150 g (5 oz, 2 cups) finely shredded sorrel, season with salt and pepper, boil again briefly then leave to cool. Just before serving, add a few drops of lemon juice to sharpen the sauce. This sauce is especially good with fish.

Sorrel velouté soup

Prepare a white roux with 40 g (1½ oz, 3 tablespoons) butter and 40 g (1½ oz, 6 tablespoons) flour. Moisten with a generous 750 ml (1¼ pints, 3¼ cups) chicken consommé. Blanch the sorrel in salted boiling water for 3–4 minutes, drain and dry thoroughly. Sweat in 40 g (1½ oz, 3 tablespoons) butter for about 15 minutes then add to the consommé, bring to the boil and cook for 15 minutes. Reduce the soup to a purée in a food processor or blender. Dilute with a little consommé, if necessary, and heat. Remove from the heat and thicken the soup with a mixture of 3 egg yolks beaten with 100 ml (4 fl oz, 7 tablespoons) double (heavy) cream. Finally, whisk in 75 g (3 oz, 6 tablespoons) butter. Reheat but do not boil.

Spinach

Botvinya

Wash and tear up 400 g (14 oz) spinach, 250 g (9 oz) beetroot (beet) leaves and 200 g (7 oz) sorrel. Cook gently in melted butter until soft, then purée in a food processor or blender. Transfer the purée to a soup tureen and stir in 250 ml (8 fl oz, 1 cup) dry white wine, 1 litre (1¾ pints, 4⅓ cups) stock, 1½ teaspoons salt, 2 teaspoons sugar, 100 g (4 oz) diced cucumber, a chopped shallot and 1 tablespoon each of chopped chervil and tarragon. Cover and chill in the refrigerator for at least 3 hours. Before serving add about 10 ice cubes, mix again and serve very cold.

Cannelloni à la florentine

Hard-boil (hard-cook) 2 eggs and remove the shells. Boil some spinach and drain it. Make a very smooth béchamel sauce. Roughly chop the spinach and heat it gently in butter, allowing 25 g (1 oz, 2 tablespoons) butter to 1 kg (2¼ lb) spinach. Finely chop the hard-boiled eggs and add to the spinach. Also add 2 raw egg yolks mixed with 100 ml (4 fl oz, 7 tablespoons) double (heavy) cream, 40 g (1½ oz, ⅓ cup) grated Parmesan cheese, salt, pepper and grated nutmeg. Gently reheat the mixture without boiling, then leave to cool. Fill fresh pasta rectangles with this mixture and roll them up. Alternatively, use bought cannelloni tubes cooked according to the packet instructions. Arrange in a buttered ovenproof dish, cover with the béchamel sauce and sprinkle with grated Parmesan cheese and a few knobs of butter. Cook in a preheated oven at 240°C (475°F, gas 9) or under a hot grill (broiler) until the surface is brown and crusty.

Fritters à la florentine

Prepare 250 g (9 oz, 1 cup) spinach purée and dry it out gently over the heat, turning it with a wooden spoon. Mix the purée with 200 ml (7 fl oz, ¾ cup) well-reduced béchamel sauce and blend in 50 g (2 oz, ½ cup) grated Gruyère cheese. Cool the mixture completely and divide it into about 15 portions. Roll each portion in flour, dip into a prepared batter and deep-fry in oil, heated to 180°C (350°F), until golden brown. Drain on paper towels, sprinkle with salt and serve very hot.

Green butter

Wring 1 kg (2¼ lb) raw crushed spinach in muslin (cheesecloth) until all the juice is extracted. Pour this juice into a dish and cook in a bain marie until separated, then filter through another cloth. Scrape off the green deposit left on this cloth and work it into the softened butter. This butter is used to garnish hors d'oeuvres and cold dishes.

Kromeskies à la florentine

Kromeskies are a type of rissole or fritter, often served as a hot hors d'oeuvre and originating in Poland, but also traditional in Russia. Thin pancakes are filled and coated in breadcrumbs or sometimes in batter.

Cook some spinach slowly in butter and mix with a well-reduced béchamel sauce and grated Parmesan cheese. Enclose the mixture in some very thin savoury crêpes, dip them in batter and deep-fry them in very hot fat.

Pannequets à la florentine

Pannequets are filled pancakes, either savoury or sweet. Prepare 8 savoury pancakes and 200 ml (7 fl oz, ¾ cup) thick béchamel sauce. Cook 400 g (14 oz) spinach in salted water, dry it thoroughly, chop it coarsely and mix it with the béchamel sauce. Add 75 g (3 oz, ¾ cup) grated Gruyère or Parmesan cheese. Spread each pancake with sauce and fold in four. Arrange these pannequets in a buttered ovenproof dish. Sprinkle with fresh breadcrumbs fried in butter and place under the grill (broiler) for 3–4 minutes or in a preheated oven at 230°C (450°F, gas 8) for 10 minutes.

Soft-boiled or poached eggs à la florentine

Slowly cook some spinach in butter and drain well. Butter some small ramekin or soufflé dishes and place a little spinach in each, making hollows to hold 2 soft-boiled (soft-cooked) or poached eggs. Coat the eggs with Mornay sauce, sprinkle with grated cheese and brown under a hot grill (broiler).

Spinach and potato soup with poached eggs

Wash and trim 1 kg (2¼ lb) spinach, cook for 5 minutes in boiling water, cool and drain. Squeeze with your hands to extract all the water, then chop. Place 150 ml (¼ pint, ⅔ cup) olive oil in a flameproof casserole, add 1 chopped onion and brown lightly, then add the spinach and stir over a low heat for 5 minutes. When the spinach is dry, add 5 potatoes cut into slices. Season with salt and pepper and a little saffron. Add 1 litre (1¾ pints, 4⅓ cups) boiling water, 2 chopped garlic cloves and 1 sprig of fennel, and cook, uncovered, over a low heat. When the potatoes are cooked, break 4 eggs, one by one, on to the surface, and allow to cook very gently. This dish can be served straight from the casserole.

Spinach au gratin

Wash, trim and parboil some spinach. Drain it in a colander or sieve and dry well. Lightly butter a gratin dish and spread out the spinach leaves in it. Cover the spinach with some light béchamel sauce flavoured with nutmeg and grated cheese. Sprinkle with more grated cheese and then with melted butter, and brown in a preheated oven at 230°C (450°F, gas 8). Hard-boiled (hard-cooked) egg halves may be arranged on top of the sauce before sprinkling with cheese, if desired.

Spinach crêpes au gratin

Prepare savoury crêpes and creamed spinach. Put about 1 tablespoon spinach on each crêpe and roll it up. Arrange the crêpes close together in a lightly buttered ovenproof dish and sprinkle them with 50 g (2 oz, ½ cup) grated cheese. Top with 25 g (1 oz, 2 tablespoons) melted butter and either brown them under the grill (broiler) or reheat them in a preheated oven at 230°C (450°F, gas 8). Serve very hot.

Spinach croquettes

Mix 2 parts chopped spinach cooked in butter with 1 part duchess potato mixture. Shape this mixture into balls the size of tangerines and gently flatten. Coat with beaten egg and breadcrumbs, deep-fry in oil heated to 180°C (350°F) until golden, then drain on paper towels. Serve with grilled (broiled) or roast meat or poultry.

Spinach in butter

Wash, trim and parboil some spinach, then drain in a colander or sieve and dry in a cloth. Melt a little butter in a frying pan and add the spinach. Season with salt, pepper and a little grated nutmeg. When all the moisture has evaporated, add more butter, allowing 50 g (2 oz, ¼ cup) butter to 500 g (18 oz, 3½ cups) cooked spinach. Arrange the spinach in a warmed vegetable dish and garnish with fried croûtons. The spinach may also be sprinkled with noisette butter, if desired.

Spinach in cream

Wash, trim, parboil and dry some spinach. Arrange it in a warm vegetable dish and pour heated crème fraîche or cream sauce over the top; stir before serving. The spinach may be slightly sweetened, and served with fried croûtons cut into the shape of sponge fingers (ladyfingers).

Spinach omelette

Braise enough spinach leaves in butter to provide 4 tablespoons cooked spinach. Mix with 8 beaten eggs and cook like a large pancake.

Spinach purée

Wash, trim, parboil and dry some spinach, then rub it through a sieve or use a blender to form a purée. Add 50 g (2 oz, ¼ cup) butter for every 500 g (18 oz, 3½ cups) cooked spinach. If desired, add one-third of its volume of potato purée, or bind with one-quarter of its volume of béchamel sauce.

Spinach salad

Plunge some prepared spinach into boiling water for a few seconds. Cool under running water, then drain and dry in a cloth. Arrange in a salad bowl, sprinkle with chopped hard-boiled (hard-cooked) eggs and dress with oil, vinegar, salt and pepper.

Raw spinach may be finely sliced and mixed with flakes of smoked haddock, sliced scallops or new potatoes.

Spinach soufflé

Chop or sieve 250 g (9 oz) blanched, drained and pressed spinach, then simmer it in butter. Incorporate 150 ml (¼ pint, ⅔ cup) béchamel sauce and 40 g (1½ oz, ⅓ cup) grated Parmesan cheese if desired. Sprinkle with nutmeg, add 3 egg yolks (use fairly large eggs) and fold in 3 egg whites whisked to fairly stiff peaks. Preheat the oven for 15 minutes at 220°C (425°F, gas 7). Butter a 20 cm (8 in) diameter soufflé mould and coat with flour. Pour in the mixture and bake in the preheated oven, reducing the temperature to 200°C (400°F, gas 6), for 25 minutes, until well risen and a deep golden-brown on top. Do not open the door during cooking.

Spinach subrics

Cook some well-washed spinach gently in a covered saucepan without water. Drain and cool it. For 500 g (18 oz, 3½ cups) pressed chopped spinach, add 150 ml (¼ pint, ⅔ cup) very thick béchamel sauce, 1 whole egg and 3 yolks, lightly beaten as for an omelette, then 2 tablespoons double (heavy) cream. Season with salt, pepper and grated nutmeg, then leave to cool completely. Mould this mixture into small balls and cook in 40 g (1½ oz, 3 tablespoons) clarified butter in a frying pan until golden (about 3 minutes). Serve piping hot, with a cream sauce well seasoned with nutmeg.

Spinach tart

Quickly blanch 1.5 kg (3¼ lb) young fresh spinach. Drain in a colander or sieve and dry well. Chop coarsely and blend with 40–50 g (1½–2 oz, 3–4 tablespoons) butter. Season with salt and pepper. Line a 20 cm (8 in) tart tin (pie pan), preferably made of cast iron for more rapid and even baking, with puff pastry rolled out to a thickness of 5 mm (¼ in). Fill it with the spinach. Drain 4 anchovy fillets canned in oil and lay them on top of the tart in a criss-cross pattern. Sprinkle the tart with a few knobs of butter and bake in a preheated oven at 220°C (425°F, gas 7) oven for 20 minutes. The anchovy fillets may be replaced by fresh sardines cooked very rapidly in a frying pan with a little olive oil.

Stuffed saveloys with spinach

Cook either 1.5 kg (3¼ lb) fresh spinach or 800 g (1¾ lb) frozen spinach in salted boiling water. Place 4 saveloys in a saucepan of cold water and heat them gently without boiling, so that they do not burst. Drain and press the spinach and reheat it with 25 g (1 oz, 2 tablespoons) butter. Scramble 6 eggs with 20 g (¾ oz, 1½ tablespoons) butter, salt, pepper and 1 tablespoon cream. Cover the serving dish with spinach. Drain the saveloys; split them along three-quarters of their length and stuff them with the scrambled eggs. Arrange the saveloys on the spinach.

Sweet potato

Sweet potatoes à l'impériale

Place equal quantities of sliced sweet potatoes, sliced dessert apples and thinly sliced bananas in a well-buttered gratin dish. Mix everything together well, add salt and sprinkle with paprika. Dot the surface with tiny pieces of butter and cook in a preheated oven at 150°C (300°F, gas 2) until tender.

This gratin is served as an accompaniment for meat, roast poultry or game; it may be coated with redcurrant jelly.

Swiss chard

To prepare

Remove the green parts of the leaves, then break off the veins and leaf stalks (it is important not to cut them with a knife) and remove the stringy parts. Divide these into sections 5–7.5 cm (2–3 in) long and cook in salted water or, better still, in a white vegetable stock. Once drained, these stalks are ready for use in various recipes. Wash the green parts, blanch for 5 minutes in boiling water (salted or unsalted), rinse in cold water, drain and pat dry. Swiss chard is prepared in the same way as spinach but it has a slightly less pronounced flavour.

Swiss chard au gratin

Prepare Swiss chard in béchamel sauce and pour into an ovenproof dish. Smooth the surface, sprinkle with grated cheese and melted butter, and brown at the hottest temperature in the oven or under the grill (broiler).

Swiss chard à la polonaise

Trim away the green parts of the leaves from the white central stalks of the Swiss chard, cut the white stalks into strips, remove the strings, then cut into pieces of the same length. Cook, covered, in a white stock for vegetables until tender. Drain thoroughly and arrange in a long buttered dish. Sprinkle with sieved hard-boiled (hard-cooked) egg yolk and chopped parsley. Lightly brown some breadcrumbs in noisette butter and pour over the chard. Serve immediately. (Cook the green part of the leaves as for spinach for a separate dish.)

Swiss chard à l'italienne

Remove the green parts of the leaves, then break off the veins and stalks (it is important not to cut them with a knife) and remove the stringy parts. Divide into 7.5 cm (3 in) lengths, put into boiling white stock, and cook for about 20 minutes. Drain the chard. Prepare enough Italian sauce to cover the chard. Put the chard and the sauce into a pan, simmer, mix well and adjust the seasoning. Before serving, sprinkle with chopped basil.

Swiss chard in béchamel sauce

Cook 800 g (1¾ lb) Swiss chard stalks in a court-bouillon and drain. Place in a deep frying pan with 400 ml (14 fl oz, 1¾ cups) fairly liquid béchamel sauce; cover and cook for about 5 minutes. Mix in 50 g (2 oz, ¼ cup) butter and serve in a vegetable dish.

Swiss chard in butter

Cook 1 kg (2¼ lb) Swiss chard stalks in salted water or white stock. Drain, put in a deep frying pan with 75 g (3 oz, 6 tablespoons) butter, cover and cook gently for 15–20 minutes. Place in a vegetable dish, pour over the butter in which the chard was cooked and sprinkle with chopped parsley. Alternatively, the chard may be blanched for 5 minutes in salted water, drained and cooked in a deep frying pan with 75 g (3 oz, 6 tablespoons) butter and 200 ml (7 fl oz, ¾ cup) water. Place in a dish and pour over the cooking liquid.

Swiss chard in cream

Boil 800 g (1¾ lb) Swiss chard stalks in white stock and drain. Fry for 5 minutes in 25 g (1 oz, 2 tablespoons) butter. Moisten with 300 ml (½ pint, 1¼ cups) boiling double (heavy) cream and cook until the volume has reduced by half. Place in a vegetable dish and pour over the cooking liquid.

Swiss chard pie

Marinate 100 g (4 oz, ¾ cup) raisins in a little brandy. Make the pastry using 500 g (18 oz, 4½ cups) strong plain (bread) flour, a pinch of salt, 4 table-spoons sugar, 1 sachet easy-blend dried yeast (1 package active dry yeast), 1 egg yolk and 200 ml (7 fl oz, ¾ cup) oil. Mix the dough, adding a few teaspoons of very cold water, knead until smooth and leave to stand, covered, in a warm place until light and risen – about 1 hour.

Blanch 500 g (18 oz) Swiss chard leaves in salted water, dry very thoroughly and chop coarsely. Peel 2 cooking apples, slice thinly and sprinkle with lemon juice. Cut 2 dried figs into quarters; crumble 1 macaroon. Mix these ingredients (including the chopped chard leaves) with the raisins, 2 eggs, a little grated lemon zest, and about 40 g (1½ oz) pine nuts (kernels).

Grease an ovenproof flan dish, 28 cm (11 in) in diameter. Line with half the pastry, spread the filling over the pastry base and coat with 3 tablespoons redcurrant jelly. Cover with the remaining pastry and pinch the edges together to seal the pie. Place a small pastry funnel in the lid. Bake in a pre-heated oven at 200°C (400°F, gas 6) for 30–40 minutes. Dust with icing (confectioner's) sugar and serve hot or cold.

Tomatoes

Andalusian sauce (cold)

Add 5 teaspoons very reduced and rich tomato fondue to 75 g (3 oz, ⅓ cup) mayonnaise. Stir in 75 g (3 oz, ½ cup) sweet (bell) peppers, seeded and very finely diced.

Andalusian sauce (hot)

Add 4 tablespoons passata or finely chopped ripe tomatoes to 3 tablespoons reduced velouté sauce. Add 2 teaspoons sweet (bell) peppers, seeded, cooked and finely diced, ½ teaspoon finely chopped parsley and. if liked, a little crushed garlic.

Cold tomato mousse

Lightly fry in butter 500 g (18 oz, 2½ cups) coarsely chopped tomato pulp (net weight after skinning and seeding). When it is well dried out, add 100 ml (4 fl oz, 7 tablespoons) velouté sauce in which 4 leaves of gelatine (first softened in cold water and drained) have been dissolved. Strain this mixture through a piece of coarse muslin (cheesecloth), then place it in a mixing bowl and whisk until smooth. When the mixture is cool, add half its volume of fresh whipped cream. Season with salt, pepper and a little cayenne pepper and add a few drops of lemon juice. Mix well, then pour the mousse into a glass dish.

The mousse can also be used as a garnish for cold dishes (particularly fish). In this case, pour into dariole moulds lined with aspic jelly, chill in the refrigerator until set, then turn out of the moulds.

Concentrated tomato glaze

Immerse some ripe tomatoes in boiling water for 30 seconds, then peel them. Pound in a mortar and cook over a brisk heat until they are boiled down by half, then press through a fine strainer. Cook once more very gently until the pulp thickens and becomes syrupy. (It can be made even smoother by straining it twice in the course of cooking.) This tomato glaze keeps well in the refrigerator. It is used in the same way as tomato purée (paste).

Croustades à la grecque

Fill some rice croustades with a tomato fondue *à la grecque*. Garnish each one with 3 onion rings, coated in batter and deep-fried.

Gnocchi with herbs and tomatoes

Wash 500 g (18 oz) potatoes and bake them in their skins in a preheated oven at 180°C (350°F, gas 4) for 40 minutes or until soft. Peel them while still hot and mash them to a purée. Arrange them with a well in the middle and allow to cool. Peel and seed 500 g (18 oz) ripe tomatoes and cut into small cubes. Chop ½ onion, 1 shallot and 1 small celery stick. Heat some olive oil in a sauté pan and stir in the onion, shallot, celery and 1 garlic clove. Remove the latter when it is golden. Add the tomatoes, fry for a few minutes, then add a little basil, rosemary, sage and mint. Season with salt and pepper and reduce the cooking juices. Then add 100 g (4 oz, 1 cup) plain (all-purpose) flour, 2 pinches nutmeg, 3 egg yolks and 50 g (2 oz, ½ cup) freshly grated Parmesan cheese to the potato purée. Add a little flour to make a ball that is neither too dry nor too moist. Divide into 100 g (4 oz) chunks and shape into cylinders on a floured surface. Cut the cylinders into small pieces and press them on to the back of a fork to make a slightly concave shape with ridges. Poach the gnocchi for 6–8 minutes in boiling salted water.

Grilled tomatoes

Cut a circle around the stalk of some round, firm, sound tomatoes. Remove the seeds with a teaspoon. Lightly season the tomatoes with salt and pepper, brush with olive oil and grill (broil) them rapidly so that they do not collapse.

Purée of tomato soup

Peel and chop 50 g (2 oz, ⅓ cup) onions. Sweat them in 25 g (1 oz, 2 table-spoons) butter, then add 800 g (1¾ lb) peeled tomatoes, 1 crushed garlic clove, 1 small bouquet garni, salt and pepper. Cook gently for 20 minutes, add 100 g (4 oz, ⅓ cup) long-grain rice and stir. Add 1.5 litres (2¾ pints, 6½ cups) boiling stock, stir, cover and leave to cook for 20 minutes. Remove the bouquet garni. Reduce to a purée in a food processor or blender, then return to the saucepan and whisk in 50 g (2 oz, ¼ cup) butter cut into small pieces. Sprinkle with chopped parsley or basil. Serve with croûtons flavoured with garlic and fried in olive oil.

Rougail of tomatoes

Using either a food processor or a mortar, make a purée of 1 large onion (chopped), a small piece of fresh root ginger, ½ teaspoon salt, 4 peeled, seeded and coarsely chopped tomatoes, the juice of lemon and 1 small red chilli. Serve this spicy condiment cold.

Royale of tomatoes

Mix 100 ml (4 fl oz, 7 tablespoons) reduced and concentrated tomato purée (paste) with 4 tablespoons consommé. Season with salt and pepper, bind with 4 egg yolks and pour into dariole moulds. Cook in a bain marie in a preheated oven at 200°C (400°F, gas 6) for 30 minutes. Cut into shapes and use to garnish clear soup.

Sautéed tomatoes à la provençale

Remove the stalks from 6 firm round tomatoes. Cut them in two, remove the seeds, then season with salt and pepper. Heat 3 tablespoons olive oil in a frying pan and put in the tomato halves cut-sides downwards. Brown them, then turn them over. Sprinkle the browned sides with a mixture of chopped parsley and garlic (3 heaped tablespoons). When the other side is browned, arrange the tomatoes on a hot serving dish. Add some breadcrumbs to the frying pan and brown lightly in the oil, then pour the contents of the pan over the tomatoes.

Alternatively, the breadcrumbs can also be added to the chopped parsley and garlic mixture; the stuffed tomatoes are then arranged in a gratin dish and the cooking finished in a hot oven.

Soufflé tomatoes

Remove the seeds from some firm, regular-shaped tomatoes. Sprinkle with oil or clarified butter and cook for 5 minutes in a preheated oven at 240°C (475°F, gas 9). Allow to cool. Make a bechamel sauce using 40 g (1½ oz, 6 tablespoons) plain (all-purpose) flour and 200 ml (7 fl oz, ¾ cup) cold milk. Season with salt, pepper and nutmeg and incorporate 250 ml (8 fl oz, 1 cup) thick fresh tomato purée and 75 g (3 oz, ¾ cup) grated Parmesan cheese. Smooth the surface, sprinkle with grated Parmesan cheese and put back in the oven at 200°C (400°F, gas 6) for 15 minutes.

Stuffed tomatoes

Choose some ripe but firm tomatoes, of medium size and regular shape. Cut a circle round the stalk end and, with a teaspoon, remove the seeds and juice. Still using the spoon, enlarge the hole slightly until it is large enough to receive the stuffing. Lightly season the inside with salt and turn the tomatoes upside down on a cloth to drain (if preferred, lightly season the inside with salt and pepper without draining). Arrange the tomatoes on an oiled baking sheet and warm them for 5 minutes in a hot oven. Drain again, then stuff them, heaping up the stuffing to form a dome. Complete according to the type of stuffing and dish, as follows.

Hot stuffed tomatoes are usually sprinkled with breadcrumbs and oil or clarified butter before being cooked.

Stuffed tomatoes à la bonne femme

For 8 medium tomatoes, mix together 250 g (9 oz, 1 cup) sausagemeat, 75 g (3 oz, ½ cup) onion lightly fried in butter, 2 tablespoons fresh breadcrumbs, 1 tablespoon chopped parsley, 1 crushed garlic clove, and salt and pepper. Stuff the tomatoes with this mixture. Sprinkle with breadcrumbs and oil or clarified butter and cook in a preheated oven at 220°C (425°F, gas 7) for 30–40 minutes, until the stuffing is cooked.

The stuffing can be precooked very gently in a frying pan for 15 minutes. The tomatoes are then stuffed and cooked *au gratin*. If this method is used, the tomatoes will not collapse.

Stuffed tomatoes à la grecque

Soak 125 g (4½ oz, scant 1 cup) sultanas (golden raisins) in a little tepid water until they swell, then drain. Heat 4 tablespoons olive oil in a saucepan and add 200 g (7 oz, 1 cup) rice; stir until the grains become transparent. Then add to the rice twice its volume of boiling water, a pinch of powdered saffron, 1 teaspoon salt, pepper, a pinch of cayenne and a bouquet garni. Bring to the boil and simmer gently until the rice is cooked. Slice off the tops of 6 large tomatoes and reserve, remove the seeds and pulp and lightly season the insides with salt. Place the tomatoes upside down in a colander to drain.

When the rice is cooked, drain and cool, add the sultanas and adjust the seasoning. Dry the tomato cases, place 1 teaspoon olive oil in the bottom of each one and fill them with the mixture of rice and sultanas. Replace the tops. Arrange the stuffed tomatoes fairly close together in an ovenproof dish. Pour a little oil in the bottom of the dish and cook in a preheated oven at 240°C (475°F, gas 9). Remove the tomatoes from the oven before they become too soft and serve immediately.

Stuffed tomatoes à la languedocienne

For 8 medium tomatoes, mix together 250 g (9 oz, 1 cup) sausagemeat, 75 g (3 oz, ½ cup) onion lightly fried in butter, 1 chopped hard-boiled (hard-cooked) egg, 2 tablespoons fresh breadcrumbs, 1 tablespoon chopped parsley, 1 crushed garlic clove, and salt and pepper. Stuff the tomatoes with this mixture. Sprinkle with breadcrumbs and olive oil and cook in a preheated oven at 220°C (425°F, gas 7) for 30–40 minutes.

Stuffed tomatoes à la niçoise

Make a stuffing consisting of equal proportions of rice cooked in meat stock and aubergine (eggplant) diced very small and tossed in olive oil. Add chopped parsley, garlic and breadcrumbs fried in olive oil. Stuff the tomatoes, put them in an ovenproof dish, sprinkle them with breadcrumbs and olive oil and cook in a preheated oven at 220°C (425°F, gas 7) for 30–40 minutes.

Stuffed tomatoes à la piémontaise

Stuff some large raw tomatoes, seasoned with salt and pepper, with risotto mixed with thick tomato sauce. Put them in a buttered gratin dish; sprinkle them with melted butter. Cook in a preheated oven at 220°C (425°F, gas 7) for about 30 minutes. Sprinkle with parsley and serve with a thick tomato coulis.

Stuffed tomatoes à la reine

Slice the tops off some large firm tomatoes; scoop out the seeds and core without breaking the skin. Make a salpicon of equal quantities of chicken breast poached in white stock and mushrooms sweated in butter; add a little diced truffle and thicken with some very thick velouté sauce. Stuff the tomatoes with this mixture and place in a buttered gratin dish. Sprinkle with fresh breadcrumbs and clarified butter and cook in a preheated oven at 240°C (475°F, gas 9) for 10–15 minutes.

Stuffed tomato nests

Prepare some tomatoes for stuffing and cook them in the oven. Break an egg into each tomato. Lightly season with salt and pepper, place a small knob of butter on top and cook in a preheated oven at 230°C (450°F, gas 8) for about 6 minutes until the eggs are set.

Tomato chaud-froid sauce

Add 350 ml (12 fl oz, 1½ cups) aspic to 500 ml (17 fl oz, 2 cups) puréed tomatoes; reduce by a third. Strain through muslin (cheesecloth) and stir until completely cooled.

Tomato coulis

Use firm ripe tomatoes. Cover them with boiling water and allow to stand for 30 seconds, then peel them. Halve the tomatoes and remove their seeds. Sprinkle the cut surfaces of the tomatoes with salt and turn them over so that the juice drains away. Then purée them in a blender with a little lemon juice and 1 teaspoon caster (superfine) sugar for each 1 kg (2¼ lb) tomatoes used. After blending, reduce the resulting purée further by boiling it for a few minutes. Press through a sieve, season with salt and pepper, and cool.

Tomatoes stuffed with cream and chives (cold)

For 6 medium-sized tomatoes, mix together 200 ml (7 fl oz, ¾ cup) double (heavy) cream and 2 tablespoons chopped chives, 2–3 very finely chopped garlic cloves and 2 tablespoons vinegar or lemon juice (or a mixture of the two). Season with salt, pepper and a little cayenne. Drain the tomatoes, lightly season with salt and pepper, pour in 1 teaspoon oil and leave to stand for at least 30 minutes. Fill the tomatoes with the cream stuffing, replace the tops and chill for at least 1 hour. The cream can be replaced by cream cheese, well-beaten until smooth.

Tomatoes stuffed with tuna

Mix together equal amounts of rice pilaf and flaked canned tuna. Add 1 tablespoon mayonnaise for every 4 tablespoons rice/fish mixture and mix in some chopped herbs and finely diced lemon pulp. Stuff the tomatoes, garnish each with a black (ripe) olive and chill until just before serving; serve with sprigs of parsley.

Tomato fondue

Peel and chop 100 g (4 oz, ¾ cup) onions. Peel, seed and finely chop 800 g (1¾ lb) tomatoes. Peel and crush 1 garlic clove. Prepare a bouquet garni rich in thyme. Soften the onions in a heavy-based saucepan with 25 g (1 oz, 2 tablespoons) butter, or 15 g (½ oz, 1 tablespoon) butter and 2 tablespoons olive oil, or 3 tablespoons olive oil. Then add the tomatoes, garlic and bouquet garni and season with salt and pepper. Cover the pan and cook over a very gentle heat until the tomatoes are reduced to a pulp. Remove the lid, stir with a wooden spatula and continue cooking, uncovered, until the fondue forms a light paste. Adjust the seasoning, press through a sieve and add 1 tablespoon chopped parsley or herbs.

Tomato fondue à la grecque

Follow the method above, using olive oil instead of butter. Add 12 coriander seeds with the tomatoes. Finish as above.

Tomato loaf

Boil down some tomato pulp or purée over a low heat until it becomes very thick. Blend in some beaten eggs – 6 eggs per 500 g (18 oz, 2 cups) purée. Season with salt, pepper and a pinch of mixed spice. Fill a round well-buttered tin (pan) or dariole moulds with this mixture and cook in a bain marie in a preheated oven at 180°C (350°F, gas 4) for 40 minutes. Allow the loaf to stand for a few moments before unmoulding. Serve coated with tomato sauce mixed with butter.

Tomato salad

Immerse some ripe, firm, sound tomatoes in a bowl of boiling water for 30 seconds. Peel the tomatoes, cut them into slices and place in a colander to drain off the liquid. Arrange the sliced tomatoes in a salad bowl. Add some finely chopped mild onion – 100 g (4 oz, ⅓ cup) onion per 1 kg (2¼ lb) tomatoes – and dress with a tarragon-flavoured vinaigrette. Leave in a cool place. Just before serving, sprinkle the salad with finely chopped chervil, parsley, basil or tarragon.

Tomato salad with mozzarella

Wash, peel and slice 4 large tomatoes. Thinly slice 200 g (7 oz) mozzarella cheese. Divide the sliced tomatoes between 4 plates and cover them with slices of mozzarella. Sprinkle with salt, pepper and chopped fresh basil, pour over a few drops of vinegar, then a trickle of olive oil, and serve at room temperature.

Tomato sauce

Cut 100 g (4 oz, 6 slices) fresh streaky (slab) bacon into small dice. Blanch, drain and lightly cook in 3–4 tablespoons oil. Add 100 g (4 oz, ¾ cup) each of diced carrots and diced onion. Cover and lightly fry for 25–30 minutes. Sprinkle in 50 g (2 oz, ½ cup) sifted plain (all-purpose) flour and lightly brown. Add 3 kg (6½ lb) fresh tomatoes, peeled, seeded and pounded, 2 crushed garlic cloves, a bouquet garni and 150 g (5 oz) blanched lean ham. Add 1 litre (1¾ pints, 4⅓ cups) white stock. Season with salt and pepper, add 1½ tablespoons sugar and bring to the boil while stirring. Cover and leave to cook very gently for 2 hours. Strain the sauce into a basin. Carefully pour some tepid melted butter on the surface to prevent a skin from forming.

Tomato sorbet

Peel 1 kg (2¼ lb) very ripe tomatoes, press them and filter the juice. Measure the volume: 250 ml (8 fl oz, 1 cup) is needed. Make a cold syrup with 150 ml (¼ pint, ⅔ cup) water and 300 g (11 oz, 1⅓ cups) preserving sugar. Mix the syrup with the tomato juice and add 2 tablespoons vodka, then pour into an ice-cream mould and freeze for at least 1 hour. Whisk 1 egg white with 50 g (2 oz, ⅓ cup) icing (confectioner's) sugar over a pan of water at about 60°C (140°F). When the sorbet begins to set, whisk it, gently fold in the beaten egg white and put back in the freezer until it sets (about 2 hours).

Tomato soufflé

Make a béchamel sauce using 40 g (1½ oz, 3 tablespoons) butter, 40 g (1½ oz, 6 tablespoons) plain (all-purpose) flour and 200 ml (7 fl oz, ¾ cup) cold milk. Season with salt, pepper and nutmeg and incorporate 250 ml (8 fl oz, 1 cup) thick fresh tomato purée and 75 g (3 oz ¾ cup) grated Parmesan cheese. Then add 4–5 egg yolks (use fairly large eggs) and fold in

4–5 egg whites whisked to stiff peaks. Preheat the oven for 15 minutes at 220°C (425°F, gas 7). Butter a soufflé mould 20 cm (8 in) in diameter and coat with flour. Pour in the mixture and bake in the preheated oven at 200°C (400°F, gas 6) for 35 minutes, without opening the door during cooking, until well risen and a deep golden-brown on top.

Tomato tart

Make some puff pastry, roll it out and use it to line a greased flan tin (pie pan); prick the bottom. Mix together 6 eggs, 100 ml (4 fl oz, 7 tablespoons) crème fraîche, 25 g (1 oz, 2 tablespoons) butter and 50 g (2 oz, ½ cup) grated Gruyère cheese. Add 1 kg (2¼ lb) tomatoes, peeled, seeded and crushed. Mix well and season with salt and pepper. Fill the tart with this mixture and bake in a preheated oven at 180°C (350°F, gas 4) for about 45 minutes.

Turnips

Poached eggs with braised turnips

Peel 4 large young turnips. Put them into a pan with a little stock, 20 g (¾ oz, 1½ tablespoons) butter, salt and pepper. Cover with foil and cook until all the liquid has evaporated. Set aside. Poach 4 eggs and keep them warm. Prepare a savoury sabayon sauce, folding in 175 g (6 oz, ¾ cup) clarified butter.

Hollow out the turnips, chop the flesh and add it to the sauce with some chopped parsley and 100 ml (4 fl oz, 7 tablespoons) single (light) cream. Place an egg in each hollowed-out turnip and coat with the sauce.

New turnip salad

Peel and quarter 1 kg (2¼ lb) small new turnips. Blanch them for 6 minutes in boiling water, drain, then cook in stock, preferably chicken stock, for about 10 minutes. Drain and leave to cool, then sprinkle with chopped herbs. Add some strips of smoked haddock poached in milk (1 part haddock to 2 parts turnips) and dress with olive oil and vinegar.

Stuffed turnips à la duxelles

Peel and hollow out some medium-sized young turnips. Cook them for 8 minutes in boiling water, then drain and refresh in cold running water. Drain again and lightly sprinkle the hollows with salt. Cook the scooped-out flesh in butter and rub it through a sieve. Prepare a mushroom duxelles (1 tablespoon per turnip), add the purée and fill the turnips with the mixture. Arrange the stuffed turnips in a buttered gratin dish. Add a few tablespoons of beef or chicken stock, sprinkle with breadcrumbs and pour on some melted butter. Cook in a preheated oven at 200°C (400°F, gas 6); the cooking time depends on how tender the vegetables are – test by pricking with a skewer.

Stuffed turnips à la piémontaise

Peel and hollow out some medium-sized young turnips. Cook them for 8 minutes in boiling water, then drain and refresh in cold running water. Drain again and lightly sprinkle the hollows with salt. Cook the scooped-out flesh in butter and rub it through a sieve. Prepare a risotto (1 tablespoon per turnip), add the purée and fill the turnips. Put them in a buttered gratin dish. Add a few tablespoons of stock, sprinkle with breadcrumbs and pour on some melted butter. Cook in a preheated oven at 200°C (400°F, gas 6); the cooking time depends on how tender the vegetables are – test by pricking with a skewer. Sprinkle with grated Parmesan and brown in the oven.

Stuffed turnips braised in cider

Peel and blanch 575 g (1¼ lb) small round young turnips. Slice off and reserve the tops, then scoop out a shallow hollow in each and cook the scooped-out flesh in boiling salted water. When soft, reduce to a purée in a blender. Sauté the hollowed-out turnips and tops in equal quantities of olive oil and butter and cook until browned. Sprinkle with salt and pepper.

Meanwhile, boil half a bottle of dry (hard) cider and reduce to half its original volume. Drain the turnips and tops well and add them to the cider. Pour in a little stock and braise in a preheated oven 190°C (375°F, gas 5) for 15 minutes. Drain them, reserving the cooking juices. Add the purée to the liquid to thicken it, and adjust the seasoning. Add 50 g (2 oz, ¼ cup) butter, beat the mixture and keep hot.

Mix together 100 g (4 oz, ½ cup) sausagemeat, 25 g (1 oz, 2 tablespoons) *à gratin* forcemeat, some basil, rosemary and thyme flowers. Shape the mixture into balls and cook in butter over a low heat. Place one ball into each hollow turnip, adding the tops to form lids. Pour the sauce over and serve.

Turnips au gratin

Peel some turnips and slice them into rounds. Blanch them in boiling salted water, drain and refresh under cold running water and braise in butter. Place the turnip rounds in a buttered gratin dish, smooth the top and coat with Mornay sauce. Sprinkle with grated cheese and brown in a preheated oven at 240°C (475°F, gas 9).

Watercress

Canapés with watercress

Spread watercress butter on some round or rectangular slices of bread. Garnish each canapé with a centre of blanched watercress leaves and a border of chopped hard-boiled (hard-cooked) egg.

Cream of watercress soup

Clean 500 g (18 oz) watercress and remove the large stems. Blanch and chop the leaves, then cook them in 40–50 g (1½–2 oz, 3–4 tablespoons) butter in a covered pan. Prepare 750 ml (1¼ pints, 3¼ cups) white sauce by adding 900 ml (1½ pints, 1 quart) milk to a white roux of 25 g (1 oz, 2 tablespoons) butter and 40 g (1½ oz, 6 tablespoons) plain (all-purpose) flour. Mix this sauce with the watercress, then simmer gently for 12–18 minutes. Purée in a food processor or blender, then press through a sieve if necessary. Dilute with a few tablespoons of white stock or milk. Heat and adjust the seasoning. Add 200 ml (7 fl oz, ¾ cup) single (light) cream and stir while heating.

Watercress brèdes

Brèdes is the name given in some of the old French colonies of the West Indies to a dish made from the leaves of various plants cooked with bacon and spices and served with rice *à la créole*.

Put some oil or lard in a cast-iron casserole and fry 150 g (5 oz, ⅔ cup) diced bacon and a chopped onion in the fat until brown. Crush 2 garlic cloves with some salt and a peeled, seeded, crushed tomato. Add them to the casserole. When the mixture is quite hot, add 275 ml (9 fl oz, generous 1 cup) water. Slightly reduce the liquid and add a bunch of washed watercress. Cook for about 30 minutes. Serve with a separate dish of rice *à la créole*.

Use the same recipe to make lettuce brèdes, but soak the leaves in cold water beforehand. Blanch spinach leaves before making brèdes.

Watercress butter

Blanch 150 g (5 oz) watercress leaves, soak in cold water and blot. Purée, then work into softened butter, season with salt and pepper. Watercress butter is used principally for canapés and sandwiches.

Watercress mayonnaise

Add 2 tablespoons very finely chopped watercress to 250 ml (8 fl oz, 1 cup) very thick classic mayonnaise. Mix well.

Watercress purée

Cook some watercress in butter for about 5 munutes, until wilted. Purée in a food processor or blender. Add one-third of its volume of either potato purée or a purée of split peas. Add some fresh butter or cream and finish with a little finely chopped raw watercress.

Watercress sauce

Remove the leaves from some watercress. Wash, drain and dry them, chop finely and blend them with a mixture of chopped hard-boiled (hard-cooked) eggs, salt, pepper, oil and vinegar.

Mixed vegetables & salads

Ali-bab salad

Turn some peeled shrimps in mayonnaise, arrange them in a mound in the centre of a serving dish or salad bowl and sprinkle with chopped fresh herbs. Surround with the following: courgette (zucchini) matchsticks, blanched in salted water; sweet potato, cut into small balls and boiled; hard-boiled (hard-cooked) egg cut into quarters; small tomatoes, peeled, seeded and quartered. Sprinkle with vinaigrette and serve garnished with nasturtium flowers.

Anchovy salad à la suédoise

Peel and dice 500 g (18 oz) cooking apples and sprinkle with lemon juice. Dice the same weight of cooked beetroot (beet). Mix these ingredients with a vinaigrette seasoned with mild mustard. Heap in a salad bowl and garnish with desalted anchovy fillets, the whites and yolks of hard-boiled (hard-cooked) eggs chopped separately and thin slices of blanched mushrooms.

Andalouse salad

Boil some rice in salted water, drain it thoroughly and mix with a well-seasoned vinaigrette containing chopped onion, parsley and a touch of crushed garlic. Place the rice in a mound in a salad bowl surrounded by mounds of thin strips of peeled green and red sweet (bell) peppers and tomato quarters, arranged so that the colours alternate around the dish. Sprinkle with chopped chervil.

Bagration salad

This dish is composed of equal quantities of blanched artichoke hearts and celeriac (celery root), cut into thin strips, and cold chopped macaroni. The ingredients are bound with tomato mayonnaise and shaped into a mound, sprinkled with chopped hard-boiled (hard-cooked) egg yolk and parsley, and garnished with a salpicon of truffles and pickled ox (beef) tongue.

Barquettes à la bouquetière

Bouquetière is the term for mixed vegetables grouped by colour as a garnish for main courses. The term is also used for a macédoine of vegetables bound with béchamel sauce.

Bind a macédoine of vegetables with béchamel sauce and use the mixture to fill barquette pastry cases. Place a small bouquet of asparagus tips on top of each barquette, sprinkle with melted butter and heat through.

Beef salad

Thinly slice 250 g (9 oz) cooked beef. Thinly slice 6 small boiled potatoes and sprinkle with salt and pepper while still warm. Pour over 150 ml (¼ pint, ⅔ cup) white wine and 1 tablespoon oil. Turn the slices so that they become well coated with this dressing. Thinly slice 3 or 4 tomatoes. Slice an onion very finely. Arrange the potatoes heaped up in a salad bowl, with the slices of beef all around. Surround with the tomato slices. Top with the sliced onion and 1 tablespoon chopped chervil. Season with vinaigrette flavoured with mustard.

Bouchées à la bouquetière

Bind a macédoine of vegetables with béchamel sauce. Gently heat some small bouchée cases in the oven and fill with the hot mixture. Garnish with chopped parsley and replace the lids on the bouchées.

Bouchées à la julienne

Cook a julienne of vegetables (carrots, parsnips, leeks, celery or fennel) in butter. Bind with cream and spoon into the cases.

Bresse chicken salad

Season some whole lettuce leaves with vinaigrette and use to line the bottom and sides of a salad bowl. Hard-boil (hard-cook) some eggs, shell them and cut into quarters. Cook and drain some asparagus tips. Finely chop the white meat of a chicken cooked in stock and season with vinaigrette. Cut some red and green sweet (bell) peppers into very thin strips. Place all these ingredients on the lettuce leaves. Prepare a mayonnaise and colour with a little sieved, well-reduced tomato sauce. Pipe a garnish of tomato mayonnaise on the salad and sprinkle with chopped parsley. Serve the remaining mayonnaise in a sauceboat (in the traditional recipe the top of the salad is garnished with slices of truffle).

Brimont salad

Cook and peel some potatoes and prepare cooked artichoke hearts. Dice both vegetables coarsely and mix with mayonnaise flavoured with sherry. Arrange in a dome in a serving dish and surround with stoned (pitted) black olives, crayfish tails and quartered hard-boiled (hard-cooked) eggs, all seasoned with olive oil and sherry vinegar. Garnish the salad with a few slices of truffle. The crayfish tails may be replaced by large peeled prawns (shrimp).

Brunoise-stuffed pancakes

Brunoise is the term for cutting vegetables into minute dice and for the resulting vegetables – individual types or a mixture of different vegetables. Stew a *brunoise* of mixed vegetables, such as celery or fennel, carrot, leek and pumpkin, in butter. Bind with a little light béchamel sauce. Make some pancakes and fill with the mixture; roll up, cut into thick slices, coat in breadcrumbs and fry.

Chinese-style duck salad

Shred 200 g (7 oz) roast duck meat (with the skin if it is crisp). Soak 7–8 black Chinese dried mushrooms and 2–3 dried shiitake mushrooms in hot water for 30 minutes. Drain and squeeze dry, then cut into quarters.

Make a dressing by mixing together 1 teaspoon each of mustard and sugar, 1 tablespoon tomato purée (paste), 1 tablespoon each of soy light sauce and cider or rice vinegar, a pinch of black pepper, ½ teaspoon ground ginger, a pinch each of thyme and powdered bay leaf, 1 small crushed garlic clove, 3 tablespoons sesame oil and, if desired, 1 tablespoon rice wine.

Mix the duck, mushrooms and 500 g (18 oz) bean sprouts together in a large bowl and pour over the dressing. Toss well, sprinkle with 1 tablespoon chopped fresh coriander (cilantro) and serve at once.

Chop suey

Prepare and mix a julienne of young vegetables in season, such as carrot, turnip, leek, onion, (bell) peppers and courgettes (zucchini). Cut some spring onions (scallions) into small sticks. Pick over and rinse some bean sprouts and drain. Chop finely 1 small garlic clove and dice some peeled and seeded tomatoes. Stir-fry the julienne of mixed vegetables in oil – 2 tablespoons for 500 g (18 oz, 4½ cups) vegetables – for 4–5 minutes. Add the bean sprouts to the pan, mix well and stir-fry for 1 minute. Finally, stir in the tomato, onion, garlic, pepper and 2 tablespoons soy sauce to 500 g (18 oz, 4¼ cups) vegetables with a little salt if necessary. Mix and serve hot. This mixture may also be seasoned with 1 teaspoon sesame oil.

Couscous with vegetables

The 'grain' made from semolina is steamed in a couscous pan: fill the pot two-thirds with water or stock and bring it quickly to the boil. Then fit the *keskès* (steamer) containing 1.5 kg (3¼ lb, 9 cups) semolina on to the pot. Tie a damp cloth around the part where the *keskès* and the pot meet so that no steam escapes. After about 30 minutes, remove the semolina, put it in a large round dish with a raised edge, coat the grains with oil and break up the lumps with the hands. Put the couscous back in the *keskès*. (Generally, this steaming is repeated twice more.) Brown 4 chopped onions in 5 tablespoons olive oil. Make sure that the onions brown without burning. Add 8 chopped carrots, 4 chopped leeks, 1 chopped fennel bulb, 6 roughly chopped tomatoes, a little tomato purée (paste) thinned with water, 4 crushed garlic cloves, a bouquet garni and a small pinch of coarse salt. Cover the ingredients with cold water and then add 225 g (8 oz, 1⅓ cups) chick peas (previously soaked for 24 hours). Put the lid on the pot and bring to the boil. Cook for 20–25 minutes.

Add 4 turnips, cut into chunks, 4 large chopped courgettes (zucchini), and 4 small trimmed and quartered globe artichokes. Put the *keskès* with the couscous on top of the pot and continue cooking for about 30 minutes.

Just before serving, enhance the flavour by seasoning with black pepper or mixed spices (*qâlat daqqāa,* or *rās al-hānout*) according to taste. Add small knobs of butter (rancid, if preferred). A wider range of vegetables can be used, such as cabbage, broad (fava) beans (preferably fresh), potatoes, beet, chard, tomatoes and peas.

Cousinette

Wash 150 g (5 oz, 1 cup) spinach leaves, 150 g (5 oz, 1 cup) Swiss chard leaves, 150 g (5 oz, 1 cup) lettuce leaves, 50 g (2 oz, ½ cup) sorrel leaves and a small handful of wild mallow leaves. Shred all the leaves finely to make a very fine *chiffonnade* and brown them gently in 50 g (2 oz, ¼ cup) butter or goose fat. Cover and braise gently for 10 minutes. Add 1.5 litres (2¾ pints, 6½ cups) water or preferably chicken stock and, if desired, 250 g (9 oz, 1¼ cups) finely sliced potatoes. Continue cooking for about 30 minutes. Just before serving, adjust the seasoning and add a knob of fresh butter. Pour the soup on to thin slices of bread that have been dried in the oven.

Crudités

Choose some very fresh raw vegetables such as small carrots, celery sticks, radish, cucumber, sweet peppers, very small artichokes known as *poivrades*, cauliflower, mushrooms and fennel.

Scrape the carrots and radishes, leaving the small green leaves on the radishes. Thoroughly remove the strings from the celery sticks, cut them into sections of about 10 cm (4 in) and split the heart into four. Peel the pepper, cut open, take out the white membrane and seeds, and cut the flesh into thin strips. Peel the cucumber and cut into sticks. Pull the cauliflower apart into small florets. Wipe and slice the mushrooms. Clean the fennel bulb and cut it into thick slices. Just before serving, break the stalks off the artichokes, cut them in four, remove the chokes and sprinkle the cut part with lemon juice.

Line a wickerwork basket with a napkin and arrange the vegetables in it, in bunches. If it is not to be served immediately, cover it with a cloth and put in a cool place. Serve accompanied by a dip, such as mayonnaise with herbs, a tarragon vinaigrette, an anchovy sauce and/or a cream cheese sauce.

Dandelion and bacon salad

Thoroughly wash and dry 250 g (9 oz) dandelion leaves. Dice 150 g (5 oz, ¾ cup) green or smoked streaky (slab) bacon and brown gently in a frying pan. In a salad bowl prepare some vinaigrette using 1 tablespoon white wine,

2 tablespoons oil, salt and pepper. Add the dandelion leaves and toss thoroughly. Pour 1 tablespoon white wine vinegar over the diced bacon and stir with a wooden spoon, scraping the bottom of the frying pan. Pour the contents of the frying pan into the salad bowl. Quartered hard-boiled (hard-cooked) eggs may be added to the bowl before adding the bacon if wished.

Garbure

In the Béarn region of France, a garbure is a kind of stew based on vegetable stock, cabbage and *confit d'oie* (preserved goose). However, there are several versions of varying richness, including mixed vegetables and different meats.

Boil some water in an earthenware pot glazed on the inside (cast-iron or iron pots spoil the delicacy of the flavour). When it is boiling, throw in some potatoes, peeled and cut into thick slices. Add other fresh vegetables in season: haricot (navy) or broad (fava) beans, peas or French (green) beans. Season with salt and pepper. Cayenne may be used in place of white pepper. Flavour with garlic, a sprig of thyme, parsley or fresh marjoram. Leave to cook, making sure that the water is constantly on the boil.

Shred tender green cabbage as finely as possible, cutting across the width of the leaves and removing any tough portions. When the rest of the ingredients are thoroughly cooked, throw the cabbage into the boiling stock. Cover the pot to keep the cabbage leaves green and, 30 minutes before serving, put in a piece of pickled meat, preferably goose (*lou trébuc*); the fat on this will be sufficient. If pickled pork *trébuc* is used, the addition of a little goose fat will enhance the flavour of the stew. Cut stale wholemeal (wholewheat) bread into thin slices and add to the stock and vegetables. The mixture must be thick enough for the ladle to stand up when it is set in the centre of the tureen.

It is possible to make a good garbure without *trébuc*, but in that case it is necessary to put a piece of ham bone or a sausage or, at the very least, lean bacon (thin flank) in the cold water. White cabbage may be used instead of green cabbage. For an everyday garbure it is usual to make do with a piece of bacon or ham, or bacon chopped with crushed garlic. According to the time of year, a few slices of swede (rutabaga) or roast chestnuts are added.

If dried beans are used, they have to be cooked in advance and drained after cooking, because their water would destroy the characteristic flavour of the garbure. To thicken the broth, the cooked beans are sometimes crushed and rubbed through a sieve. The meat is served separately from the broth, either by itself or with the vegetables. Some cooks brown the *trébuc* in a pan before putting it in the stock. In this case, some fat must be added, but the fat in which the *trébuc* was browned should not be used.

Green vegetable puffs

Fill some small cooled choux buns or fingers with a thick purée of green peas, French (green) beans and asparagus tips, seasoned and bound with whipped double (heavy) cream, crème fraîche or yogurt. Snipped chives can be added to the purée.

Julienne salad with orange and horseradish dressing

Pare the zest from ½ orange and cut it into fine julienne. Cook the strips of orange zest in boiling water for about 5 minutes or until tender. Drain and set aside. Squeeze the juice from the orange and place it in a large bowl. Add 1 teaspoon caster sugar, 2 teaspoons creamed horseradish, salt and pepper, and whisk until the sugar has dissolved. Gradually whisk in 4 tablespoons olive oil. Then stir in the orange zest.

Cut ½ celeriac into julienne and add to the dressing in the bowl, tossing well to coat the celeriac evenly and prevent it from discolouring. Cut

4 carrots into julienne and add to the celeriac. Finely chop 4 spring onions (scallions) and add to the salad with 2 tablespoons chopped mint. Toss well and chill lightly before serving.

Maharajah salad

Prepare some rice *à la créole* and flake some crabmeat. Mix together, dress with Indian-style vinaigrette, then pile up in a salad bowl. Around this, arrange some shredded celeriac, alternated with blanched and diced courgettes (zucchini) and tomato quarters. Sprinkle with sieved hard-boiled (hard-cooked) egg yolk and chopped chives. Pour some more of the same vinaigrette over the garnish just before serving.

Mikado salad

Boil 800 g (1¾ lb) unpeeled potatoes in salted water. Allow them to cool, remove the skin and dice them. Season 3 tablespoons mayonnaise with a little soy sauce. (If making the mayonnaise, use soy sauce instead of salt as the seasoning.) Remove the seeds from a green (bell) pepper and cut it into very fine strips. Peel, seed and dice the flesh of 3 firm tomatoes. Blanch 6–7 small chrysanthemum flowers for 2 minutes in boiling water, drain, dry and season lightly with vinaigrette. Mix the diced potatoes with the mayonnaise and 150 g (5 oz, scant 1 cup) peeled prawns (shelled shrimp). Arrange the mixture in a dome in a salad bowl and garnish the top of the salad with chrysanthemum petals. Surround the salad with clusters of finely shredded green (bell) pepper and diced tomato.

Mimosa salad

Boil some unpeeled potatoes, then peel them, cut into cubes and keep warm. Poach some artichoke hearts in salted water and cut them into quarters. Boil and chop some French (green) beans. Mix the ingredients and season them with a very spicy vinaigrette. Rub the yolks of some hard-boiled (hard-cooked) eggs through a coarse sieve and sprinkle over the salad.

Minestrone

Cook 300 g (11 oz, 1¾ cups) small white haricot (navy) beans in a large amount of water, seasoned with 1 garlic clove, 1 bunch sage and 1 tablespoon extra-virgin olive oil. Purée half the haricot beans by crushing through a sieve. Heat some olive oil in a large saucepan and fry in it 1 slice of chopped uncooked ham, 1 celery stick, 1 bunch parsley, 1 chopped onion and 1 sprig thyme. Add 2 sliced leeks and 2 courgettes (zucchini), cut into cubes, 1 cabbage, cut into thin strips, and 500 g (18 oz) spinach. Then, after 10 minutes, add tomato sauce. When everything has simmered, add all the haricot beans together with their cooking juices and the puréed haricot beans. Add 1 litre (1¾ pints, 4⅓ cups) stock to obtain an unctuous consistency. Simmer for another hour. Season with salt and pepper. Pour 1 glass olive oil into a small frying pan and add 2 crushed garlic cloves, 1 sprig thyme and 2 sprigs rosemary. Place over the heat and when the garlic starts to turn golden pour this flavoured oil on to the minestrone through a sieve. Serve hot or cold.

Montfermeil salad

Put the juice of 1 lemon in a saucepan with 2 tablespoons flour, a generous pinch of salt and 2–3 litres (3½–5 pints, 9–13 cups) water. Peel 500 g (18 oz) salsify, cut into small pieces and cook for about 1 hour in this liquid – it should be tender but not disintegrating. Scrub 250 g (9 oz) potatoes and boil them. Drain and peel while still warm, then leave to cool completely and cut into dice. Leave the salsify to cool in its cooking liquid, then drain and refresh.

Wash and chop a small bunch of parsley and a few sprigs of tarragon and mix with 2 roughly chopped hard-boiled (hard-cooked) eggs. Drain and then dice 400 g (14 oz) canned artichoke hearts and put them in a salad bowl. Add the diced potatoes and the salsify. Pour over a vinaigrette flavoured with mustard and sprinkle with the chopped eggs and herbs.

Mussel and potato salad

Trim, scrape and wash some mussels. Peel and chop 1 large shallot per 1 kg (2¼ lb) mussels. Put the chopped shallots in a buttered pan with 2 table-spoons chopped parsley, a small sprig of thyme, ½ bay leaf, 200 ml (7 fl oz, ¾ cup) dry white wine, 1 tablespoon wine vinegar and 2 tablespoons butter (cut into small pieces). Add the mussels, cover the pan and cook over a high heat, shaking the pan several times, until all the mussels have opened. Remove the pan from the heat. Drain them and remove their shells. Set aside.

Boil, without peeling, 675 g (1½ lb) potatoes; peel while still hot and cut into cubes. Finely dice or shred 2–3 celery sticks. Peel and chop 1 shallot and 1 garlic clove and mix with plenty of chopped parsley. Mix all the ingredients together in a salad bowl.

Make a vinaigrette with 2 tablespoons hot vinegar, 6 tablespoons oil, 1 tablespoon Dijon mustard, salt and pepper. Pour this dressing over the salad and serve immediately.

Pistou soup

Pistou is a condiment from Provence, made of fresh basil crushed with garlic and olive oil. The word (derived from the Italian *pestare*, to pound) is also used for the vegetable and vermicelli soup to which it is added. The condiment, sometimes supplemented by Parmesan cheese and tomatoes, is similar to the Italian *pesto*.

Soak 500 g (18 oz, 3 cups) mixed white and red haricot (navy) beans for 12 hours in cold water. Drain and place in a large saucepan together with 2.5 litres (4½ pints, 11 cups) cold water and a bouquet garni. Bring to the boil, boil rapidly for 10 minutes then reduce the heat and cook gently. String 250 g (9 oz) French (green) beans and cut them into short lengths. Cut 2 or 3 courgettes (zucchini) into dice. Scrape and dice 2 carrots and peel and dice 2 turnips. When the haricots have been cooking for 1½ hours, add the French beans and carrots to the soup and season to taste with salt and pepper. After a further 15 minutes, add the courgettes and turnips. Cook for another 15 minutes, then stir in 200 g (7 oz) large vermicelli and cook for a further 10 minutes.

Meanwhile, pound together the pulp of 2 very ripe tomatoes, 5 peeled garlic cloves, 3–4 tablespoons fresh basil leaves and 75 g (3 oz, ¾ cup) grated Parmesan cheese, gradually working in 4 tablespoons olive oil. Add this mixture to the soup while it is still boiling, then remove from the heat and serve immediately.

Quartered artichoke hearts or potatoes may be added 30 minutes before the end of cooking, if wished.

Potage cultivateur

Cut 2–3 small carrots and 1 small turnip into large dice; prepare 6 table-spoons diced leeks (white part only) and 2 tablespoons diced onions. Season with salt and a pinch of sugar. Cook the prepared vegetables together in 50 g (2 oz, ¼ cup) butter in a covered pan. Moisten with 1.5 litres (2¾ pints, 6½ cups) white consommé and cook for 1¼ hours. About 25 minutes before serving, add 150 g (5 oz, ¾ cup) sliced potatoes and 75 g (3 oz, ½ cup) well-blanched diced bacon.

The potatoes can be replaced by rice.

Potage julienne à la cévenole

Prepare 450 g (1 lb) julienne of carrots, turnips, white of leek, celery and onions, in equal proportions; cook gently in butter for about 30 minutes. Pour in 1 litre (1¾ pints, 4⅓ cups) consommé and cook for a further 30 minutes. Add 500 ml (17 fl oz, 2 cups) salted chestnut purée, mix thoroughly, and boil for 5 minutes. Just before serving, blend in 50 g (2 oz, ¼ cup) butter, cut into small pieces.

Rachel salad

Clean and string some celery sticks and cut them into chunks. Cook some potatoes and some artichoke hearts in salted water and cut them into small dice. Mix equal amounts of these ingredients and dress them with a well-flavoured mayonnaise. Pile into a salad bowl and garnish with asparagus tips, cooked in salted water and well drained. If desired, the salad can be garnished with slices of truffle.

Raphael salad

Line a shallow salad bowl with shredded lettuce dressed with mayonnaise and seasoned with paprika. Arrange on top slices of peeled cucumber (previously sprinkled with salt and left to stand, then rinsed and drained), white asparagus tips (boiled and well drained), small tomatoes (peeled, seeded and cut into quarters), small lettuce hearts and sliced pink radishes. Dress with vinaigrette made with olive oil, lemon juice and chopped chervil.

Ratatouille niçoise

Trim the ends of 6 courgettes (zucchini) and cut them into rounds (do not peel them). Peel and slice 2 onions. Cut the stalks from 3 green (bell) peppers, remove the seeds and cut them into strips. Peel 6 tomatoes, cut each into

6 pieces and seed them. Peel and crush 3 garlic cloves. Peel 6 aubergines (eggplants) and cut them into rounds. Heat 6 tablespoons olive oil in a cast-iron pan. Brown the aubergines in this, then add the peppers, tomatoes and onions, and finally the courgettes and the garlic. Add a large bouquet garni, containing plenty of thyme, salt and pepper. Cook over a low heat for about 30 minutes. Add 2 tablespoons fresh olive oil and continue to cook until the desired consistency is reached. Remove the bouquet garni and serve very hot.

Raw vegetable salad

Wash and thinly slice 2 tomatoes, 3 celery sticks and 1 head of fennel. Peel and finely dice 1 beetroot (beet). Halve 2 sweet (bell) peppers, remove the seeds and cut the flesh into thin strips. Wash and chop a small bunch of parsley. Wash 1 lettuce and line the base of a shallow dish with the lettuce leaves. Top with small heaps of fennel, beetroot, celery and sweet peppers. Arrange 10 green and black (ripe) olives in the centre and place the tomato slices all around the side. Pour some vinaigrette over the salad and sprinkle with the chopped parsley.

Russian salad

Boil and finely dice some potatoes, carrots and turnips; boil some French (green) beans and cut into short pieces. Mix together equal quantities of these ingredients and add some well-drained cooked petits pois. Bind with mayonnaise and pile up in a salad bowl. Garnish with a julienne of pickled tongue and truffles and add some finely diced lobster or langouste meat.

For a more elaborate dish, the ordinary mayonnaise can be replaced by thickened mayonnaise and the salad is poured into mould lined with aspic and garnished with slivers of truffle and pickled tongue. Chill in the refrigerator for 4 hours and remove from the mould just before serving.

Salad à la favorite

Arrange in a salad dish, in separate heaps, asparagus tips, shelled crayfish and sliced white truffles. Season with oil, lemon juice, salt and pepper. Sprinkle with chopped celery and herbs.

Salad à l'orientale

Cook some long-grain rice in salted water to which saffron has been added, keeping it fairly firm; drain thoroughly. Mix the rice with some peeled and finely chopped onion and season with vinaigrette well spiced with paprika. Pile the rice in a dome in a salad bowl. Turn some red and green (bell) peppers under a hot grill (broiler), then skin them, cut them open, take out the seeds and cut the flesh into strips. Peel, seed and chop some tomatoes. Garnish the rice with the peppers, tomatoes and some stoned (pitted) black (ripe) olives.

Salade gourmande

Cook 175 g (6 oz) fine French (green) beans topped and tailed, in plenty of salted water until *al dente*. Remove the beans with a slotted spoon and plunge them into icy cold water for 10 seconds, then drain thoroughly. Using the same cooking water, cook 12 asparagus tips for 5–6 minutes.

Using a small whisk, mix together salt, pepper, 1 teaspoon olive oil, 1 teaspoon lemon juice, 1 teaspoon groundnut (peanut) oil, 1 teaspoon sherry vinegar, 1 teaspoon chopped chervil and 1 teaspoon chopped tarragon. Season separately the French beans, asparagus tips and 20 g (¾ oz) sliced truffle with a little of the dressing.

Place a few leaves of radicchio, frisée or other salad leaves on each plate and arrange the beans on top. Add a little chopped shallot and the asparagus tips. Cut 50 g (2 oz) foie gras into fine slices and place on the vegetables. Garnish with the slices of truffle.

Salade niçoise

Separate the leaves of 1 lettuce or use 100 g (4 oz) mesclun (mixed salad greens). Cut 10 very firm tomatoes into 8 equal wedges. Place in a colander in the refrigerator, over a plate, and sprinkle with salt to extract the water. Hard boil (hard cook) 6 eggs, then cool, shell and cut into quarters. Peel 2 small mild salad onions and chop very finely. Wash and fillet 6 anchovies preserved in salt. Seed 1 (bell) pepper and cut into strips. Finely chop 3 celery sticks with their leaves. Sprinkle 3 artichoke hearts, preferably from purple Provençal artichokes, with lemon juice and slice very finely. In a shallow serving dish, place a few lettuce leaves, a layer of tomatoes, slivers of artichoke hearts, a few strips of pepper, shredded tuna, chopped celery and onions. Repeat the layers until all these ingredients have been used up. Prepare a vinaigrette with oil, vinegar and pepper. Season the salad, toss and add a little salt if necessary. Garnish with the quarters of hard-boiled egg, some black (ripe) olives and anchovy fillets.

Saveloys in salad

Cut some cold cooked saveloys into slices. Slice a cucumber and several seeded tomatoes into half rounds. Cut the heart of a head of celery into small rounds, and quarter some artichoke hearts that have been cooked in a court-bouillon. Arrange all the ingredients in a salad bowl, moisten with a well-seasoned vinaigrette containing white mustard, sprinkle with chopped parsley and chives, and serve chilled.

Scallop and cucumber salad

Hard boil (hard cook) some eggs, then quarter them. Shape the flesh of a cucumber into little ovals. Poach some scallops and let them cool. Shred some lettuce and season it with vinaigrette, then line the rounded halves of the scallop shells with this. Slice the scallops thinly, put them in a bowl with the cucumber, add some vinaigrette and mix well. Place the scallop slices and the cucumber into the lettuce-lined shells. Garnish with the egg quarters and corals, and sprinkle with mixed herbs. Crème fraîche with a little ketchup may be added to the scallop slices, with lemon juice, salt and pepper.

Scallop salad

Clean 1 lettuce heart, ½ bunch of watercress and the white part of 2 leeks. Slice the lettuce and the leeks and cook all these vegetables very gently in 1 tablespoon oil with salt and pepper until well reduced. Slice the flesh and corals of 12 scallops and seal them by steaming. Place the scallops on the tepid vegetables and sprinkle with a little olive oil and the juice of 1 lemon.

Seville gazpacho

Put 4 crushed garlic cloves, 1 teaspoon salt, ½ teaspoon ground cayenne and the pulp of 2 crushed medium-sized tomatoes in a bowl. Thoroughly mix these ingredients and add 4 tablespoons olive oil, drop by drop. Then add a Spanish onion cut into slices as thin as tissue paper, a green or red (bell) pepper (cored and diced), a cucumber (peeled, seeded and diced) and 4 tablespoons croûtons. Add 750 ml (1¼ pints, 3¼ cups) water and mix well. Serve chilled.

Solferino soup

Wash, trim and chop the white part from 100 g (4 oz) leeks and 100 g (4 oz) carrots and sweat in 25 g (1 oz, 2 tablespoons) butter for 15 minutes. Make about 20 potato balls using a melon baller, and cook in salted boiling water for 15 minutes, without allowing them to break up. Set aside. Peel, seed and crush 800 g (1¾ lb) tomatoes and add the pulp to the sweated vegetables with

1 bouquet garni and 1 garlic clove. Season, cover and cook gently for 15 minutes, then add 1.5 litres (2¾ pints, 6½ cups) stock and 250 g (9 oz) peeled potatoes cut into pieces. Cook for 30 minutes.

Remove the bouquet garni and purée the vegetables in a blender or food processor. Dilute with a little stock if necessary and reheat. Remove from the heat, whisk in 50–75 g (2–3 oz, 4–6 tablespoons) butter in small pieces, then add the potato balls. Serve sprinkled with chopped chervil.

Stuffed provençal vegetables

Trim the tops off 6 onions, 6 small aubergines (eggplants), 6 round courgettes (zucchini), 6 sweet (bell) peppers and 6 medium-sized tomatoes to reduce them to three-quarters of their original height, and cut the aubergines and peppers in half. Use a teaspoon to hollow out the vegetables and mix the pulp with the trimmings. Fry the pulp lightly in a little olive oil, then leave to cool. Cut 5 slices of bread into small dice and soak in 100 ml (4 fl oz, 7 tablespoons) milk. Mix with the vegetable pulp and add 400 g (14 oz) sausagemeat, 5 garlic cloves, chopped, 75 g (3 oz, 1¼ cups) finely chopped parsley, 3 tablespoons chopped basil, 3 eggs (beaten), 100 g (4 oz, 1 cup) grated Parmesan cheese, salt and pepper. Stir the mixture until smooth with a wooden spatula.

Bring a saucepan of water to the boil and cook the onions lightly, followed by the courgettes, peppers and aubergines, cooked separately. Drain each batch on a cloth or paper towels.

Stuff all the vegetables with sausagemeat mixture and arrange them in a roasting pan (tin), greased with olive oil.

Carefully remove the flowers of 6 courgettes and set aside. Chop the courgettes finely and fry gently in 2 tablespoons olive oil for 5–8 minutes, stirring often. Remove from the heat and add 2 chopped basil leaves, 1 tablespoon finely chopped parsley and 1 finely chopped garlic clove. Cool, then incorporate 1 tablespoon fresh breadcrumbs and half a beaten egg.

Fill the flowers with the sausagemeat mixture, fold over the petals and place the flowers side by side in a second roasting pan (tin). Pour over a mixture of 120 ml (4½ fl oz, ½ cup) boiling water, 1 chicken stock (bouillon) cube and 2 tablespoons olive oil. Cover with foil.

Cook both batches of vegetables in a preheated oven at 200°C (400°F, gas 6) for 15–20 minutes. The stuffed vegetables and courgette flowers may be eaten hot or cold.

Soup à la fermière

Finely shred 2 or 3 small carrots, 1 small turnip, 1 leek (white part only), 1 onion and 75 g (3 oz, 1¼ cups) cabbage heart. Season and cook gently in 50 g (2 oz, ¼ cup) butter in a covered pan. Add 750 ml (1¼ pints, 3¼ cups) water in which white beans have been cooked, and 600 ml (1 pint, 2½ cups) white consommé. Cook gently for 1¼ hours. Add 100 ml (4 fl oz, 7 tablespoons) single (light) cream, 4 tablespoons cooked white beans and some chervil leaves.

Soup à la paysanne

For 4 servings, peel and dice the following ingredients and place them in a large pan: 200 g (7 oz, 1¾ cups) carrots, 100 g (4 oz, 1 cup) turnips, 75 g (3 oz, ¾ cup) leeks (white part), 1 onion and 2 celery sticks. Cover the pan and sweat the vegetables in 40 g (1½ oz, 3 tablespoons) butter.

Add 1.5 litres (2¾ pints, 6½ cups) water and bring to the boil. Blanch 100 g (4 oz, 1½ cups) cabbage cut into small squares; refresh, drain and add them to the pan. Leave to cook gently for 1 hour, then add 100 g (4 oz, ⅔ cup) diced potatoes and 100 g (4 oz, ¾ cup) small fresh peas. Cook for a further 25 minutes.

Crisp a long French stick in the oven. Just before serving the soup, add 25 g (1 oz, 2 tablespoons) butter and sprinkle with chopped chervil. Serve with the hot French bread.

Soupe à la bonne femme

Heat 40 g (1½ oz, 3 tablespoons) butter in a saucepan, but do not let it brown. Add the cleaned white part of 4 finely sliced leeks and cook gently until quite soft. Then add 3 litres (5 pints, 13 cups) ordinary consommé and bring to the boil. Add 350 g (12 oz, 1¾ cups) thinly sliced potatoes, bring to the boil again, season with salt and pepper, then lower the heat and leave to cook for 1 hour. Just before serving, remove the saucepan from the heat and whisk in 50 g (2 oz, ¼ cup) butter and 1 tablespoon chervil leaves.

Terrine of vegetables Fontanieu

Cook separately, in very lightly salted water, 7 fluted carrots, 300 g (11 oz) French (green) beans, and 150 g (5 oz, ¾ cup) petits pois. Cut the following vegetables into sticks and cook separately: 500 g (18 oz) turnips, 500 g (18 oz) courgettes (zucchini) and 1 small root of celeriac. Peel, halve and seed 3 tomatoes. Cool the vegetables and dry them thoroughly.

Bring 1 litre (1¾ pints, 4⅓ cups) double (heavy) cream just to the boil, then blend in 500 g (18 oz, 6 cups) shredded button mushrooms. Season with salt and pepper. Remove the mushrooms after 5 minutes and chop them. Do not boil down the cream, but blend in, while it is still hot, 25 g (1 oz, 4 envelopes) powdered gelatine, 5 tablespoons dry vermouth and the chopped mushrooms. Keep the mixture warm.

Pour a thin layer of this mixture into the bottom of a china terrine or mould. Arrange the French beans lengthways, covering the whole of the bottom of the terrine, then mask them with a little of the mushroom cream.

In this way, build up the terrine, alternating the layers of vegetables according to colour. (The purpose of the cream mixture is simply to bind the ingredients – it should not take precedence over the vegetables.) Place the tomato halves in the middle. When the terrine is full, settle the ingredients by lightly tapping the bottom and refrigerate for at least half a day. When serving, turn out of the mould and serve with small diced tomatoes sprinkled with chopped basil. Sprinkle the terrine with a dash of raspberry vinegar and olive oil. Season with salt and pepper.

Toulouse salad

Using a melon baller, scoop balls of melon from the flesh of a medium-sized melon. Cook 2 artichoke hearts in water and lemon juice, cool, then cut into thin strips. Thinly slice the white and green parts of a very tender leek; shred a thick slice of unsmoked ham. Mix together all these ingredients. Make a well-seasoned vinaigrette, adding chopped parsley, chives and sage, and blend it with 1 teaspoon cream. Pour over the salad and toss gently. Place a large leaf of raw spinach, washed and patted dry, on each plate. Divide the salad between the plates and grate a little fresh root ginger over them.

Vegetable achar with lemon

An achar is a pickle of vegetables or fruit and vegetables steeped in spices and seasoning. The flavour may be sharp or sweet, and piquant or mild.

Cut thin-rinded lemons into quarters and remove the seeds. Cut some carrots, sweet (bell) peppers and seeded cucumbers into strips about 4 cm (1½ in) long, and cut some thin green beans and cabbage leaves into small pieces. Separate a cauliflower into tiny florets. Steep the lemons and the vegetables separately in coarse salt. After 12 hours, wash the lemons and soak them in cold water for 24 hours, changing the water several times, then boil them in water until the quarters have become soft. Drain and dry them. When the vegetables have been steeping for 36 hours, drain and dry them too. Finely mince or grate some onion and fresh root ginger (or use a blender). Add cayenne pepper, vinegar and powdered saffron, then some best-quality olive oil. Place the lemon quarters and vegetables in a jar and cover with the aromatized oil. Seal and store in a cool place.

Vegetable macédoine with butter or cream

A macédoine is a mixture of vegetables or fruit cut into small dice. Peel and dice 250 g (9 oz) each of new carrots, turnips, French (green) beans and potatoes. Prepare 500 g (18 oz, 3½ cups) shelled peas. Add the carrots and turnips to a pan of boiling salted water. Bring back to the boil and add the beans, then the peas and finally the potatoes. Keep on the boil but do not cover. When the vegetables are cooked, drain and pour into a serving dish and add butter or cream (keep the cooking water for a soup base). Sprinkle with chopped herbs.

Vegetable ragoût à la printanière

Generously grease a large flameproof casserole with butter. Prepare and wash the following new vegetables: 250 g (9 oz) baby carrots, 250 g (9 oz) baby turnips, 12 button onions, 250 g (9 oz) very small new potatoes, 2 lettuce hearts, 250 g (9 oz) finely sliced French (green) beans, 250 g (9 oz, 1½ cups) shelled peas and 3 trimmed artichoke hearts quartered and sprinkled with lemon juice. Separate half a very white cauliflower into tiny florets.

Put the carrots, beans, artichoke hearts and onions into the buttered casserole; just cover with chicken stock and bring to the boil. Boil for 8 minutes, then add the turnips, potatoes, peas, cauliflower and lettuce hearts; adjust the seasoning and continue cooking for about 20 minutes. Drain the vegetables and arrange them in a dish. Reduce the cooking liquid, whisk in 50 g (2 oz, ¼ cup) butter and pour over the vegetables.

Vegetable salpicon with mayonnaise

A salpicon is a mixture of finely diced ingredients bound with a sauce or dressing. Use any or a mixture of the following vegetables: artichoke hearts cooked in white stock, patted dry and diced; asparagus tips or French (green) beans cut into short pieces, boiled in salted water and patted dry; peeled, diced celeriac, boiled in salted water and patted dry; mushrooms cooked in butter, drained and diced; or potatoes, boiled in their skins, peeled and diced.

Cook the chosen vegetable completely and leave to cool. Cut into small dice and bind with classic mayonnaise, which may be flavoured, coloured or thickened.

Vegetable salpicon with vinaigrette

Use any or a mixture of the following vegetables: diced cooked beetroot (red beet) with chervil and parsley; raw cucumber, sprinkled with salt, left to stand, rinsed, patted dry and diced, with fresh mint or tarragon; tomatoes, blanched for 20 seconds, peeled, seeded and diced, with basil or tarragon.

Cook the chosen vegetable completely. Leave to cool, dice and dress with seasoned vinaigrette flavoured with finely chopped aromatic herbs.

Vegetables à la grecque

Choose very fresh tender vegetables, such as aubergines (eggplants), cardoons, mushrooms, cauliflower, courgettes (zucchini), fennel, artichoke hearts and small onions. Small onions may be left whole, but the other vegetables should be washed thoroughly and cut into fairly small pieces so that they can be cooked properly. They should be sprinkled with lemon juice if there is a risk of discoloration. Make a court-bouillon by boiling 6 tablespoons olive oil, 750 ml (1¼ pints, 3⅛ cups) water and the strained juice of 2 lemons with a bouquet garni (consisting of parsley, celery, fennel, thyme and bay leaf), 12–15 coriander seeds and 12–15 peppercorns for 20 minutes. Lightly brown the vegetables in a little olive oil, then pour over the very hot court-bouillon and finish cooking. Add 2 tablespoons concentrated tomato purée (paste) to the court-bouillon if desired. Leave to cool in the cooking liquor, then drain and serve moistened with a little of the liquor, if desired.

Basic recipes & classic additions

Batters

Buckwheat crêpes or galettes

Mix 250 g (9 oz, 2¼ cups) buckwheat flour and 250 g (9 oz, 2¼ cups) plain (all-purpose) flour (or, alternatively, use all buckwheat flour) in a bowl with 5–6 beaten eggs and a large pinch of salt. Add, a little at a time, 500 ml (17 fl oz, 2 cups) milk and 750 ml (1¼ pints, 3¼ cups) water and then 3–4 tablespoons oil. Leave the batter to stand for 2 hours at room temperature so that the air bubbles disperse, preventing the crêpes from bubbling. Just before making the crêpes, thin the batter with up to 100 ml (4 fl oz, 7 tablespoons) water if necessary.

Coating batter

This batter is suitable for coating food before deep-frying. Sift 200 g (7 oz, 1¾ cups) plain (all-purpose) flour into a large mixing bowl. Add 2 teaspoons baking powder, 2 tablespoons groundnut (peanut) oil, a pinch of salt and 250 ml (8 fl oz, 1 cup) warm water. Mix the ingredients together thoroughly and beat until smooth, then leave the batter to rest in a cool place for at least 1 hour. Just before using the batter, carefully fold in 2 stiffly whisked egg whites.

Fritter batter (1)

Sift 250 g (9 oz, 2¼ cups) plain (all-purpose) flour into a mixing bowl. Heat 200 ml (7 fl oz, ¾ cup) water until it is just lukewarm. Make a well in the centre of the flour and add 150 ml (¼ pint, ⅔ cup) beer, the warm water and a generous pinch of salt. Mix, drawing the flour from the sides to the centre. Add 2 tablespoons groundnut (peanut) oil and mix. Leave to rest for 1 hour if possible. When required for use, stiffly whisk 2 or 3 egg whites and carefully fold them into the batter. Do not stir or beat. For sweet fritters, the batter can be flavoured with Calvados, Cognac or rum. The batter may also be sweetened with 1½ teaspoons sugar and the oil replaced with the same amount of melted butter.

Fritter batter (2)

Put 250 g (9 oz, 2¼ cups) sifted plain (all-purpose) flour in a mixing bowl. Make a well in the centre and add 1 teaspoon salt, 2 eggs and 300 ml (½ pint, 1¼ cups) groundnut (peanut) oil. Whisk the eggs and oil together, incorporating a little of the flour. Add 250 ml (8 fl oz, 1 cup) beer and, stirring well, gradually incorporate the rest of the flour. Allow to stand for about 1 hour. A few minutes before using the batter, whisk 3 egg whites stiffly and fold into the batter.

Pannequet pancake batter

Pannequets can have sweet or savoury fillings. Make a batter with 250 g (9 oz, 2¼ cups) plain (all-purpose) flour, a pinch of salt, 3 beaten eggs, 250 ml (8 fl oz, 1 cup) milk, 250 ml (8 fl oz, 1 cup) water and 1 tablespoon melted butter. For sweet pancakes, add 1 tablespoon caster (superfine) sugar mixed with the eggs. Prepare some fairly thick pancakes. Pile them in a covered dish and keep hot over a saucepan of boiling water.

Savoury crêpe batter

Mix 500 g (18 oz, 4½ cups) plain (all-purpose) flour with 5–6 beaten eggs and a large pinch of salt. Gradually add 1 litre (1¾ pints, 4⅓ cups) milk or, for lighter pancakes, 500 ml (17 fl oz, 2 cups) milk and 500 ml (17 fl oz, 2 cups) water. Equal quantities of beer and milk may also be used, or the milk may be replaced by white consommé. Finally, add 3 tablespoons oil, either one with little taste, such as groundnut (peanut) oil or sunflower oil or, if the recipe requires it, use olive oil; 25 g (1 oz, 2 tablespoons) melted butter may also be added. Leave the batter to stand for 2 hours. Just before making the crêpes, dilute the batter with a little water (100–200 ml, 4–7 fl oz, ½–¾ cup).

Butters

Beurre manié

To thicken 500 ml (17 fl oz, 2 cups) stock or sauce, work together 25 g (1 oz, 2 tablespoons) butter and 25 g (1 oz, 4 tablespoons) plain (all-purpose) flour. Add this paste to the boiling liquid and whisk over the heat for 2 minutes.

Clarified butter

Melt some butter gently in a heavy saucepan; do not stir. Continue to heat gently until the butter ceases spitting – this shows that the water content has evaporated. There should be a small white residue in the bottom of the pan. Carefully pour the butter into another container so that the whitish sediment stays in the pan. Clarified butter is used for frying and for emulsified sauces.

Maître d'hôtel butter

Work 200 g (7 oz, generous ¾ cup) butter to a smooth paste with a wooden spoon, add ½ teaspoon fine salt, a pinch of pepper, a squeeze (about 1 tablespoon) of lemon juice and 1 tablespoon chopped parsley. This butter can be kept in the refrigerator for 2 or 3 days.

Noisette butter

Gently heat some butter in a frying pan until it is golden and gives off a nutty smell. Serve scalding hot with lambs' or calves' sweetbreads, fish roe, vegetables (boiled and well drained), eggs or skate poached in stock. Noisette butter is known as meunière butter when lemon juice is added.

Tarragon butter

Blanch 150 g (5 oz) stripped tarragon leaves, soak in cold water and blot. Purée, then work into the finely softened butter, season with salt and pepper. Tarragon butter is used to finish sauces or garnish cold hors d'oeuvres.

Dressings & mayonnaise

Mayonnaise

Half an hour before making the mayonnaise, ensure that all the ingredients are at room temperature. Put 2 egg yolks, a little salt and white pepper, and a little vinegar (tarragon, if available and suitable) or lemon juice in a medium mixing bowl; 1 teaspoon white mustard can also be added. Stir quickly with a wooden spoon or whisk and as soon as the mixture is smooth use a tablespoon to blend in about 300 ml (½ pint, 1¼ cups) olive oil. Add the oil slowly drop by drop, with a few drops of vinegar, taking care to beat the sauce against the sides of the bowl. The whiteness of the sauce depends on this continued beating. As the mayonnaise increases in volume, larger quantities of oil can be added in a thin trickle and also more vinegar or lemon juice. It is essential to add the ingredients slowly and sparingly in order to avoid curdling.

The mayonnaise can be flavoured with any of the following, adding them sparingly and tasting to check the intensity and suitability for the dish. Grated lemon zest; crushed garlic; anchovy essence or finely chopped or puréed anchovy fillets; finely chopped watercress leaves; finely chopped herbs, such as tarragon, chives, dill, parsley or chervil; tomato purée (paste) or ketchup; chopped gherkins; chopped capers; or chopped truffle.

Vinaigrette

Dissolve a little salt in 1 tablespoon vinegar (salt does not dissolve in oil). Add 3 tablespoons oil and some pepper. The vinegar can be replaced by another acid, such as the juice of a lemon, orange or grapefruit. In that case, the ratio is half lemon, half oil.

Olive, sunflower, grapeseed or other light oils can be used. Strongly flavoured and light oils can be combined; nut oils, such as walnut, hazelnut, pistachio or macadamia oils, can be added with olive or sunflower oil for a richly flavoured vinagrette.

Other flavouring ingredients, such as herbs, mustard or garlic, may be added to taste. The mixture may also be placed in a screw-top jar and shaken vigorously to form an emulsion. For a creamy dressing, the oil can be replaced by crème fraîche.

Mirepoix, forcemeats & sausagemeat

À gratin forcemeat

Fry 150 g (5 oz, 1 cup) finely chopped unsmoked bacon until soft. Add 300 g (11 oz) chicken livers, 2 thinly sliced shallots, 50 g (2 oz, ⅔ cup) finely chopped mushrooms, a sprig of thyme and ½ bay leaf. Season with a generous pinch of salt, some pepper and a little mixed spice. Sauté quickly over a high heat. Allow to cool completely, then pound in a mortar and press through a fine sieve. Cover with buttered or oiled greaseproof (wax) paper and chill until needed. A gratin forcemeat is spread on croûtons of fried bread that are used as a base for small roast game birds or served with salmis or *civets*.

Bread panada

A panada is a paste used for thickening or as a base for some mixtures, such as soufflé. Bread panada is useful for thickening and binding forcemeats; other thick pastes of flour or potatoes may also be used. Soak 250 g (9 oz, 4½ cups) fresh white breadcrumbs in 300 ml (½ pint, 1¼ cups) boiled milk until the liquid is completely absorbed. Pour into a saucepan and let it thicken over the heat, stirring with a wooden spoon. Pour into a buttered dish and leave to cool.

Forcemeat for poultry

This consists of fine sausagemeat mixed with one-fifth of its weight each of fresh breadcrumbs and finely chopped onion cooked in a little butter until soft, together with chopped parsley. Chill until required.

Forcemeat for vegetable terrine

Peel 500 g (1 lb 2 oz) celeriac (celery root) and cut into quarters. Steam, drain and purée in a blender. Dry slightly in a warm oven but do not allow the celeriac to colour. In the bowl of a mixer, combine the celeriac purée with 2 egg yolks, 150 ml (¼ pint, ⅔ cup) single (light) cream and 2 stiffly whisked egg whites. Season to taste with salt, pepper and nutmeg. Other vegetables, in equal quantities, may be added to the stuffing: diced carrots, petits pois, green beans, blanched or cooked in steam. The vegetable terrine can then be cooked in the oven or in a bain marie.

Mirepoix

Peel and finely dice 150 g (5 oz) carrots, 100 g (4 oz) onions and 50 g (2 oz) celery. Heat 25 g (1 oz, 2 tablespoons) butter in a saucepan and add the vegetables, with a sprig of thyme and ½ bay leaf. Stir the ingredients into the butter, cover and cook gently for about 20 minutes until they are very tender.

Mirepoix with meat

Prepare the mirepoix as above, cutting the celery into fine strips instead of dice and adding 100 g (4 oz) raw ham or blanched streaky bacon.

Mushroom forcemeat

Sauté 2 peeled and finely chopped shallots and 175 g (6 oz, 2 cups) button mushrooms, also finely chopped, over a high heat in a frying pan, with 40 g (1½ oz, 3 tablespoons) butter and a generous pinch of grated nutmeg. When cooked, allow to cool. Make 100 g (4 oz) bread panada and purée it in a blender, adding the mushrooms and shallots. Finally, add 3 egg yolks and mix thoroughly (it is not necessary to sieve this forcemeat). It is used to stuff vegetables, poultry, game and fish.

Sausagemeat

Weigh out equal quantities of lean pork and fat bacon. Mince (grind) finely and add 3 tablespoons salt per 1 kg (2¼ lb) mince. Chopped truffle or truffle peelings may be added, or the mince may be seasoned with finely chopped onions, garlic, salt, pepper and herbs. Chopped mushrooms, wild or cultivated, may also be added.

Sausagemeat – fine – or fine pork forcemeat

Using the same mixture as for the sausagemeat recipe, finely mince (grind) the ingredients twice, or chop once and sieve. The seasonings are the same.

Veal forcemeat

Pound 1 kg (2¼ lb) lean minced (ground) veal in a mortar (or reduce to a purée in a blender). Season with 1 tablespoon salt, some white pepper and grated nutmeg. Purée 300 g (11 oz) flour panada; when really soft, add the veal, together with 65 g (2½ oz, 4½ tablespoons) butter, and beat the mixture well. Finally, beating continuously, add 5 whole eggs and 8 yolks, one by one. Then add 1.25 litres (2¼ pints, 5½ cups) thick béchamel sauce. Press through a fine sieve and work with a spatula to make the forcemeat smooth. Chill until required. This forcemeat is used for borders and large quenelles.

Pastry

Basic shortcrust pastry

Sift 225 g (8 oz, 2 cups) plain (all-purpose) flour into a mixing bowl and stir in a pinch of salt, if required. Add 50 g (2 oz, ¼ cup) chilled butter and 50 g (2 oz, ¼ cup) chilled lard or white vegetable fat (shortening). Cut the fat into small pieces, then lightly rub the pieces into the flour using your fingertips until the mixture resembles breadcrumbs. Sprinkle 3 tablespoons cold water over the mixture, then use a round-bladed pastry knife to mix it in. The mixture should form clumps: press these together into a smooth ball. Chill the pastry in the refrigerator for 30 minutes before baking. Roll out and use as required.

Bouchée cases

These small puff pastry cases with savoury fillings are generally served hot. Lightly dust the work surface with flour and roll out some puff pastry to a thickness of about 5 mm (¼ in). Using a round, crinkle-edged pastry (cookie) cutter, 7.5–10 cm (3–4 in) in diameter, cut out circles of pastry and place them on a damp baking sheet, turning them over as you do so. Use a 7.5–10 cm (3–4 in) ring cutter to stamp out rings of pastry. Brush the edge of the pastry bases with beaten egg and place the pastry rings on top. Chill the cases in the refrigerator for about 30 minutes. Bake in a preheated oven at 220°C (425°F, gas 7) for 12–15 minutes. Using the point of a knife, cut out a circle of pastry from inside each bouchée, lift it out and set aside to use as a lid. If necessary remove any soft pastry inside the case. The bouchées are now ready to be filled.

Choux paste

To make about 40 small buns, 20 larger buns or éclairs, measure 250 ml (8 fl oz, 1 cup) water or milk and water (in equal proportions) into a saucepan. Add a large pinch of salt and 65 g (2½ oz, 5 tablespoons) butter cut into small pieces. Add 2 teaspoons caster (superfine) sugar for sweet choux. Heat gently until the butter melts, then bring to the boil. As soon as the mixture begins to boil, take the pan off the heat, add 125 g (4½ oz, 1 cup) plain (all-purpose) flour all at once and mix quickly. Return the saucepan to the heat and cook the paste until it thickens, stirring: it takes about 1 minute for the paste to leave the sides of the saucepan. Do not overcook the mixture or beat it vigorously as this will make it greasy or oily. Remove from the heat and cool slightly. Beat in 2 eggs, then 2 more eggs, one after the other, continuing to beat hard until a smooth glossy paste is obtained.

Transfer the pastry to a piping bag fitted with a plain nozzle, 1 cm (½ in) in diameter, and pipe small balls, 4–5 cm (1½–2 in) in diameter, on to a lightly oiled baking sheet, spacing them out so they do not stick to each other as they swell during cooking. Alternatively, pipe the paste into larger buns or fingers to make éclairs.

Bake choux pastries in a preheated oven at 220°C (425°F, gas 7) for 10 minutes. Reduce the temperature to 180°C (350°F, gas 4) and continue to cook, allowing a further 10 minutes for small buns or up to 25 minutes for large puffs. Transfer cooked choux pastries to a wire rack to cool and split them immediately to allow steam to escape, so that they stay crisp outside, but slightly moist on the inside.

Pâte à foncer

This is a lining pastry for flans and tarts; it is a basic shortcrust made by the French method. Sift 250 g (9 oz, 2¼ cups) plain (all-purpose) flour on to a board. Make a well in the centre and add ½ teaspoon salt and 125 g (4½ oz, ½ cup) butter (softened at room temperature and cut into pieces). Start to mix the ingredients and then add 2 tablespoons water (the quantity of water required may vary depending on the type of flour used). Knead the dough gently, using the heel of the hand, shape it into a ball, wrap it in foil and set aside in a cool place for at least 2 hours if possible.

A richer pastry can be made by increasing the quantity of butter to 150 g (5 oz, ⅔ cup) and by adding 1 small egg and 2 tablespoons caster (superfine) sugar.

Pâte brisée

This is the French equivalent of shortcrust pastry (basic pie dough) which can be made with, or without, a little sugar. Sift 250 g (9 oz, 2¼ cups) plain (all-purpose) flour into a bowl or on to a board. Add a pinch of salt and 1½ tablespoons caster (superfine) sugar (to taste). Spread the mixture into a circle and make a well in the centre. Add 125 g (4½ oz, ½ cup) softened butter and a beaten egg, and knead the ingredients together as quickly as possible with 2 tablespoons very cold water. Form the dough into a ball, even if there are still some whole pieces of butter visible. Wrap it in foil and leave it to rest for at least 1 hour in the refrigerator. Knead the dough, pushing it down gently with the heel of the hand, and roll it out on a lightly floured worktop to the required thickness.

Puff pastry

Put 500 g (18 oz, 4½ cups) plain (all-purpose) flour on a board in a circle, making a well in the middle. Since flours differ, the exact proportion of water to flour is variable. Into the centre of this circle put 1½ teaspoons salt and about 300 ml (½ pint, 1¼ cups) water. Mix and knead until the dough is smooth and elastic. Form into a ball and leave to stand for 25 minutes.

Roll out the dough into square, mark a cross in the top and roll out the wedges to form an evenly thick cross shape. Put 500 g (18 oz, 2¼ cups) softened butter in the middle of this dough. (The butter should be softened with a wooden spatula until it can be spread easily.) Fold the ends of the dough over the butter in such a way as to enclose it completely. Leave to stand for 10 minutes in a cold place, until rested and firmed slightly.

The turning operation (called *tournage* in French) can now begin. Roll the dough with a rolling pin on a lightly floured board in such a way as to obtain a rectangle 60 cm (24 in) long, 20 cm (8 in) wide and 1.5 cm (⅝ in) thick. Fold the rectangle into three, give it a quarter-turn and, with the rolling pin at right angles to the folds, roll the dough out again into a rectangle of the same size as the previous one. Again fold the dough into three and leave to stand for about 15 minutes and chill if too sticky. Repeat the sequence (turn, roll, fold) a further 4 times, leaving the dough to stand for about 15 minutes after each folding. After the sixth turn, roll out the dough in both directions and use according to the recipe.

Rich shortcrust pastry

Follow the recipe for shortcrust pastry, using 175 g (6 oz, ¾ cup) butter instead of butter and lard or white vegetable fat (shortening). Bind with water or beat 1 egg yolk with 1 tablespoon water and use to bind the pastry, adding a further 1 tablespoon water if necessary.

Sauces & purées

Anchovy sauce

Thoroughly desalt 6–8 anchovy fillets by soaking them in milk. Drain, wipe and purée them in a blender with 1 tablespoon capers, 100 ml (4 fl oz, ½ cup) oil, the juice of ½ lemon and salt and pepper. Serve as a dip with an assortment of raw vegetables – small artichokes, cauliflower florets, small sticks of carrot and seeded cucumber, thin slices of green or red sweet (bell) peppers, small quarters of fennel or raw mushrooms – or with fish poached in a court-bouillon, either hot or cold.

Béarnaise sauce

Put 1 tablespoon chopped shallots, 2 tablespoons chopped chervil and tarragon, a sprig of thyme, a piece of bay leaf, 2½ tablespoons vinegar, and a little salt and pepper in a pan. Reduce by two-thirds; cool slightly. Mix 2 egg yolks with 1 tablespoon water, add to the pan and whisk over a very low heat. As soon as the egg yolks have thickened, add 125 g (4½ oz, ½ cup) butter in small pieces, a little at a time, whisking continuously. Adjust the seasoning, adding a dash of cayenne if desired, and a little lemon juice. Add 1 tablespoon each of chopped chervil and tarragon. The sauce can be kept in a warm bain marie until required, but it must not be reheated once it has cooled.

Béchamel sauce

Gently heat 500 ml (17 fl oz, 2 cups) milk with 1 bay leaf, a thick slice of onion and 1 blade of mace. Remove from the heat just as the milk boils, cover the pan and set aside for at least 30 minutes. Strain the milk and discard the flavouring ingredients. Melt 40 g (1½ oz, 3 tablespoons) butter over a low heat in a heavy saucepan. Add 40 g (1½ oz, 6 tablespoons) flour and stir briskly until the mixture is smoothly blended, without allowing it to change colour. Slowly stir in the milk and bring to the boil, beating well to prevent lumps forming. Add salt and pepper and (according to the use for the sauce) a little grated nutmeg. Simmer gently for 3–5 minutes, stirring occasionally.

Breton sauce

Cut the white part of 1 leek, ¼ celery heart and 1 onion into thin strips. Soften gently in a covered pan with 1 tablespoon butter and a pinch of salt for about 15 minutes. Add 2 tablespoons thinly sliced mushrooms and 175 ml (6 fl oz, ¾ cup) dry white wine. Reduce until dry. Add 150 ml (¼ pint, ⅔ cup) thin velouté sauce and boil vigorously for 1 minute. Adjust the seasoning and stir in 1 tablespoon double (heavy) cream and 50 g (2 oz, ¼ cup) butter. Serve at once. If the sauce is to be served with braised fish, cook the sliced vegetables with the fish, adding 175 ml (6 fl oz, ¾ cup) fish stock or white wine and finishing with cream and butter.

Brown roux

Melt the butter in a heavy saucepan, then clarify it. Add the same weight (or a little more) of sifted plain (all-purpose) flour – up to 125 g (4½ oz, 1 cup) flour for 100 g (4 oz, ½ cup) butter.

Mix the butter and flour, and cook very gently for 15–20 minutes, stirring constantly until the roux becomes light brown. Take the pan off the heat and leave it to cool until time to add the liquid (milk, white stock, fish stock). To avoid lumps forming this must be poured boiling on to the cold roux. Use a whisk to mix the roux and heat gradually while whisking constantly. (Alternatively, the cold liquid may be whisked gradually into the warm roux.)

Butter sauce (1)

Mix 25 g (1 oz, 2 tablespoons) melted butter, 25 g (1 oz, ¼ cup) plain (all-purpose) flour and 250 g (8 fl oz, 1 cup) salted boiling water in a heavy-based saucepan. Whisk vigorously, blending in 1 tablespoon ice-cold water. Place the pan on the hob (stove top) over a low heat and gradually incorporate 100 g (4 oz, ½ cup) butter, cut into small pieces, stirring constantly. Season with salt and pepper, and strain if necessary. This sauce is served with fish and boiled vegetables.

Butter sauce (2)

Put 1 scant tablespoon flour and a little butter into a heavy-based saucepan and place over a gentle heat. Blend together the flour and butter with a wooden spoon, remove from the heat and add 4½ tablespoons water or consommé, a little salt, some grated nutmeg and the juice of ½ lemon. Stir constantly over a brisk heat, and as soon as it comes to the boil, remove the sauce. Stir in a large piece of butter. The sauce should be velvety and very smooth, with a rich but delicate flavour.

Chervil-leaf butter sauce

In a saucepan, boil a generous ladleful of butter sauce, adding to it a little salt, pepper, grated nutmeg, the juice of ½ lemon, a large knob of butter and 1 tablespoon small blanched chervil leaves.

Chicken purée

Remove the sinews from the cooked meat of chicken and reduce the flesh to a purée in a food processor or blender. Incorporate the same weight of rice cooked in meat stock and purée again quickly. Taste and adjust the seasoning.

This purée is used as an *à gratin* forcemeat.

Cream sauce

Add 100 ml (4 fl oz, 7 tablespoons) double (heavy) cream to 200 ml (7 fl oz, ¾ cup) béchamel sauce and boil to reduce by one-third. Remove from the heat and add 25–50 g (1–2 oz, 2–4 tablespoons) butter and 60–100 ml (2–4 fl oz, ¼–scant ½ cup) double (heavy) cream. Stir well and strain. This sauce is served with vegetables, fish, eggs and poultry.

Curry or Indian sauce

Cook 4 large sliced onions slowly in 5 tablespoons ghee, butter or oil. Add 1 tablespoon each of chopped parsley and chopped celery, a small sprig of thyme, half a bay leaf, a pinch of mace, salt and pepper. Sprinkle with 25 g (1 oz, ¼ cup) flour and 1 generous tablespoon good-quality curry powder and stir. Then add 500 ml (17 fl oz, 2 cups) chicken stock, stir and bring to the boil, stirring. Reduce the heat, cover and cook slowly for about 30 minutes. A quarter of the stock can be replaced by coconut milk for a coconut-flavoured curry. Rub the sauce through a sieve, add 1 teaspoon lemon juice and 5 tablespoons cream, and reduce a little. Adjust the seasoning.

Demi-glace

To make this rich brown sauce, boil down to reduce by two-thirds a mixture of 500 ml (17 fl oz, 2 cups) espagnole sauce and 750 ml (1¼ pints, 3¼ cups) clear brown stock. Remove from the heat, add 3 tablespoons Madeira and strain. A handful of sliced mushroom stalks may be added during cooking.

Devilled sauce (1)

(English recipe) Add 1 tablespoon chopped shallots to 150 ml (¼ pint, ⅔ cup) red wine vinegar and reduce by half. Then add 250 ml (8 fl oz, 1 cup) espagnole sauce and 2 tablespoons tomato purée (paste). Cook for 5 minutes.

Just before serving, add 1 tablespoon Worcestershire sauce, 1 tablespoon Harvey sauce or spiced vinegar, and a dash of cayenne pepper. Strain the sauce. This sauce is generally served with grilled (broiled) meat.

Devilled sauce (2)

Mix 150 ml (¼ pint, ⅔ cup) dry white wine with 1 tablespoon vinegar, then add 1 tablespoon finely chopped shallots, a sprig of thyme, a small piece of bay leaf and a generous pinch of pepper. Reduce the sauce by two-thirds, then add 200 ml (7 fl oz, ¾ cup) demi-glace and boil for 2–3 minutes. Strain through a sieve. Just before serving, add 1 teaspoon chopped parsley and check the seasoning, adding a little cayenne pepper if liked. Alternatively, omit straining the sauce and add 1 tablespoon butter or beurre manié.

English butter sauce

Make a white roux with 25 g (1 oz, 2 tablespoons) butter and 25 g (1 oz, ¼ cup) plain (all-purpose) flour. Then whisk in vigorously 250 ml (8 fl oz, 1 cup) salted boiling water. Season with salt and pepper, and whisk in 100 g (4 oz, ½ cup) butter cut into pieces.

Espagnole sauce (1)

(From Carême's recipe) Put 2 slices of Bayonne ham into a deep saucepan. Place a noix of veal and 2 partridges on top. Add enough stock to cover the veal only. Reduce the liquid rapidly, then lower the heat until the stock is reduced to a coating on the bottom of the pan. Remove it from the heat. Prick the noix of veal with the point of a knife so that its juice mingles with the stock. Put the saucepan back over a low heat for about 20 minutes. Watch the liquid as it gradually turns darker.

To simplify this operation, scrape off a little of the essence with the point of a knife. Roll it between the fingers. If it rolls into a ball, the essence is perfectly reduced. If it is not ready, it will make the fingers stick together.

Remove the saucepan from the heat and set it aside for 15 minutes for the essence to cool. (It will then dissolve more readily.) Fill the saucepan with clear soup or stock and heat very slowly.

Meanwhile prepare a roux: melt 100 g (4 oz, ½ cup) butter and add to it enough flour to give a rather liquid consistency. Put it over a low heat, stirring from time to time so that gradually the whole mixture turns a golden colour. As soon as the stock comes to the boil, skim it, and pour 2 ladles into a roux. When adding the first ladleful of stock, remove the roux from the heat, then replace it and stir in the second ladleful until the mixture is perfectly smooth. Now pour the thickened sauce into the saucepan with the veal noix. Add parsley and spring onions (scallions), ½ bay leaf, a little thyme, 2 chives, and some mushroom trimmings. Leave the sauce to simmer, stirring frequently. After 1 hour skim off the fat, then 30 minutes later, skim off the fat once again.

Strain the sauce through a cloth into a bowl, stirring from time to time with a wooden spoon so that no skin forms on the surface, as easily happens when the sauce is exposed to the air.

Espagnole sauce (2)

Make a brown roux in a heavy-based saucepan using 25 g (1 oz, 2 tablespoons) butter and 25 g (1 oz, ¼ cup) plain (all-purpose) flour. Add 1 tablespoon mirepoix, 50 g (2 oz, ⅔ cup) chopped mushrooms and 1 kg (2¼ lb) crushed tomatoes. Stir in 2.25 litres (4 pints, 10 cups) brown stock and simmer gently for 3–4 hours, skimming the sauce occasionally. Pass the sauce through a very fine sieve, or preferably strain through muslin (cheesecloth), when cold.

Game purée

Remove the sinews from the cooked meat of pheasant, duck, young rabbit or partridge and reduce the flesh to a purée in a food processor or blender. Incorporate the same weight of rice cooked in meat stock and purée again quickly. Adjust the seasoning.

This purée is used as an *à gratin* forcemeat.

Italian sauce

Clean and chop 250 g (9 oz, 2 generous cups) button mushrooms, 1 onion and 1 shallot. Heat 5 tablespoons olive oil in a saucepan, add the chopped vegetables and cook over a high heat until the juices from the mushrooms are completely evaporated. Add 150 ml (¼ pint, ⅔ cup) stock, 6 tablespoons tomato purée (paste), salt, pepper and a bouquet garni and cook gently for 30 minutes. Just before serving, add 1 tablespoon diced lean ham and 1 tablespoon chopped parsley.

Lyonnaise sauce

Cook 3 tablespoons finely chopped onions in 15 g (½ oz, 1 tablespoon) butter in a heavy-based saucepan. When the onions are well softened, add 500 ml (17 fl oz, 2 cups) vinegar and 500 ml (17 fl oz, 2 cups) white wine. Reduce until the liquid has almost evaporated, then add 200 ml (7 fl oz, ¾ cup) demi-glace. Boil for 3–4 minutes, then strain the sauce or serve it unstrained if you prefer. A tablespoon tomato purée (paste) can be added to this sauce if liked.

Alternatively, sprinkle the cooked onions with 1 tablespoon flour and cook until golden, deglaze with 175 ml (6 fl oz, ¾ cup) vinegar and 175 ml (6 fl oz, ¾ cup) white wine, then add some meat stock or pan juices. Boil for a few minutes and serve as above.

261

Mornay sauce

Heat 500 ml (17 fl oz, 2 cups) béchamel sauce. Add 75 g (3 oz, ¾ cup) grated Gruyère cheese and stir until all the cheese has melted. Take the sauce from the heat and add 2 egg yolks beaten with 1 tablespoon milk. Bring slowly to the boil, whisking all the time. Remove from the heat and add 2 tablespoons double (heavy) cream (the sauce must be thick and creamy). For browning at a high temperature or for a lighter sauce, the egg yolks are omitted. If the sauce is to accompany fish, reduced fish stock is added.

Parsley sauce

Make 250 ml (8 fl oz, 1 cup) butter sauce, add 1 tablespoon chopped blanched parsley and a little lemon juice. This sauce is served with poached chicken, boiled rabbit, boiled ham and braised veal.

Parsley sauce for fish

Prepare a sauce with 25 g (1 oz, 2 tablespoons) roux and 250 ml (8 fl oz, 1 cup) freshly cooked fish stock that is strongly flavoured with parsley. Cook for 8 minutes and strain. Just before serving, add 1 tablespoon chopped blanched parsley and a dash of lemon juice. This sauce is particularly suitable to serve with salmon and mackerel.

Poor man's sauce

Make a golden roux with 1 tablespoon butter and 1 heaped tablespoon flour. Deglaze with 3 tablespoons vinegar, boil to reduce and add 200 ml (7 fl oz, ¾ cup) stock (or use water with a little added meat glaze or extract). Season with salt and pepper and boil for a few minutes. Just before serving, add 1 tablespoon chopped chives or blanched shallots or a mixture of both, 1 tablespoon chopped parsley and 2 tablespoons dried white breadcrumbs.

Poulette sauce

Whisk 2 or 3 egg yolks with 400 ml (14 fl oz, 1¾ cups) white veal or poultry stock (or fish fumet if the sauce is to be served with fish or mussels). Heat in a heavy-based saucepan for about 10 minutes, whisking all the time, adding lemon juice (from ½ or 1 lemon) and 50 g (2 oz, ¼ cup) butter. Remove the saucepan from the heat when the sauce coats the spoon. Keep the sauce warm in a bain marie until required, stirring it from time to time to stop a skin from forming on the top.

Rémoulade sauce

Make some mayonnaise using 250 ml (8 fl oz, 1 cup) oil, replacing, if desired, the raw egg yolk with 1 hard-boiled (hard-cooked) egg yolk rubbed through a fine sieve. Add 2 very finely diced gherkins, 2 tablespoons chopped herbs (parsley, chives, chervil and tarragon), 1 tablespoon drained capers and a few drops of anchovy essence (optional).

Sauce à la bretonne

Peel and slice 6 large onions, break them up into rings and brown in clarified butter in a sauté pan. Drain and add 2 ladles each of consommé and thickened espagnole sauce. Season with a little sugar and a touch of white pepper, then add a little butter and a little chicken stock. Finally, press this sauce through a fine sieve.

Sauce with fines herbes

Make 250 ml (8 fl oz, 1 cup) demi-glace sauce or brown stock and add 2 tablespoons chopped parsley, chervil and tarragon. Reduce, press through a very fine sieve, add a few drops of lemon juice and adjust the seasoning. This sauce is served with poached poultry.

Savoury sabayon sauce

Whisk 4 egg yolks with the grated zest of ½ lemon and 2 tablespoons champagne until pale. Place over a bain marie and gradually whisk in 200 ml (7 fl oz, ¾ cup) champagne, adding it a little at a time until the sauce is thick and foamy. Season with salt aand pepper. Remove from the heat and fold in whipped double (heavy) cream – up to half the volume of sauce – or 175 g (6 oz, ¾ cup) clarified butter.

Soubise purée

Soubise is the name given to dishes containing an onion sauce (a béchamel to which onion purée has been added) or an onion purée (usually thickened with rice). It is particularly applied to dishes of eggs, served on the purée or sometimes covered with the sauce. The purée may also be used to garnish cuts of meat or as a stuffing for vegetables.

Peel and thinly slice 1 kg (2¼ lb) white onions and place them in a saucepan with plenty of salted water. Bring to the boil, then drain the onions and place in a saucepan with 100 g (4 oz, ½ cup) butter, salt, pepper and a pinch of sugar. Cover and cook over a gentle heat for 30–40 minutes (the onions should not change colour). Then add to the onions a quantity of boiled rice or thick béchamel sauce equal to one quarter of the volume of the onion. Mix together thoroughly and cook for a further 20 minutes. Taste and adjust the seasoning, press through a very fine sieve and stir in 75 g (3 oz, 6 tablespoons) butter.

Soubise sauce

Prepare a Soubise purée using béchamel sauce. When the sauce is well thickened, stir in 100 ml (4 fl oz, 7 tablespoons) whipping cream and blend thoroughly.

Suprême sauce

Prepare a velouté with a white roux, comprising 40 g (1½ oz, 3 tablespoons) butter and 40 g (1½ oz, 6 tablespoons) plain (all-purpose) flour and 750 ml (1¼ pints, 3¼ cups) well-seasoned and well-reduced chicken consommé. Add 500 ml (17 fl oz, 2 cups) white chicken stock and reduce it by at least half. Add 300 ml (½ pint, 1¼ cups) crème fraîche and reduce the sauce to about 600 ml (1 pint, 2½ cups), at which point it should coat the spoon. Remove from the heat and stir in 50 g (2 oz, ¼ cup) butter. Strain through a very fine sieve and keep warm in a bain marie until ready to use.

Tarragon cream

Boil 100 g (4 oz, 2 cups) chopped fresh tarragon with 150 ml (¼ pint, ⅔ cup) dry white wine. When almost completely dry, add 350 ml (12 fl oz, 1½ cups) thick béchamel sauce, season with salt and pepper, bring to the boil for a few seconds, then rub through a sieve. Reheat and add a little butter.

This purée is used as a filling for small vol-au-vents, barquettes or canapés and also for stuffing vegetables such as artichoke hearts or mushrooms.

Tarragon purée (cold)

Blanch 100 g (4 oz, 2 cups) tarragon leaves and cool under running water. Wipe them and pound in a mortar (or use a blender) with the yolks of 6 hard-boiled (hard-cooked) eggs, 2 tablespoons butter, salt and pepper.

Tarragon purée (hot)

This is prepared in the same way as tarragon cream, but with a very reduced béchamel sauce. It can also be made by adding a purée of tarragon leaves (blanched, cooled under running water, drained, pounded in a mortar and sieved) to twice its volume of mashed potatoes.

Tarragon sauce for poached fowl

Add a large handful of tarragon to the white stock in which the chicken was poached. Skim the fat from the stock, strain, reduce and thicken with arrowroot. Add some freshly chopped tarragon just before serving.

Tarragon sauce for soft-boiled or poached eggs

Coarsely chop 100 g (4 oz, 2 cups) washed and wiped tarragon leaves, add 100 ml (4 fl oz, 7 tablespoons) white wine, then boil down. Add 200 ml (7 fl oz, ¾ cup) demi-glace or thickened brown veal stock and boil for a few moments. Strain through a very fine sieve. Add 1 tablespoon fresh coarsely shredded tarragon just before serving.

Velouté sauce

Stir 2.75 litres (4¾ pints, 12 cups) white veal or chicken stock into a pale blond roux made with 150 g (5 oz, ⅔ cup) butter and 150 g (5 oz, 1¼ cups) plain (all-purpose) flour. Blend well together. Bring to the boil, stirring until the first bubbles appear. Cook the velouté very slowly for 30 minutes, skimming frequently. Strain through a cloth. Stir until it is completely cold.

Velouté may be prepared either in advance or just before it is required. As the white stock used for making it is seasoned and flavoured, it is not necessary to add other flavourings. An exception is made for skins and trimmings of mushrooms, which may be added when available, this addition making the sauce yet more delicate.

Vierge sauce

Beat 125 g (4½ oz, ½ cup) butter until soft, then beat in 2 tablespoons lemon juice and some salt and pepper. Continue to beat well until the mixture is fluffy. This sauce is served with asparagus, leeks and boiled vegetables.

White roux

Melt the butter in a heavy-based saucepan, then clarify it. Add the same weight (or a little more) of sifted plain (all-purpose) flour – up to 125 g (4½ oz, 1 cup) flour for 100 g (4 oz, ½ cup) butter. To make 1 litre (1¾ pints, 4⅓ cups) béchamel sauce, the roux should contain 75 g (3 oz, ¾ cup) flour and the same weight of butter; to make 1 litre (1¾ pints, 4⅓ cups) velouté sauce, use 50–65 g (2–2½ oz, ½–⅔ cup) flour and the same weight of butter.

Mix the butter and flour, stirring constantly with a wooden spoon and covering the whole bottom of the saucepan, so that the roux does not colour unevenly and become lumpy. Continue to cook in this way for 5 minutes, until the mixture begins to froth a little. Take the pan off the heat and leave it to cool until time to add the liquid (milk, white stock, fish stock). To avoid lumps forming this must be poured boiling on to the cold roux. Use a whisk to mix the roux and heat gradually while whisking constantly. (Alternatively, the cold liquid may be whisked gradually into the warm roux.)

Yogurt sauce

Mix 1 small pot of natural yogurt with 1 teaspoon paprika; season with salt and pepper, then add 1 teaspoon lemon juice and the same quantity of chopped chervil and chopped chives.

Use to dress a salad of cucumber, tomatoes, courgettes (zucchini), sweet (bell) peppers, cauliflower, green beans or potatoes.

Stocks,
consommés & glazes

To prepare

A white stock is prepared by placing the ingredients directly into the cooking liquid; in a brown stock, the ingredients are first browned in fat.

White and brown stocks, which used to be essential bases for almost all the great classic sauces, take a long time to make and are often expensive. In practice, they belong to the realm of the restaurant and their use has been considerably reduced in domestic cookery. The advent of stock (bouillon) cubes and of commercial ready-made stocks have reduced the use of traditional stocks.

- FISH STOCK: this is made with fish trimmings, including bones, skin and heads (excluding the gills as they are bitter). They are simmered for 30–45 minutes with aromatic vegetables and herbs. Overcooking spoils the flavour of fish stock.

- WHITE STOCK: this is made with white meat or poultry, veal bones, chicken carcasses and aromatic vegetables. It is used to make white sauces, blanquettes, fricassées and poached chicken dishes.

- BROWN STOCK: this is made with beef, veal, poultry meat and bones, and vegetables that have been browned in fat and then had the liquid added to them. It is used to make brown sauces and gravies, braised dishes and brown stews, for deglazing fried meats and for making glazes by reduction.

- VEGETABLE STOCK: this is made by boiling vegetables and aromatic herbs that have first been gently fried in butter.

Beef consommé

Cut up 2 kg (4½ lb) lean beef and 1.5 kg (3¼ lb) shin of beef (beef shank) (with bone) and put them into a big stockpot. (To extract the maximum amount of flavour from the bones, ask the butcher to break them into chunks.) Add 7 litres (12 pints, 7½ quarts) cold water. Bring to the boil and carefully remove the scum that forms on the surface. Season with coarse salt (it is better to adjust the seasoning at the end than to add too much at the beginning). Add 3 or 4 large carrots, 400 g (14 oz) turnips, 100 g (4 oz) parsnips, 350 g (12 oz) leeks tied in a bundle, 2 celery sticks, sliced, 1 medium-sized onion with 2 cloves stuck in it, 1 garlic clove, a sprig of thyme and ½ bay leaf. Simmer very slowly so that boiling is hardly perceptible, for 4 hours. Remove the meat and very carefully strain the stock. Remove surplus fat carefully.

Clarify the consommé, if required; alternatively clear consommé can be prepared following clear beef consommé.

Beef stock

Coarsely chop 100–150 g (4–5 oz) beef, a small carrot, a white leek, a small celery stick and 1 onion. Place all the ingredients in 1.5 litres (2¾ pints, 6½ cups) water, add 1 clove and simmer gently for 20 minutes. Strain.

Brown veal stock

Bone 1.25 kg (2¾ lb) shoulder of veal and the same amount of knuckle of veal. Tie them together and brush with melted dripping. Crush 500 g (18 oz) veal bones as finely as possible. Brown all these ingredients in a large heavy-based saucepan. Peel and slice 150 g (5 oz) carrots and 100 g (4 oz) onions, then add them to the pan. Cover and leave to sweat for 15 minutes. Add 250 ml (8 fl oz, 1 cup) water and reduce to a jelly-like consistency. Repeat the process. Add 3 litres (5 pints, 13 cups) water or white stock and bring to the boil. Skim and season. Leave to simmer very gently for 6 hours. Skim off the fat and strain through a fine sieve or, better still, muslin (cheesecloth).

Chicken consommé

Proceed as for beef consommé, but replace the lean beef by a small chicken and 3 or 4 giblets browned in the oven, and the shin of beef (beef shank) by 800 g (1¾ lb) veal knuckle. For clarification, proceed as for clear beef consommé, using 4 or 5 chopped chicken giblets instead of the chopped beef. The chicken may then be used for croquettes or patties.

Chicken stock (quick)

Coarsely chop 400–500 g (14–18 oz) chicken wings, 1 small carrot, 1 white leek, 1 small celery stick, 1 onion and add 1 clove. Place the ingredients in 1.5 litres (2¾ pints, 6½ cups) water and simmer gently for 20 minutes. Strain.

Clear beef consommé

For 3 litres (5 pints, 13 cups) stock, use 800 g (1¾ lb) lean beef, chopped and trimmed, 100 g (4 oz) carrots, 100 g (4 oz) leeks and 2 egg whites. Clean the vegetables and cut into small dice. Put them into a pan with the chopped beef and the egg whites. Add the stock cold, or at most, tepid. Heat gently, stirring constantly, until the stock is just boiling. Then reduce the heat, if necessary, to prevent the stock from boiling, and simmer slowly for 1½ hours. Remove surplus fat and strain the consommé through a damp cloth.

Consommé à la brunoise

For 4 servings, finely dice 200 g (7 oz) carrots, 100 g (4 oz) new parsnips, 100 g (4 oz) leeks (white part only), 25 g (1 oz) onions and 75 g (3 oz) well-trimmed celery sticks. Braise gently in 25 g (1 oz, 2 tablespoons) butter, then add 750 ml (1¼ pints, 3¼ cups) consommé and cook for 15 minutes. Just before serving, adjust seasoning and add 150 g (5 oz) each cooked green peas and green beans (cut into short lengths).

Consommé julienne

Make a julienne of 100 g (4 oz) carrot (discarding any hard core), 75 g (3 oz) turnip, and 40 g (1½ oz) each of white of leek, onion and celery. Sprinkle with a pinch of salt and a pinch of sugar. Soften the vegetables in 50 g (2 oz, ¼ cup) melted butter over a low heat, with the pan covered, for 10 minutes. Cut 50 g (2 oz) white cabbage into julienne strips and blanch for 10 minutes in boiling water, then refresh and drain; do the same with the heart of a medium-sized lettuce; add these to the other vegetables.

Cook them all together, covered, for 15 minutes. Pour in 300 ml (½ pint, 1¼ cups) consommé and simmer for 5 minutes; add 25 g (1 oz) sorrel cut into fine ribbons and 1 tablespoon fresh peas, and cook for a further 25 minutes. Add another 1.25 litres (2¼ pints, 5½ cups) consommé and boil for a few seconds; skim the consommé, and at the last moment add some small chervil leaves.

The consommé can be garnished with pearl barley, rice, semolina, tapioca or vermicelli, or with quenelles, profiteroles or royales.

Giblet bouillon

Put the giblets from 2 chickens in a heavy-based saucepan with 2 litres (3½ pints, 9 cups) cold water and bring to the boil. Chop 4 carrots, 2 turnips, 3 leeks (white part only), 2 celery sticks and a small piece of parsnip. Skim the liquid, then add the vegetables together with an onion stuck with cloves, a bouquet garni, salt and pepper. Simmer gently until completely cooked (about 1½ hours). Just before serving, bone the giblets and return the meat to the bouillon, adding the juice of ½ lemon and some chopped parsley. Taste and adjust the seasoning.

If desired, this bouillon can be prepared in the Greek way by cooking 2 handfuls of rice in the stock and thickening with a beaten egg yolk or, preferably, a whole beaten egg.

Herb broth

Use 40 g (1½ oz) fresh sorrel leaves, 20 g (¾ oz) lettuce leaves, 10 g (¼ oz) fresh chervil leaves, ½ teaspoon sea salt, 5 g (¼ oz, 1 teaspoon) butter and 1 litre (1¾ pints, 4⅓ cups) water. Wash the vegetables and cook them in the water. Then add the salt and butter. Strain.

Beetroot (beet) or spinach leaves may be added to the stock if desired and, just before serving, parsley and lemon juice can be included.

Light brown stock

Scald 150 g (5 oz) fresh pork rind and 125 g (4½ oz) knuckle of ham for 4–5 minutes. Bone 1.25 kg (2¾ lb) lean stewing beef (leg or blade) and cut into cubes, together with the same amount of knuckle of veal. Peel 150 g (5 oz) carrots and 150 g (5 oz) onions, cut them into slices, then brown on the hob (stove top) in a large flameproof casserole with all the meat, 500 g (18 oz) crushed veal or beef bones and the pork rind. Add 1 bouquet garni, 1 garlic clove, 500 ml (17 fl oz, 2 cups) water and reduce to a jelly-like consistency. Add another 500 ml (17 fl oz, 2 cups) water and reduce to a jelly once again. Add 2.5–3 litres (4¼–5 pints, 11–13 cups) water and 2 teaspoons coarse salt; bring to the boil and simmer very gently for 8 hours. Skim off the fat and strain the stock through a fine sieve or, better still, through a piece of muslin (cheesecloth).

Meat aspic

Brown 1 kg (2¼ lb) leg of beef and 500 g (18 oz) knuckle of veal, cut into pieces, 1 calf's foot, 500 g (18 oz) veal bones, and 250 g (9 oz) bacon rind, trimmed of fat, in a preheated oven at 200°C (400°F, gas 6). Peel and shred 2 onions, 4 carrots and 1 leek. Place all these ingredients in a stockpot together with a large bouquet garni, 1 tablespoon salt and pepper. Add 3 litres (5 pints, 13 cups) water and bring to the boil. Skim, then add a ladleful of very cold water and simmer for 5 hours. Carefully strain the liquid through a strainer lined with muslin (cheesecloth), let it cool completely and put it in the refrigerator so that the fat which solidifies on the surface can be removed easily. Clarify the stock with 200 g (7 oz) lean beef, 2 egg whites and a small bouquet of chervil and tarragon.

The aspic can be flavoured with Madeira, port, sherry or with any other liquor. If this is done, the flavouring is added just before straining the aspic. White aspic is obtained in a similar fashion, but the meat and bones are not browned. Game aspic is obtained by adding to meat aspic 1.25 kg (2¾ lb) game carcasses and trimmings, which have been previously browned in the oven, and several juniper berries.

Chicken aspic is obtained by adding to meat aspic either a whole chicken or 1.5 kg (3¼ lb) chicken carcasses and giblets, both browned in the oven.

Meat glaze

This is known as *glace de viande*. Remove all the fat from a brown stock. When it is as clear as possible, boil it down by half. Strain through a muslin cloth (cheesecloth), then boil it down again and strain. Continue this process until it will coat the back of a spoon, each time reducing the temperature a little more as the glaze becomes more concentrated. Pour the meat glaze into small containers and keep them in the refrigerator.

A similar method is used with a poultry or game stock to obtain a poultry or game glaze.

By boiling down a fish fumet to a syrupy consistency, then decanting it and straining it through muslin, a light-coloured fish stock is obtained, which is used to enhance the flavour of a fish sauce or to pour over fish before putting it in the oven.

Tapioca consommé

Sprinkle 75–100 g (3–4 oz, ⅔–¾ cup) tapioca in 1.5 litres (2¾ pints, 6½ cups) boiling consommé and cook for 10 minutes. Serve piping hot.

Tarragon-flavoured consommé

Use chicken consommé. Add 20 g (¾ oz, ¼ cup) fresh tarragon leaves to the consommé after it has been clarified and before straining, and leave to infuse.

Veal stock

Coarsely chop 100–150 g (4–5 oz) lean veal (haunch or shoulder), 1 small carrot, 1 white leek, 1 small celery stick, and 1 onion and add 1 clove. Place all the ingredients in 1.5 litres (2¾ pints, 6½ cups) water and simmer gently for 20 minutes. Strain.

Vegetable bouillon or stock

Use vegetables that are generally included in a stockpot – carrots, onions, leeks, celery, garlic cloves, tomatoes and turnips are typical. Potatoes and parsnips tend to make the stock cloudy; strongly flavoured vegetables give the stock a distinctive flavour – for example, broccoli, cauliflowers, swede (rutabaga) or fennel. Using a large proportion of red vegetables, such as carrots, swede (rutabaga), tomatoes and red (bell) peppers, gives the stock a good colour. Onion skins give stock a brown colour. For a white stock carrots can be included with a large proportion of pale vegetables. Chop the vegetables, cook gently in butter, then pour boiling water over them to cover. A bouquet garni, salt and pepper (optional) are added and the broth is simmered until the vegetables are cooked. Alternatively, simply add all the ingredients to boiling water and simmer until cooked, either conventionally or using a pressure cooker. In both cases, the broth must be strained before it can be served.

White stock

Bone an 800 g (1¾ lb) shoulder of veal and a 1 kg (2¼ lb) knuckle of veal, then tie them together with string. Crush the bones. Place the bones, meat and 1 kg (2¼ lb) chicken giblets or carcasses in a saucepan. Add 3.5 litres (6 pints, 3½ quarts) water, bring to the boil and skim. Add 125 g (4½ oz) sliced carrots, 100 g (4 oz) onions, 75 g (3 oz) leeks (white part only), 75 g (3 oz) celery and 1 bouquet garni. Season. Simmer gently for 3½ hours. Skim off the fat and strain through a very fine sieve or muslin (cheesecloth).

Index

Picture acknowledgements

Cabanne P. et Ryman C. *Coll. Larousse* colour plates 3, 4; **Daniel de Nève** *Coll. Larousse* colour plate 1; **Magis J.-J.** *Coll. Larousse* colour plates 2, 6, 8; **Magis J.-J.** *La Photothèque culinaire* colour plate 7; **Sudres J.-D.** *Coll. Larousse* colour plate 5.

Editorial Director **Jane Birch**

Executive Editor **Nicky Hill**

Design Manager **Tokiko Morishima**

Editorial team **Anne Crane, Lydia Darbyshire, Bridget Jones, Cathy Lowne**

Index **Hilary Bird**

Cover design **Tokiko Morishima**

Senior Production Controller **Ian Paton**

Picture Research **Jennifer Veall**

Typesetting **Dorchester Typesetters**